Lenin and the Problem
of Marxist Peasant Revolution

LENIN AND THE PROBLEM OF MARXIST PEASANT REVOLUTION

ESTHER KINGSTON-MANN

New York Oxford
OXFORD UNIVERSITY PRESS
1983

Library of Congress Cataloging in Publication Data
Kingston-Mann, Esther.
Lenin and the problem of Marxist peasant revolution.
Includes index.
1. Lenin, Vladimir Il'ich, 1870–1924.
2. Peasantry—Soviet Union—History—20th century.
3. Communism—Soviet Union—History—20th century.
I. Title. HX312.L43K56 1983 320.5′322 82–14314
ISBN 0–19–503278–0

The following journals have kindly granted permission to include in this book articles that were first published in their pages in somewhat different form:

Soviet Studies – "Proletarian Theory and Peasant Practice: Lenin, 1901–1904" (October 1974): 522–39

Russian Review – "Lenin and the Challenge of Peasant Militance: From Bloody Sunday, 1905, to the Dissolution of the First Duma," vol. 38, no. 4 (October 1979): 435–55

Journal of Peasant Studies – "A Strategy for Marxist Bourgeois Revolution: Lenin and the Peasantry, 1907–1917," vol. 7, no. 2 (January 1980): 132–52. By permission of Frank Cass & Co., Ltd.

Russian History – "Problems of Order and Revolution: Lenin and the Peasantry in March and April, 1917" (1979:6): 39–56.

American Historical Review – "Marxism and Russian Rural Development: Problems of Evidence, Experience, and Culture," vol. 86, no. 4 (October 1981): 745–49.

Slavonic and East European Review – "Lenin and the Beginnings of Marxist Peasant Revolution: July–October, 1917," vol. L, no. 121 (October 1972): 570–88.

Fried. 19.95/17.50/8/12/83

Printing (last digit): 9 8 7 6 5 4 3 2 1

Printed in the United States of America

To my father, Echiel Kingston, who first alerted me to problems of Marxist theory and practice.

Preface

The questions addressed in this book have played an important role in my own personal history, and they also form part of the experience which I share with many students of working-class origin who attend the university where I teach. We start, all of us, from an initial vantage point outside the great cultural traditions which not only shaped but also provided tools of debate and analysis for Marx, Lenin, and other political theorists. From this position, we make our way, misunderstanding much and being misunderstood with at least equal frequency. Our troubled and exhilarating encounter with the ideas and structures created by a highly educated minority of the world's population seems to me significant on more than a personal level; it has a social and historical resonance as well. It is no accident, as the Soviets are fond of saying, that when I became a Russian historian I wanted more than anything else to investigate the relationship between Marxists and a peasantry whose culture and institutions were apparently quite alien to the categories of Marxist analysis. Russian Marxism was, after all, a minority perspective aimed at an urban proletarian minority. After years of struggle, Lenin was able to transform it into an ideology which in 1917 appealed to the peasants who comprised the overwhelming majority of the Russian population. The cultural, political, and economic issues which he confronted were historically specific. But for those of us with special reasons for concern with the change process itself, Lenin's solution carries lessons and warnings which go far beyond the limits of the Russian situation.

I have many people to thank for encouragement and suggestions. The most immediately helpful words came from Ralph Miliband, and the earliest source of intellectual aid and comfort was Owen Lattimore. David Hunt and Linda Gordon have provided critical support and intellectual stimulation of a rare order during the many years of our friendship, and Carmen Sirianni was a source of many helpful comments. Clifford Garber, Nancy Farrell, and Jack Treanor were invaluable as research assistants, Patricia Denault fulfilled what is every writer's fantasy of excellence in a typist, and Tessa DeCarlo has given me the benefit of her considerable skills as copy editor for Oxford University Press.

Most of all, I want to thank my husband Jim Mann, who brought a composer's sense of form and structure and an extraordinarily empathic intelligence to the reading of a study which could not be more distant from his own field. Without the sustaining warmth he generously provided, this book would never have been completed.

Boston   E.K.-M.
February 1983

Contents

*Lenin and the Problem
of Marxist Peasant Revolution*

Introduction

BETWEEN 1893 AND 1917, Lenin developed a strategy for peasant
revolution which was crucial to the first Marxist political success of the
twentieth century. The history of his efforts is filled with contradiction
and inconsistency; enthusiastic response to the demands of an increasingly revolutionary peasantry coexists throughout with the denial that
peasants possess a culture, a sense of solidarity, or any constructive
economic potential. Like other Marxists before him, Lenin believed
that peasants were a transient social element, soon to disappear before
the onslaught of commercial capitalism. But Lenin was wrong. If
peasants are nothing else, they are survivors. Long before and after the
advent of Lenin, they have endured as the majority of the world's
population. Low in social status, forced to relinquish a portion of their
crop to a lord, a landlord, or the state before their own consumption
needs are met, peasants have managed to survive on their small plots of
land by relying on their families, their communities, and their
knowledge of the land they work.[1] The peasantry's stubborn persistence
in nineteenth- and twentieth-century Russia as a commune-oriented
majority who neither hired labor nor hired themselves out to work for
others confronted Lenin with the most serious challenge he would ever
face as a revolutionary activist.

After making such a categorical statement, I must also admit that
few scholars have agreed with it; Lenin's peasant policy has attracted
very little attention on the part of Western historians even though the
importance of this topic is never denied.[2] For example, in Marcel

Liebman's valuable study *Leninism under Lenin*[3] we find Lenin's assertion in September 1917 that the peasants' revolt constituted "the most outstanding fact of present-day Russian life," but Liebman gives us not a single discussion of the peasant question in Leninist theory or practice for the period 1893 to 1917. While it is usually a thankless task to survey all of the reasons why this or any other topic is *not* dealt with, it is nevertheless worth noting that Western Lenin scholars have been primarily concerned with character studies, with the role of urban institutions and social elements, or with ideological disputes within the Russian Social Democratic Labor Party. In certain respects, Neil Harding's *Lenin's Political Thought*[4] constitutes an exception in the field of Lenin scholarship. Harding considers Lenin neither a fanatic political manipulator nor the all-wise teacher of an assortment of more or less grateful Russian radicals. With great empathy, he has understood Lenin as Lenin would himself have preferred to have been understood. By downplaying the vicious and destructive polemics which pervade Lenin's writings, Harding has been able to construct a better case for Lenin's ideas than Lenin did himself. But Harding's is not a critical study. On the subject of peasants and Russian agriculture which concerns us, for example, he is able to demonstrate that Lenin's position in the 1890s was serious and even original, but he fails to indicate that Lenin's carefully selected data and conclusions were contradicted by most of the economic evidence available at the time.[5]

In contrast to Western investigators, Soviet scholars have not ignored Lenin's peasant policy, and their work contains much useful data. But even at best, as in the work of S. P. Trapeznikov, for example,[6] they have been more concerned to praise than to understand and critically evaluate his achievement. The Soviet Lenin does not grow or change; he is from the beginning to the end of his life correct and miraculously insightful on every possible issue, including the peasant question. In my view, the peasant majority of the Russian population posed a fundamental challenge to Lenin as a Marxist dedicated to the triumph of an urban proletarian minority. And as far as I can tell, the nature of that challenge has never been systematically investigated.

During most of the years between 1893, when Lenin began his political career, and the triumphant Bolshevik victory of October 1917, Lenin was in exile or in prison. Autocratic Russia did not willingly provide him or any of its leading critics with opportunities to perfect their political skills by engaging in long-term grass-roots organizational activities among workers or peasants. But it was not only the force of state coercion which placed the peasantry so far out of reach. Russian peasants were enserfed until 1861, and isolated from the rest of the population before and after that time by a separate set of laws and uniquely peasant institutions. Although peasants were in no sense unchanging—freedom from serfdom and the development of a money economy were only two of the most striking transformations to take place in nineteenth-century rural life—neither the patterns of their opposition to authority nor their economic and social traditions had ever been significantly shaped or influenced by the conscious efforts of educated Russians. By the middle of the nineteenth-century the staying power of these patterns and traditions had become a source of increasing frustration, for reasons which were closely related to the issue of economic backwardness. As radicals and other critics and supporters of the tsarist regime observed the subjugation of peasant societies the world over by advanced capitalist nations, they came to fear that Russia might suffer the fate of India or Ireland unless she somehow became a capitalist and peasantless "England." Lenin's strategy for Marxist peasant revolution developed within this cultural context and in the context of a European Marxist movement which considered England as a model for the less developed nations of the world, and placed the predominantly peasant population at the periphery of its concerns.

This book is organized in four parts: In Part I, "The Tradition," an attempt is made to locate both Marx and Lenin within the urban-centered Western European culture which shaped the theories and behavior of so many capitalists, anti-capitalists, democrats, and statists of the nineteenth-century. Part II, "Peasant Militance and Petty Bourgeois Capitalism, 1901–16," details the repeated clash between Lenin's enthusiastic response to revolutionary peasant action and his dogmatic Marxist belief that small producers were economic reactionaries. In exile and in increasing political isolation, Lenin was at pains to devise a peasant strategy for economic development as well as revolution. The components of his success as a revolutionary activist in 1917, as well as the seeds of future difficulty, emerge clearly during this period. In Part III, "Peasant Revolution in Theory and Practice," Lenin's peasant strategy is tested by the events of 1917. His insight into the policies followed by his Menshevik and SR rivals, and his constructive response to the peasant violence which raged unchecked in the countryside, not only contributed to the growth of "Bolshevism" among peasant elements who had never heard of *What Is To Be Done?* but convinced his fellow party members to lay claim to the right and the responsibility to shape a new social order. Part IV sets out the meaning and the implications of Lenin's success as spokesman for Russia's peasant revolution of 1917.

I

The Tradition

I

The Lessons of the Marxist Classics

> If the revolution is to occur at the end of
> two parallel movements, the unlimited
> shrinking of capital and the unlimited
> expansion of the proletariat, it will not
> occur or ought not to have occurred.
>
> ALBERT CAMUS

WE BEGIN WITH MARX, because his insights and cultural assumptions so profoundly defined and limited Lenin's understanding of the peasant question. A prototype of the revolutionary as urban intellectual, Marx was all the more a product of his time for his failure to recognize the extent to which he shared its most anti-peasant assumptions. Like other nineteenth-century European progressives, Marx took for granted the "idiocy of rural life." Certain that his passionate faith in the power and prerogatives of urban social elements was scientific and objective, he produced economic and political studies which documented the widespread contemporary belief that peasants the world over would inevitably be replaced by entrepreneurs and wage laborers. As impressed by conflict models of behaviour as Thomas Malthus or Herbert Spencer, Marx developed a penetrating critique of Romantic idealizations of the "Christian" peasant and the social harmonies of the peasant community. His own compassionate vision of prosperity, freedom, and creativity for working people was emphatically *not* rooted in the communal traditions and practices which other observers had discovered among subsistence peasantries. While Marx was confident that there was a new socialist world to be won, he believed that urban-centered class struggle rather than the collective efforts of small producers would bring it into being.[1]

Despite his commitment to scientific inquiry and his gift for systematic and wide-ranging empirical research, Marx was notably unrigorous in his references to the peasantry.[2] In his major works, tillers of the soil were portrayed either as the pathetic remnants of feudal society or as incipient capitalists and proletarians. In the first instance they were an ineffective obstacle to modern capitalist development, and in the second, a temporary phenomenon whose sympathies lay with the exploiters and whose fate, in most cases, was to be oppressed. The social relations which existed among peasants themselves did not interest Marx. He found more fruitful subjects for study in the conflicts which took place between peasants and their feudal or capitalist exploiters.

Before Capital

As a young radical concerned with the overthrow of the German social order, Marx wrote about the most active rather than the most numerous social elements. In *The German Ideology* (1845–46) and in his other early writings, we find not only a devastating critique of capitalism, but a pervasive assumption that capitalists were a dynamic, economically rational, and revolutionary social class within any feudal or semi-feudal society. In contrast, the peasantry appear as denizens of a stagnant medieval world, brutalized primitives who live out their lives in hopeless and unending poverty. From a revolutionary point of view, the most repellent defect of the peasant economy was its lack of dynamic tension. As Marx saw it, the unity of industry and agriculture within unspecialized rural communities bred a myopic resistance to progress. Unskilled and apathetic, peasants could not be expected to welcome the painful and destabilizing process which created rational entrepreneurs and mobile, productive, potentially revolutionary proletarians. It was fortunate, therefore, that progress did not depend on the preferences of the peasantry; Marx pointed out that a lack of capital and scientific knowledge would eventually doom them just as surely as it had the feudal landlords. The peasant commune, the peasant farm, and the feudal estate were all fated to disappear in an unequal struggle against more progressive and efficient large-scale capitalist enterprise.[3]

In the "Communist Manifesto" (1848), the peasantry's hopeless economic situation became an explanation for the illusions and errors which pervaded their political efforts. French and German farmers were found to be so limited in knowledge and perspective by the local character of their economic activities that they either fought in vain to restore an obsolete pre-capitalist order or aspired with equally dismal results to become prosperous bourgeois exploiters of hired labor. Marx argued that in the past and in his own time, peasant interests could be identified with those of the urban artisans, the intellectuals, and the small shopkeepers. As members of the petty bourgeoisie, peasants were obsessed by the tiny properties which made them into owners without ever protecting them from the threat of poverty. Trapped within an insecure class position, they were never confronted by the clear choices which faced the big capitalist or the alienated proletarian. For these reasons, although oppressed and exploited peasants might engage in violence against the existing order, they attained the status of true revolutionaries only when they *deserted their interests* as peasants in order to unite with the urban proletariat. They were therefore in no sense revolutionaries with nothing to lose but their chains.[4]

To Marx, the ideological and political defenders of the peasantry seemed to reflect the objective inconsistencies of an unstable, never really capitalist or proletarian social element. "Petty bourgeois" socialists like Sismondi deplored the poverty of the masses, but demanded either a return to "outmoded" property relations or a delay in the capitalist development which alone could create the material basis for socialism. "Utopians" like Fourier and Owen eloquently protested the cruelty of capitalist exploitation and proposed the establishment of model communities without ever recognizing that class antagonism would inevitably doom any efforts to establish socialist alternatives within the framework of a capitalist society.[5]

The "sentimental moralizing" of Proudhon and Herzen on the subject of the peasantry seemed to Marx equally futile. In his view, fundamental change could not be expected to follow from the power of example, from logic or rational arguments, or from the power of moral appeals to the upper class. Capitalist exploitation was after all not a matter of the evil impulses or the ignorance of wealthy individuals; it was the central feature of a system based upon the conflict between producers (the workers) and those who appropriated the product of proletarian labor (the capitalists). While a concern for logic, morality, or knowledge might be praiseworthy or hypocritical depending on the circumstances, Marx never considered such motives as reliable or certain as the force of class struggle. In the long run, he did not believe that commitments to morality or reason could ever permanently triumph over class interest. Poverty did not exist because the rich were ignorant of the consequences of their actions. And petty bourgeois intellectuals who hoped for miracles of benevolence from a conscience-stricken gentry or bourgeoisie would in his view only end as dupes or unconscious apologists of the exploiting classes.[6]

Although Marx did not believe that the bourgeoisie would allow itself to be led or guided by more radical elements, he did not completely rule out the possibility of joint action between the peasantry and the urban proletariat. Particularly after the failure of the European revolutions of 1848, Marx took more seriously the popular support given to "petty bourgeois democrats" in Germany, France, England, and Italy. Cautiously, he suggested that in specific and limited instances the working class might form temporary anti-feudal alliances with the rest of the town population, and even with peasants and agricultural laborers. This did not mean that peasants were to be "merged" with the proletariat; there was to be no blurring of the class distinctions between the unreliable petty bourgeoisie and the steadfast urban worker. Because their common interests were so short-lived, Marx argued that German workers had to imitate the Frankfurt liberals of 1848, who betrayed their allies among the poor at the very moment of their joint success. In order for a worker–peasant alliance to succeed, the proletariat would have to deal with the peasantry in similar fashion, with the Frankfurt liberals' sort of tough-mindedness: ". . . from the first moment of victory we must no longer direct our distrust against the beaten reactionary enemy, but against our former allies, who are about to exploit the common victory for their own ends only."[7] In his view, the only reliable allies for the urban proletariat were the agricultural laborers who had been "misled" into joining the ranks of the petty bourgeoisie. Although he did not present any evidence that rural proletarians were ever actually willing to fight in opposition to the rest of the peasantry, Marx argued nevertheless that rural proletarians could join with their urban counterparts to establish a revolutionary government which would exist alongside the official government and protect their interests.[8]

For revolutionaries in peasant societies, Marx's brief "Address to the Communist League" (1850) was significant because he so rarely dealt with the politics of the peasant question. Yet it should be noted that

Marx was quite guarded and cautious in his references to the possibility of constructive action by any rural social element. Here as elsewhere in his writings, he was far more sensitive to the danger of excessive faith in the petty bourgeoisie than he was to the benefits of cooperation. (In later years, his meager comments would be cited by Lenin and by other Marxists in their arguments for a worker–peasant alliance. True to the letter and spirit of Marx's approach, his Russian disciples would interpret cooperation to mean proletarian domination of the peasantry.)

The reasons why domination was so necessary were spelled out in Marx's historical studies of revolution and counterrevolution of the 1850s. In *The Class Struggles in France* and *The Eighteenth Brumaire of Louis Bonaparte*, the defects of the peasantry were catalogued in detail, with the negative aspects of peasant action everywhere given particular weight. While the bourgeoisie was portrayed as oppressive, reactionary, or "incurably barren"[9] and the democrat as a ridiculous figure who emerged from "disgraceful defeat as immaculate as he went innocently into it, and with the refreshed conviction that he must win,"[10] the peasant embodied the worst aspects of both bourgeois and democrat. Reactionary, greedy, and stupid, the wealthy peasant stubbornly opposed any threat to the security of his property, while the poor were only "revolutionary" in their efforts to get hold of the land of their richer neighbors.[11]

Although he undertook no empirical investigation of peasant social life, Marx assumed that French peasants were nothing more than a "sack of potatoes," a vast atomized mass of small proprietors who found in the "great dignitaries of property the defenders of their small property and their petty prejudices."[12] Quite selective in his contempt for Louis Napoleon's admirers, he considered peasant Bonapartism typically petty bourgeois, but did not find working-class support for "President" Bonaparte typically proletarian. It was only the peasants who were castigated for finding in Louis Napoleon their master and protector. Marx even discovered an appalling resemblance between the oafish cunning of the peasants and the leader they had chosen. Louis Napoleon symbolized for him the peasantry's "entry into the revolutionary movement, doltishly sublime, an undecipherable hieroglyph for the understanding of the civilized—this symbol bore the unmistakable features of the class that represented barbarism within civilization."[13]

While peasants were responsible for Louis Napoleon's triumph, Marx argued that Bonapartist dictatorship would not halt their precipitous economic decline. As a system of capitalist usury and mortgages inexorably replaced traditional feudal obligations, the French social order became a kind of "vampire that sucks out [the land allotment's] heartblood and very brains, and throws it into the alchemist's pot of capital."[14] In this process, small farmers were driven from the land. And although the level of consciousness created by life and work in an isolated village made it unlikely that they would be capable of understanding the reasons for their ruin, Marx argued that if peasants could somehow find in themselves the sense to abandon their "property fanaticism" and support the proletariat, they might win a better life. Their only hope was to reject the leadership of Louis Napoleon and allow themselves to be led by the proletariat.[15]

The views expressed in Marx's historical studies were eloquently supported by the works of Friedrich Engels, his first disciple. In *The Peasant War in Germany* and *Germany in 1848* (1851), Engels found medieval and modern German peasants geographically isolated from one another, traditionally obedient to authority, and variously exploited by the ruling classes. In time of social crisis they were therefore both fragmented and incapable of independent revolutionary initiative, with each sector of the rural populace following the lead of the more advanced urban element which appeared to represent its position. With little concrete evidence and a substantial measure of wishful thinking, Engels claimed that in 1848 the agricultural laborers had supported the revolutionary city artisans, while the small farmers followed the dissatisfied small shopkeepers of the towns. In his view, peasants were paralyzed in typical petty bourgeois fashion by the concrete implications of their professed willingness to risk life and property for the sake of "liberty" and the "republic,"[16] and were sorely in need of guidance from a highly organized urban proletariat.[17]

Capital: The Peasantry's Death Sentence

Unlike Marx's historical studies, which focused primarily on the political struggles of traditional and modern elites, *Capital* dealt in detail with the process of economic change as it affected working people. Although it was not a treatise on the general nature of all societies but a study of England's economic development, *Capital* was widely understood as a work with much broader implications because it contained so many universalistic statements. As Marx had put it, an industrialized society simply "showed to the less developed the image of its own future."[18] Just as English capitalism had crushed the small producer, peasants the world over were apparently to be ruined by the same invincible capitalist process. According to Marx's "law of concentration," peasant property systems, like older communal forms of tenure, inevitably gave way to more productive, larger-scale enterprise, just as peasants gave way to more economically and politically rational social groups like the bourgeoisie and the proletariat. In this process, the village would supply raw materials and labor to the city in return for decent social values, rational models for economic development, and the culture it lacked (not, it should be emphasized, in return for material welfare, which was promised at some future date). Although Marx explicitly denied that he had discovered any general laws which were the same for all historical phases of social development,[19] he did claim that there were "natural laws of capitalist production."[20] Insofar as agriculture was based on commodity production, Marx assumed that it would experience the same sort of evolution as industry. But his comparisons between industry and agriculture were not very rigorous and careful; too often he took for granted that what "worked" for industry (concentration and centralization of production, for example) would automatically serve to increase productivity in agriculture.

Marx's treatment of the peasant in *Capital* in no way contradicted the conclusions reached in his historical studies. With a powerful mixture of pity and contempt, he argued that "small property in land creates a class of barbarians standing halfway outside society, a class suffering all the tortures and all the miseries of civilized countries in addition to the crudeness of primitive forms of society."[21] Although Marx suggested in the third volume of *Capital* that subsistence farmers or "associated producers" helped the capitalist system to survive its incessant cyclical crises, he saw these crises as an inevitable, brutal, and progressive component of rural economic development.[22] Where Marx had claimed in 1844 that the low degree of division of labor in traditional peasant communities functioned to stabilize the feudal order,[23] he argued in 1867 that associated peasant producers sustained an exploitative capitalist system. In both cases, Marx judged the strength of the peasantry an obstacle to progress.

According to Marx, agricultural growth and development might take unusual forms, occurring sometimes without landlords, tenants, or even the institution of private property. Arguing that the purchase price paid by the landowner and the rent paid by the tenant were *in principle* diversions of capital from its more economically rational investment function, he concluded that state ownership of land was quite compatible with capitalist economic growth. He pointed out that in the American West the abolition of rent, like the abolition of private landownership, had brilliantly served the interests of bourgeois proponents of economic development.[24]

Such arguments for the staying power of associated small producers or for progress without the ownership of land were profoundly suggestive to Marx's disciples and critics,[25] but it was significant that Marx did not himself explore their implications at length or in depth. As in his earlier writings, the scheme of historical development outlined in *Capital* held out no hope for peasants or peasant institutions. Certain that peasant farms functioned only to block the concentration of capital and the application of technology to agriculture, Marx argued that with or without private property or "associations," the peasantry would eventually give way before the capitalist agricultural magnate. Therefore, to preserve the small proprietor was to decree a kind of "universal mediocrity." According to Marx the system of small proprietorship

> must be annihilated. Its annihilation, the transformation of individual and scattered means of production into socially concentrated ones, of the pygmy property of the many into the huge property of the few . . . this fearful and painful expropriation of the mass of the people forms the prelude to the history of capital.[26]

Once peasants were transformed into proletarians and capitalists, it would be necessary to proceed to the task of expropriating the capitalists.

It has been justly argued that Marx understood much more than this about problems of rural transformation. And in the following chapter, it will become evident that when Marx began to consider the problems and prospects of Russia, he became far more aware of the limits to the analysis he had put forward in *Capital*. But it is nonetheless understandable that Marx's scholarly and intellectual scruples (admirable as they were) were not taken as a substitute for the arguments which he had made in his masterwork. In its treatment of the peasant question, *Capital* reflected the conventional disgust of an urban intellectual for the backward and stagnant provinces, where unproductive, patriarchal peasants suffered feudal exploitation, ignorantly rejected modern agricultural methods, and disappeared beneath the capitalist juggernaut. *Capital* provided as well a chilling account of the rural idiocy which deprived the peasantry of the will and the intelligence necessary to create a modern and productive agriculture, much less a successful revolutionary movement against the exploitative capitalist system. In this context, peasant cooperation and mutual aid were for Marx a Romantic idealization of the "universal mediocrity" created by the system of small property relationships.

The Lessons To Be Learned:
The Challenge of Revolutionary Practice

The straightforward economic determinism of *Capital* appeared to leave little room for constructive action by radicals in predominantly peasant societies. Yet it was significant that in practice, Marx would respond positively to revolutionary outbreaks even when peasants were major participants. The relationship between his determinism and his revolutionary spirit was at its most instructive in 1871, when the Communards of Paris launched a struggle to establish a socialistic republic. On the eve of this attempted revolution, Marx had written quite explicitly that any effort at proletarian revolution in France was doomed to failure.[27] But once the Commune was established, Marx did not dwell upon the hopelessness of its prospects. Throughout the Commune's brief existence he remained enthusiastic and hopeful. He refused to denounce the Communards for opportunism when they attempted to formulate a program to satisfy the common interests of peasants and proletarians. Instead, Marx claimed that by enacting measures (1) to break the power of wealthy landlords and (2) to compel the rich to pay the French war debt, the Commune provided a revolutionary model for peasant participation in the transformation of a capitalist society. And two days after the Commune's fall, he wrote of the "heroic" Communards who had "stormed heaven" and provided future generations with the example of their courage, initiative, and social creativity.[28]

Marx had not, of course, lost his urban bias: he emphasized that the Commune and its constitution were progressive and revolutionary because the peasant had been brought under the intellectual leadership

of the town, while the constitution "secured to [the peasants] in the
working men the natural guardians of their interests."[29] He remained
certain that wherever peasants were in the majority, they would cause
the defeat of any workers' revolution which failed to act immediately to
improve the peasants' material lot. Nevertheless, however grudging
and contemptuous his remarks, Marx had for the first time held out the
possibility that the peasant (as small producer and not as future
proletarian) might be a positive auxiliary force in an anti-capitalist
revolution led by the working class.

Marx's enthusiasm for the unexpected and unsuccessful struggle of
the Communards suggested that he did not intend his theories to be
used as an excuse for the imposition of "prudent" constraints upon
popular initiatives which radicals had judged premature. On the
contrary, his Commune writings implied that it was incumbent upon
revolutionaries to support even ill-timed popular movements. To
activists like Lenin, Marx's attempts to derive constructive lessons from
the Commune experience were particularly inspiring. In his struggle
against the caution of his Menshevik political rivals between 1905 and
1917, he would repeatedly refer to the example which Marx had set in
his writings on the Paris Commune.[30]

At the same time, Marx's revolutionary enthusiasm was no substitute for a systematic explanation of why the backward petty
proprietor might come to fight alongside the proletariat in a revolution
against capitalism. In early twentieth-century Russia and elsewhere, a
number of Marxist intellectuals found the systematic economic analysis
provided by *Capital* far more easy to assimilate than Marx's revolutionary spirit. As we shall see, they did not study Marx in order to learn about
the economic and social life of the peasantry. Instead, they found in
Capital the image of a future filled with merchants and bankers who
penetrated every corner of the non-Western world in their search for
profits. The undogmatic enthusiasm which Marx expressed for "inappropriate" revolutionary upheavals did in fact offer his followers an
escape from the political passivity which economic determinism might
have seemed to require, as peasant societies underwent a more or less
lengthy period of bourgeois preparation for a socialist future. But the
failure of Marx to incorporate "revolutionary" peasants into his
theoretical framework would leave future Marxist peasant policies to
bear a painful resemblance to opportunism.

2

Populists and Marxists: The "Russian" and "Western" Paths to Socialism

LIKE EDUCATED PEOPLE in technologically backward societies the world over, nineteenth-century Russians who read Marx were both dazzled and terrified by Western wealth, military might, and cultural achievements. The tension between admiration and the fear of domination was evident as early as the 1840s, in the debates between Russia's Slavophiles and "Westernizers." On one level, educated Russians faced a choice between "progress" and "reaction." On another, they were like the former colonial peoples of today, attempting to discover whether national survival required a wholesale adoption of Western economic, social, and political institutions, as well as the total repudiation of their own. In the course of the late nineteenth century, Russian Marxists, government modernizers, and a host of tough-minded intellectuals came to consider both of these choices inevitable and necessary. Despite the reservations of Marx himself, Russian Marxists grew steadily more confident that Russia was in the process of recreating the experience of England.[1] Certain that the peasant majority of the population could neither survive nor change the shape of the modern world, they would consider themselves justified in focusing their attention upon the elements which most closely resembled the urban entrepreneur and proletarian. The evolution of such attitudes is the subject of this chapter.

The Origins of "Peasant" Socialism

Driven by an awareness of the contempt which Western Europeans felt for less "civilized" peoples, Slavophile intellectuals in the reign of

Nicholas I (1825–55) developed a wide-ranging critique of Western ideas and institutions, and claimed superiority for the values they held to be peculiarly Russian. In the 1830s I. V. Kireevskii argued that Western achievements were founded upon morally reprehensible and socially dangerous economic and political principles. In England and France he found many examples of unprecedented material wealth accumulated by individuals obsessed with private gain and unrestrained by any sense of social obligation.[2] To A. S. Khomiakov, the ideal of equality before the law meant in practice a callous disregard for individual differences in wealth, intelligence, or moral character. The discoveries of Western science were recognized as a legitimate source of pride, but even these achievements were viewed by Slavophiles as the product of a fragmented and overspecialized culture.[3] In place of a Western world filled with dissatisfied and isolated profit-seekers, constantly at war with one another, Slavophiles conjured up an ancient Russia where Orthodox peasants were at one with their tsar, and the time-honored Russian commune sustained Christian forms of social life.

The peasant commune (*mir*, or *obshchina*) had been a subject of controversy long before the emergence of the Slavophile movement, perhaps because few educated Russians had ever seemed to need much empirical evidence in order to pass judgment on its evident defects or striking virtues. Except for the west and south, where forms of hereditary (*podvornoe*) tenure prevailed, most nineteenth-century Russian peasants belonged to communes which periodically redistributed scattered strips of land to members according to family size, the number of able-bodied workers per household, or some other collectivist social principle. Within each commune, a patriarchal village assembly (the *skhod*) which included the head of each family and one or more village elders decided how and when repartition, planting, and harvesting would take place. While the *skhod* could seldom withstand the demands of the gentry or the state, in the absence of outside intervention it established most of the rules for local social and economic life. A place where the strong, the wealthy, or the cunning were frequently able to exert undue influence, the commune served also as a framework for economic decision-making, for the implementation of mutual guarantees of security, and—in time of particularly serious discontent—for the organization of resistance to external authority.[4] As we shall see, the strategies for change developed by educated Russians in the course of the nineteenth century were deeply affected by their assessment of the commune's economic, political, and social significance.

In the 1840s I. V. Kireevskii held that the security of livelihood provided by the Russian commune was morally and socially more valuable than the security of property guaranteed by English laws and parliaments. In his view, unrestricted property rights transformed the individual into nothing more than an appendage of his property. In contrast, the commune showed its concern for the individual by ensuring that he did not starve to death.[5] From such a perspective, Western freedom was an idealization of selfishness, defined by the Slavophiles as the refusal to subordinate human activity to a common moral purpose. The lowly Russian peasant, humble and uncompetitive, sharing a collectivist social and economic tradition, stood for the Slavophiles as the antithesis of such shoddy conceptions of progress.

In the Slavophile love of tradition Russia's early Westernizers found obscurantism and a justification for reactionary government policies. It seemed obvious to Belinskii and the young Herzen that autocratic, serf-ridden, and backward Russia would not be improved by a return to the past. In their view, a society worth defending needed as a minimum such Western achievements as equality before the law, civil liberties, and constitutional and representative government. At the same time, it should be emphasized that even the most fanatic of these early Westernizers were unwilling to believe that Russians had to imitate and recreate *every* aspect of Western experience. Their ambivalence about the need for total Westernization was evident in the writings of Belinskii, who denounced the "money-grubbing" European bourgeoisie with the passion of a medieval schoolman, while agonizing all the while over the possibility that progress might be dependent upon just such contemptible social elements.[6] But in general, Westernizers were less concerned with economics than they were with politics and culture. They assumed that substantial, Western-style progress in the latter areas could not help but bring an end to serfdom as well as an increased measure of social justice for all.

Populism as a specifically Russian form of socialism developed out of a painful recognition that such easy assumptions were untenable. As an exile in Paris during the "June Days" of 1848, the Westernizer Alexander Herzen watched in disbelief and horror as the democratically elected French National Assembly sanctioned General Cavaignac's massacre of the rebellious Paris poor, rejected all social welfare programs, and supported the rise to power of Louis Bonaparte. By emancipating political democracy from any commitment to the material welfare of the masses, the French National Assembly demonstrated to many idealists of the time that democratic politics could be a morally and socially neutral process. A system which could be used to build a more decent society, political democracy could also, apparently, function to render powerless and obliterate concern for all social groups whose interests were not bourgeois. Like Marx, Herzen came to believe that political democracy in France was essentially a "dictatorship by the bourgeoisie." But unlike Marx, Herzen went on to argue that if political democracy permitted the rule of a socially irresponsible elite, there was no reason to suppose that it would necessarily prepare the way for socialism. Without abandoning his love and admiration for European culture and science, Herzen noted what he called Europe's "surprising incapacity for social revolution,"[7] and looked again to his native land for possible solutions. Herzen's experience of the France of Cavaignac led him to hope that even backward Russia might contain some potentially valuable social institutions and values.

In the 1850s Herzen took from the Slavophiles and the studies of Haxthausen a belief in the repartitional land commune[8] and rejected the Slavophile tendency toward religious and political mythmaking on such topics as Russian Orthodoxy and the beauties of autocratic rule. Herzen appealed to his fellow landowners to recognize the evils of their privileged position, to abolish serfdom, and to act as "apostles" to a long-suffering peasantry. In Marx's terms, Herzen was typically utopian in his moral appeals and petty bourgeois in his defense of obsolete institutions like the peasant commune. At the same time, it was significant that Herzen took seriously, as Marx did not, the social relations of peasant production. According to Herzen, the peasants' ability to work in common according to unwritten but all the more powerful "laws," and their solidarity against the myriad impositions of bureaucrats and policemen, provided important lessons to the peasantry's social betters. In contrast to the parliaments of Western Europe, communes directly involved the majority of the population in a democratic decision-making process which was vital to their immediate interests. For these reasons, Herzen believed that educated Russians could learn more from the commune than they could from the machinations of a profit-hungry bourgeoisie against a demoralized and degraded urban proletariat. Herzen's populism was essentially a commitment to the commune as an indigenous, morally superior social institution whose traditions could serve as the foundation for Russian socialism.[9]

The emancipation of the Russian serfs in 1861 provided rich material for the disillusionment of those (Herzen among them) who had hoped that the government had at last recognized its debt to the long-suffering rural populace. According to the terms of the emancipation, peasants were freed not as individuals but as commune members, and were provided with land allotments which they were required to purchase from their former masters. Through a complicated series of arrangements intended to preserve the gentry from financial ruin, ex-serfs were granted far less land than they had previously cultivated. In some of the rich Black Earth districts of the south, peasants lost 25 per cent of their former holdings. In the less fertile north, peasants received larger allotments for which they paid nearly double the market value.[10] Stringent measures were taken to force peasants to accept the loss of the *otrezki* (the lands "cut off" from the original allotments). One of the more striking methods was to chain the peasant to the plow and compel him to cultivate his new holding, to demonstrate publicly his willingness to labor on and lay claim to the shrunken allotment of land which was now his.

During the period of the "Great Reforms" N. G. Chernyshevskii came to speak for a younger and more indigent generation of radicals, who ridiculed the trust that wealthy social critics like Herzen had placed in the goodwill of Russian landowners and in Alexander II, the "Liberator Tsar." From the first, Chernyshevskii's view of Russian society and the West was more complex than Herzen's. For Chernyshevskii the commune was not the embodiment of decent human relationships. His memories of childhood in the provincial town of Saratov made it impossible for him to believe that peasants miraculously preserved any particular moral and social virtue under the degrading circumstances of Russian rural life.

However, Chernyshevskii's refusal to claim superiority for any Russian social group or institution did not make him into an uncritical champion of the West. The immense gulf which divided the European bourgeoisie from the proletariat appeared to him neither temporary nor a sign that revolution was imminent in Germany, France, or England. And while Chernyshevskii did not consider Russia in any sense immune to capitalism, his reading of English economists did not convince him that Russia was simply England in embryo, with commune peasants inevitably destined for replacement by tenants or hired hands. If a revolutionary political upheaval drastically altered the autocracy's current economic policies, Chernyshevskii believed, it might yet be possible for the commune to provide the basis for a non-capitalist economic development.[11]

To Chernyshevskii, the peasants were as battered, as heavily burdened, but still potentially as vital as their communes. He insisted that Russian radicals look to the peasants as a revolutionary force, while recognizing at the same time that ignorance, irrational violence, and drunkenness were dominant features of peasant life. Unlike Herzen's noble savage, Chernyshevskii's peasant was an ignorant, poorly armed fighter against a hostile material and social environment. As he wrote in 1861, "Only a few clearsighted persons who love the people fiercely can muster the resolution to lay before us these [negative] traits without mitigation."[12] Chernyshevskii's emphasis on the role of violence in peasant life did not lead him to claim, like Bakunin, that the urge to destruction was a creative passion. He argued instead that violence was an inevitable component of any social or political change involving groups which benefited little from civilized patterns of behavior. It was with the acceptance of such difficult truths that Chernyshevskii wrote from Saratov in the 1860s that unlike his kindhearted friend, the novelist Kostomarov, "I am not afraid of dirt, nor of drunken peasants with sticks, nor of massacres."[13]

While Chernyshevskii insisted that the masses were neither helpless victims nor moral teachers for a corrupt intelligentsia, many of his contemporaries felt constrained to choose between these difficult and unsatisfactory alternatives. In the process, they experienced all of the problems which arise when educated people attempt to revolutionize "primitives." G. E. Eliseev insisted that intellectuals unconditionally accept the wisdom of the peasant, and S. N. Nechaev argued that the true revolutionary was a master manipulator of the uninformed masses. P. L. Lavrov assumed, like Nechaev, that peasants were ignorant children,[14] but claimed that educated people had an obligation to enlighten them and develop their hidden talents. According to Lavrov, once peasants were humanized by the efforts of their dedicated teachers, it might be possible to rekindle the spirit of earlier peasant uprisings, which "contained more vital social principles, more solid promises, more threatening and certain prophecies for the future, than all the liberal and radical prophecies against throne and altar that echoed along the banks of the Thames, the Seine, and the Delaware."[15]

Inspired by the writings of Lavrov and Chernyshevskii, more than a thousand young students set forth in 1874 to break down the barriers which divided them from the peasantry they wanted to liberate. In this "movement to go to the people," student radicals tried at all costs to look and sound like peasants; some learned useful trades, others converted to Orthodoxy so as to more easily win the peasants' confidence. They descended upon an astonished peasantry with socialist pamphlets, questionnaires about rural life, and information about agricultural improvements. But peasants proved difficult either to convince or to manipulate. (Both strategies were tried.) For the peasant whose experience of outsiders was limited to the landlord, the tax collector, the police official, or some other urban agent for the imposition of heavier burdens and restrictions, students were simply another object of suspicion. In areas where peasants remembered the beatings inflicted by government punitive expeditions, there was little willingness to risk illegal action on the advice of strangers. At the same time, radicals like Vera Figner and Catherine Breshko-Breshkovskaia were able to gain a substantial measure of trust and support for their efforts. They and others like them evoked a sort of protective response in peasants who spoke with pride of "our radical" and refused to betray their naive and mysterious benefactors to the police. But it was only in Chigirin that Lev Deutsch was able to incite peasants to open rebellion in 1876 by distributing forged manifestos from the tsar.[16]

The response of the state was not as complicated as the reactions of the peasantry. From 1873 onward the police and the army loyally carried out their orders to arrest student radicals. The effectiveness of police efforts led even the saintly Vera Figner to believe that if revolutionaries were to organize peasants, they first had to check the power of the state's machinery of repression. The terrorist strategy adopted by the *Narodnaia Volia* (Peoples' Will) was a result of deeply felt political frustration, combined with a desperate hope that the "disorganization of the state" by means of political assassination would undermine traditional peasant habits of obedience. As the terrorist Stepniak put it,

> the agricultural class is like a latent and mysterious volcano, upon the edge of which the oppressors are heedlessly dancing. . . . This class is so

desperate, so unfortunate, so miserable, that it only needs a spark to make
its hatred burst out into an immense flame which would destroy the
entire edifice of the State and the modern economic order, and with it,
also everything wearing the impress of civilization. . . .[17]

While the terrorists hoped that a politically democratic and socialistic
order would eventually emerge from such a confrontation, the populist
G. V. Plekhanov ridiculed the idea that socialism could result from a
terrorist coup d'état and a primitive peasant rebellion à la Pugachev. It
was obvious to Plekhanov that peasants had to be organized and
educated so that they could reasonably be expected to act as a mass
revolutionary force, capable of building a decent society. To accomplish this purpose, he, Vera Zasulich, and Lev Deutsch set up a non-
terrorist propaganda group called *Cherny Peredel* (Black Repartition) to
oppose the political strategy of the *Narodnaia Volia*. But in fact neither
the terrorist group nor the *Cherny Peredel* was successful. Plekhanov's
organization was unable to develop any real ties with the countryside,
and although the bombs and daggers of the *Narodnaia Volia* put an end
to the reign of Alexander II in 1881, Stepniak's peasant "volcano"
failed to erupt.

The repeated failure of efforts to organize or even appeal to the
peasantry did not weaken the populist commitment of most Russian
radicals. Unable to succeed in their attempts to rapidly politicize the
rural populace, they nevertheless continued to believe that the peasant
majority of the population was the key to Russia's future. Those who
remained in the countryside and managed to escape the police and the
punitive detachments were eventually able to achieve some notable
successes. In the 1880s and 1890s they organized unions of rural
schoolteachers to serve as a kind of bridge between the outside world
and the life of the village. In Tambov and Saratov provinces networks
of mobile libraries were established, where peasants borrowed and
avidly read the stories of Tolstoi and translations of French novels about
the Revolution of 1789, and perused (with substantially less interest) a
variety of pamphlets on socialism and agronomy.[18] The evidence does
not in general suggest that such populist efforts to make contact with the
countryside were based upon a naive faith in peasants or in the all-
emcompassing virtues of the repartitional land commune. Activists like
I. N. Myshkin and P. A. Kropotkin explicitly refused to lay claim to any
uniquely Russian path to socialism, but hoped instead that Russia's

communal peasantry might participate in what the First International had defined as a worldwide socialist movement of working people.[19]

In contrast, the intellectuals who became Marxists believed that Russia would recreate the economic experience of "peasantless" England. They interpreted their failure to gain immediate and grateful popular acceptance as proof that peasants were hopelessly irrational, brutalized, passive, and doomed. Other conclusions were clearly as plausible: Plekhanov might, for example, have taken his disillusioning experience as an indication that Russian radicals understood little about the process of rural political organization. Even the perceptions of political failure and peasant apathy may have been premature, since the areas where students were active in the 1870s became centers of recurrent unrest in later decades—the scene of agrarian strikes by field workers in the 1880s, the formation of populist groups in the 1890s, and the establishment of peasant brotherhoods in the 1900s. The "movement to go to the people" coincided with a massive over-enrollment in local *zemstvo* schools, as the supposedly traditional-minded peasantry spent a healthy percentage of their meager commune funds on education.[20] But the bitterness of anti-peasant feeling expressed by populists on the road to Marxism revealed how thin was the layer of benevolence which covered deeper feelings of contempt for the primitive. By the 1880s a small number of populist intellectuals were already willing to discard the peasant majority of the population in a political sense and to reject peasant institutions as a basis for Russia's economic development. A rather romantic disillusionment with the peasantry led them to turn from the Russian countryside to the cities of the West for models of revolution and progress, and to a new and "active" Russian proletarian class which Marx had defined as revolutionary.[21]

Marxism in Russia

Because the government's censors considered their work "harmless, abstract speculation," the writings of Marx and Engels had long been available to educated Russians. As on so many other occasions, the censors were mistaken in their judgment; the influence of Marxism in Russia would be particularly wide-ranging. Among academic economists and industrialists, there were those who found in *Capital* a source of powerful arguments for the brutally progressive virtues of free enterprise and long working hours. The economist N. I. Ziber celebrated Marxism as the culmination of Ricardian economics, while Moscow factory owners sponsored lectures on the Marxist "proof" that unfettered capitalist initiative represented a step forward in Russia's historical development.[22] In contrast, populists found it easy to accept and use Marxism as a critique of capitalism. Chernyshevskii had written a defense of Engels's study of the English working class, and in 1869 the populist Daniel'son (whose pseudonym was Nikolai ____on) completed the first Russian translation of *Capital*. In 1870, when a Russian factory owner claimed that restrictions on child labor delayed the economic advance which brought civilization to the factory worker, the populist Mikhailovskii based his refutation upon the descriptions of child labor which appeared in *Capital*.[23]

But most populists did not become Marxists. Those who were receptive to his writings did not accept them as a body of comprehensive, scientific laws of social development. It was obvious to the populists that Russia's fate would not be decided by a tiny urban proletariat; Marxism had not been developed with Russian problems in mind. Even Daniel'son, who called himself a Marxist, did not consider it *lèse majesté* to ask Marx to broaden his theoretical framework so that it might better apply to the Russian situation. No populist, not even Daniel'son at the height of his enthusiasm for Marx's work, accepted the dialectical reasoning which made the evils of capitalism the source of future good. Impressed by the Marxian analysis of the horrors of capitalism, they could not bring themselves to believe that the introduction of capitalism was a prerequisite for socialism, or that industrial proletarians constituted the only revolutionary social class. Populists accepted the aspects of Marx's work which corresponded to their hatred of capitalism and their sense of obligation to the poor, and especially to the Russian peasant. Despite the tough-mindedness of Chernyshevskii, and Nechaev's dreadful parody of revolutionary firmness and lack of compromise, most populists were warmhearted individuals who did not separate their interest in economic materialism from a belief in appeals to conscience. Daniel'son, Vorontsov (who used the pseudonym V.V.), and other leading populists assumed that the proletariat was only one of the exploited elements which would eventually carry out a socialist revolution.

The problematic implications of Marxist theory for the Russian situation were particularly evident in 1875, when Friedrich Engels entered into a bitter polemical dispute with the Russian Jacobin P. N. Tkachev. Tkachev argued that a dedicated band of revolutionary conspirators could carry out a coup d'état, halt the advance of capitalism, and build socialism on the basis of collectivist peasant traditions and practices. As a historical materialist, Engels found it easy to ridicule both the idea that peasants were socialist "by instinct" and the hope that the revolutionary determination of a few conspirators could nullify the laws of historical development. It was clear to Engels that Russia lacked the material foundations for socialism (although he granted that Russia might avoid capitalism if a proletarian socialist revolution took place in the West). At the same time, it should be noted that for all his materialism Engels was quite willing to ignore the material reality of the institutions and social classes which dominated Russian life. He did not believe that the ubiquitous peasant commune created any politically significant patterns of behavior; the majority of commune peasants were less important to him than the minority of kulaks and proletarians created by Russia's capitalist development.

Tkachev rejected Engels's arguments, but his very insistence on immediate revolutionary action, whatever the degree of Russia's preparedness for socialist revolution, was a direct response to the horrifying descriptions of exploitation which Engels had provided in his study of the English working class. Tkachev wrote as a revolutionary burdened by a "Marxist" conception of historical development which suggested that the evils of capitalism were all that Russians could hope to experience for a long time to come. His voluntarism was generated by precisely the same fears which later drove Lenin to what his critics called "adventurism" and opportunism. Tkachev found the implications of Marxian economic determinism both heartless and politically irresponsible. He denounced Russian Marxists for their callous and inhuman ability to

> understand that under present economic and political conditions, in Russia a correct and in any way reasonable organization of workers' groups is absolutely impossible. But this does not disturb them. Why then, they will wait. They do not lack patience! The people's grief, the people's tears are not their grief, their tears! Why should they compromise themselves in risky enterprises? They want to act only when it is a sure thing. It is impossible to act now and be certain. We, all the

revolutionaries, understand this very well, and they understand it better than we. But we are not afraid of the risk. Neither we nor the people have anything to regret, anything to lose![24]

In 1877, when the populist Mikhailovskii wrote to Marx to ask him to spell out the precise implications of *Capital* for Russia, Marx replied quite frankly that his studies of West European capitalism offered Russia's revolutionaries no unconditional solutions. As Marx put it, his work was not to be considered a "historico-philosophical theory of the general path fatally imposed upon all peoples, whatever their historical circumstances." He admitted that "history offered Russia" a chance to avoid capitalism if its relentless advance were somehow checked.[25]

The reluctance of Marx to make definitive pronouncements on either the subject of the commune or the prospects for revolution in Russia was made unmistakably clear in his letter of 1881 to Vera Zasulich. Zasulich, troubled by the paralyzing implications of a capitalist- and proletarian-centered Marxism for radical activists in a peasant society, had written to ask if Marx believed that Russian socialists could do nothing but watch as peasants were driven from the land to the streets of the cities in search of wages. Were radicals simply to live for the future, calculating all the while how many decades had to pass before the peasants' land was in the hands of the bourgeoisie, and how many "centuries, perhaps" before Russia's economic and social development made it appropriate to fight for socialism? Responding in a manner which has been described as "aussi peu 'Marxiste' que possible," Marx suggested that in Russia

> thanks to an extraordinary concatenation of circumstances, the peasant commune, still existing on a national scale, can gradually shake off its primitive qualities and develop directly as an element of collective production on a national scale. Precisely because it is a coeval of capitalist production, it is in a position to assimilate its positive achievements without going through all its horrors.

While the analysis given in *Capital* proved nothing for or against the viability of the peasant commune, Marx concluded,

> the special research into this subject which I conducted, the materials for which I obtained from original sources, has convinced me that this community is the mainspring of Russia's social generation, but in order that it might function as such one would first have to eliminate the

deleterious influences which assail it from every quarter and then to ensure the conditions normal for spontaneous development.[26]

Marx's researches were undertaken with the advice and aid of Daniel'son, and his letter to Zasulich reflected a clear acceptance of Daniel'son's populist argument that commune peasants were still desperately holding their own against the encroachments of capitalism.[27] More importantly, Marx's writings indicated that he had begun at last to move beyond the history of England's economic experience to reflect upon a contemporary problem of economic development. He had concluded that "even from the purely economic point of view only the development of the commune can lead Russia's agriculture out of its blind alley; other means, such as, for instance, the English system of capitalist landholding, would surely prove unsuccessful. The English system is completely incapable of fulfilling the conditions on which the development of Russia's agriculture depends."[28]

Marx was as impressed by the political strategy of the *Narodnaia Volia* as he was by the economics of Daniel'son. Although it may have been that Marx and Engels considered terrorism the best that Russia could do in the absence of a revolutionary proletariat, Marx nevertheless called the *Narodnaia Volia* "the leading detachment of the revolutionary movement in Europe."[29] In contrast, he wrote of the exiled members of Plekhanov's *Cherny Peredel* that most of them "had abandoned Russia voluntarily—in contrast to the terrorists whose heads are at stake—to form a so-called propaganda party. In order to carry on propaganda in Russia, they come to Geneva. How is that for *quid pro quo?*"[30] Marx's reflections on Russian problems formed a striking contrast to his earlier writings, and to the dogmatic certainties of Plekhanov, who would emerge as his foremost Russian disciple.

Plekhanov has been called the "father of Russian Marxism," and if Marxism is defined as an ideology derived above all from the economic example of England and the political traditions of England and France, the designation is accurate. A romantic about Western achievements, a disillusioned populist and a selective materialist, Plekhanov refused to confront the issues raised by Marx's correspondence with Daniel'son, Mikhailovskii, and Zasulich. For Plekhanov, the laws of history as they were embodied in the history of British capitalism could not be discarded at will or arbitrarily "chosen" by populists of high moral character. Regardless, therefore, of what seemed humane and desirable to noble-minded idealists, "capitalism goes on its way, dislodging the independent producers from their unstable conditions and creating an army of workers in Russia by the same tried and true methods which had created modern English society."[31]

Plekhanov considered himself an heir of the Westernizers, although it must be said that he was far less critical of the bourgeoisie than Belinskii had been. In his Westernism, and in his bitter rejection of Russian society as barbaric (or in nineteenth-century terminology "Asiatic," or "semi-Asiatic"), there was something of the impassioned romantic's rejection of a false religion and conversion to the only true faith. For Plekhanov, all hopes for Russian socialism rested on the further development of Western political traditions, economic institutions, and culture. Certain that the emancipation of 1861 had drawn Russia into the world of bourgeois civilization, he believed that before long a revolutionary Russian bourgeoisie would come forward to champion the "Rights of Man" just as the French had done in 1789.[32] Plekhanov attributed all delays in this process to what he termed the "Asiatic" character of Russian society. From the 1880s onward "Asia" became for Plekhanov a kind of shorthand explanation for Russia's backwardness. Russia was labeled an "Oriental despotism," while primitive commune peasants were "Asiatic" in their indifference to the outside world and in their lack of "solidarity, broad social interests, or ideas." Accordingly, Plekhanov found the Russian peasant no better than the Chinese, a "barbarian-tiller of the soil," cruel and merciless, "a beast of burden" whose life provided no opportunity for the luxury of thought.[33]

It was in the context of such hopes for the bourgeoisie and fears of the peasantry that Plekhanov rejected Marx's correspondence with the populists, and focused instead upon Marx's analysis of Western European history. In 1883, when Plekhanov formed the Marxist "Emancipation of Labor" group, he proposed a "radical reconsideration" of agrarian relations, one which took into account the inevitable development of progressive, Western-style capitalism.[34] The explicitly proletarian and "pro-capitalist" emphasis of the new Marxist group served to set off a controversy over the peasantry, the proletariat, and the forms of capitalist progress which would continue through the revolutions of 1917. The protests of L. N. Tikhomirov exemplified populist attitudes toward Plekhanov's brand of Marxism. In Tikhomirov's words, "We must not deprive the peasant of his land; we must not develop the proletariat; not implant capitalism but increase the strength of the people economically, intellectually and morally."[35]

In response, Plekhanov made use of Russian agricultural statistics which suggested (1) that capitalism had taken deep root in Russia, (2) that the commune was disintegrating, and (3) that peasants were hopelessly conservative. His use of evidence was extremely selective and his tone was imbued with anger at wrongheaded populists and disgust with peasants who rejected the enlightenment offered them by a generation of revolutionaries. Plekhanov relied in particular upon the work of V. I. Orlov, a *zemstvo* statistician whose work documented the existence of economic inequalities among commune peasants in Moscow province. Like most Russian economists and statisticians of the time, Orlov believed that the evidence indicated that the commune was still a viable institution whose members were more equal and whose agricultural practices were no more backward than in non-commune districts.[36] It was therefore particularly significant that Plekhanov took Orlov's investigations as conclusive evidence that the central fact of Russian rural life was the emergence of kulaks and proletarians. Although Plekhanov did not make the claim that either group was numerically dominant, the populist focus on the peasant majority who neither hired labor nor hired themselves out to others would nevertheless become his proof that populists were ignorant of the realities of Russian rural life.

In some of his early writings Plekhanov was scrupulous enough to refer to Marx's favorable comments on the commune, but he no longer did so in *Our Differences* (1885), his Marxist polemic against the populists. In this work he vilified the populists for their supposed denial that capitalism existed in Russian agriculture.[37] According to Plekhanov, it was the populists' beloved *obshchina* which no longer existed. Since rural differentiation had already made a mockery of the claims made for "eternal" commune principles, efforts to preserve those principles would only strengthen the kulaks who were currently engaged in the task of ruining their poorer commune "brothers." According to Plekhanov, economic competition among the petty bourgeoisie was eventually bound to result in the complete triumph of a kulak elite over a proletarianized peasantry. Indifferent to the evidence of commune-based economic innovation cited by the leading economists of his day, Plekhanov claimed that one of capitalism's great historical merits was to destroy the weakness and inertia which, as he put it, "give such pain to educated people in any agricultural society."[38] According to Plekhanov, the fruitless populist search for signs of progress and vitality in the obsolete institutions of small producers revealed a typically narrow, petty bourgeois determination to ignore the lessons of England's historical experience.

Critical of the political terrorism of the *narodovoltsi*, Plekhanov ridiculed the naiveté of Daniel'son's attempt to develop a strategy for economic modernization without raising the question of political revolution: "Let us suppose that the peasant commune is really our anchor of salvation. But who will carry out the reforms postulated by Nikolai ___ on? The tsarist government? Pestilence is better than such reformers and their reforms! Socialism being introduced by Russian policemen—what a chimera. . . ."[39]

As the defender of a new Marxist orthodoxy, Plekhanov found himself more "Marxist" than Engels, who coolly distanced himself from the launching of anti-populist crusades and suggested that Plekhanov attempt "serious research work" on the agrarian question instead of "polemical articles."[40] On political grounds, Engels feared that Plekhanov's vicious denunciations might weaken the terrorist efforts of surviving *narodovoltsi*, whom he considered still capable of carrying out a populist revolution in Russia. It should of course be noted that for Engels such a revolution would inevitably be petty bourgeois, while for the populists it would be socialist, or at least "socialistic."[41] But Plekhanov did not waver, and in an article written in 1887 he succinctly expressed what was thereafter to be the orthodox Russian Marxist position on the peasant question. In his view, the Russian revolutionary movement, which had tried to minister to the needs of the peasantry, had met with no peasant support, sympathy, or understanding. Their political indifference and intellectual backwardness, claimed Plekhanov, were proof that peasants were traditionally the strongest supporters of Russian absolutism.[42]

The harshness of such statements would return to haunt Plekhanov in the famine year of 1891, when one-third of a million Russian peasants died of hunger and disease. The explanations offered for the famine disaster reflected the growing bitterness of the conflict between the allegedly heartless Russian Marxists and their allegedly naive populist opponents. Plekhanov and "legal Marxists" like Struve, Tugan-Baranovskii, and Bulgakov attributed the famine to Russian backwardness, and in particular to the indisputable facts of low agricultural productivity and rapid population increase. The populists Daniel'son and Vorontsov blamed the equally indisputable fall in world grain prices and a government modernization policy which encouraged industry at the expense of agriculture, education, and the general popular welfare. N. K. Mikhailovskii, aware by this time that Russian Marxism was taking shape as a proletarian-centered movement, argued that honest and consistent Marxists would callously welcome the famine as a progressive historical phenomenon which hastened the separation of the producer from the means of production.[43]

For the populists, the ruin of the peasantry was an unmitigated evil. Even aside from the incalculable human tragedy involved, they did not believe that entrepreneurs and farmhands were necessarily more progressive in an economic sense than the small producers. In 1892 V. P. Vorontsov published a massive summary of *zemstvo* statistical investigations of rural life which suggested that neither communal institutions, nor illiteracy, nor superstition posed serious obstacles to rational decision-making when peasants faced what they considered viable alternatives. Making use of a far wider range of empirical evidence than had any Russian Marxist of the time, Vorontsov argued that the peasantry were to be distinguished from other social elements not by the abstractions of "Asiatic" backwardness but by the disproportionate financial burdens they carried and by their limited access to knowledge and capital. The kulak, so deplorably necessary to the Marxist analysis, was apparently no more enlightened in his economic behavior than the poorer peasants. Vorontsov presented abundant evidence to suggest that kulak wealth was based above all on usury, rather than the use of modern tools and techniques. Commune peasants introduced new methods of field use, Vorontsov reported, and in areas where improved plows were cheap and easily available there was no evidence of peasant reluctance to use them.[44]

According to Daniel'son, when the autocracy weakened the commune by forcing the peasant majority to suffer for the sake of a government-aided minority of industrialists and financiers, it was "gratuitously" submitting to doctrinaire Marxist laws of economic development. Daniel'son quoted from Marx's letter to Mikhailovskii and argued that the Russian economy could still be based upon the commune:

> We do not have to wait until all the peasants are deprived of their land, and replaced by a capitalist agriculture. . . . We must graft scientific

agriculture and modern large-scale industry onto the commune, and at
the same time give the commune a form that will make it an effective tool
for the organization of large-scale industry and the transformation of the
form of that industry from a capitalist to a public one.[45]

Plekhanov dismissed such arguments as subjective, romantic, and
economically naive, but he did not undertake a serious economic
investigation of his own in order to counter them. Instead, he ridiculed
the populist willingness to reject the painful reality of capitalism in
order to wallow in unassailably moral but futile regrets for the peasants'
tragic plight. According to Plekhanov, Marxists did not "welcome" the
famine. Famines were the inevitable result of an economic backwardness which could only end with the further development of capitalism,
the only mechanism which history had provided for the modernization
of a peasant society. Plekhanov argued that no Marxist wanted the ruin
of the peasantry:

> the better the condition of the peasantry, the sooner would the commune
> break up. Moreover, that breakup can take place in conditions which are
> either more or less advantageous for the people. The "pupils" [of Marx]
> must "strive" to see to it that the breakup takes place in the conditions
> most advantageous for the people.[46]

Since Plekhanov never spelled out what he meant by "advantageous"
conditions for the *mir*'s disappearance, there remained a contradiction
between this vague philanthropic statement and his repeated assertions
that peasants had no future in a modern society. In 1892 Plekhanov
irritably warned that if peasants did not listen to Social Democratic
warnings of their coming expropriation by the forces of capital, they
had only themselves to blame. Under the system advocated by Social
Democrats, there would be no poor peasants and no landlords.[47]

Plekhanov's arguments were quite consistent with the analysis
implicit in the major works of Marx and Engels. In general, Marx and
Engels had been content to assume that only the socialized industrial
process of capitalist production could provide the basis for a socialist
revolution. Toward the end of his life, when Marx began to take
seriously the Russian peasant experience of collective decision-making
and common labor, he did not go on to revise his major theoretical
works so that they would reflect the change in his position. In
Plekhanov's writings the prevailing assumptions of Marx and Engels
became more doctrinaire and explicit, as the peasant majority became

historically irrelevant, or a stubborn obstacle to human progress. Although such attitudes were hardly conducive to the development of a constructive revolutionary peasant strategy, they nevertheless became widespread in the late nineteenth century. In the 1890s Plekhanov proudly boasted that he would make of *Capital* a "Procrustean bed" for the populists.[48] But his real accomplishment may have been to perform that task for the Russian Marxist movement.

3

Lenin as an Orthodox Marxist

> We have all of us sufficient courage
> to bear the pains of others.
>
> LA ROCHEFOUCAULD

BY THE LATE NINETEENTH CENTURY many capitalist and non-capitalist modernizers were agreed that peasants had to pay the costs of economic development, even if they were destroyed in the process. In Russia at least, the first half of this proposition was more openly recognized than the second. Particularly after the famine disaster of 1891, no government official was willing to publicly echo Finance Minister Vyshnegradskii's notorious "We shall eat less, but we will export grain." But "eating less" remained the unavoidable choice of many peasants even after such tactless government statements became impolitic. Under Sergei Witte, who replaced Vyshnegradskii in 1892, peasants were still disproportionately taxed to pay for Russia's economic development program. The government continued to fear that taxing potential entrepreneurs would weaken incentives for investment, while taxing the gentry was avoided because it might weaken the autocracy's most reliable political supporters. Rural education and the supply of cheap credit to small producers remained low-priority items in the state budget. Instead of changing the basic outlines of the Vyshnegradskii strategy, Witte and his supporters argued that peasant poverty and backwardness were a consequence of the survival in Russia of the outmoded repartitional land commune. Like their Marxist contemporaries, "progressive" state officials looked to the West for proof that rural development could only be the task of private landowners acting on their own.[1]

These were audacious claims, in view of traditional government policies and contemporary economic research. Within the autocracy, the fear that peasants deprived of communal land guarantees might become lawless, even revolutionary, had traditionally served to moderate the influence of commune critics. In the 1890s K. P. Pobedonostsev, Witte's archenemy, would continue to argue for the commune as a bulwark against Western-style proletarian revolution. Russia's professional economists were generally still agreed that the commune was an economically viable institution; although the existence of rural inequality was widely recognized, it was believed that the flawed security of the commune served nevertheless to ease some of the initial pressures and burdens imposed by rapid economic development.[2] But by the turn of the century, pro-commune arguments and the evidence which supported them appeared less and less convincing both to the government and to its Marxist critics. Within the bureaucracy, time-honored commitments to guarantees of social security gradually gave way to the more compelling fear that Russia would suffer the fate of nineteenth-century China or India unless urban and rural entrepreneurs took on the task of modernization. Only after a more or less painful capitalist transformation (so the argument went) could the problem of rural poverty be effectively dealt with.

Such arguments were quite consistent with the European Marxist "orthodoxy" which had taken shape after the death of Marx in 1883. Neither Engels nor any of the other Marxists who rose to prominence in the last decades of the nineteenth century had shown any eagerness to pursue the implications of Marx's correspondence with the Russian populists. The more constructive comments which Engels and Marx had made on the transformation of rural life were forgotten. Instead, Engels insisted that peasants had to "recognize that they are lost beyond saving"; an inexorable dialectic of historical development was held to require peasant ruin as a precondition for the achievement of socialism.[3] In the 1880s, the obsoleteness of peasants and peasant institutions began to attain for Marxists the status of an axiomatic truth, requiring elucidation and illustration rather than empiral proof.

European Marxists who did not accept the peasantry's death sentence came to be called revisionists. The revisionist movement, a product of the hope for peaceful reform generated by the growth of legal political opportunities in late nineteenth-century Western Europe, was also a response to the curious fact that despite a worldwide agrarian crisis, the supposedly obsolete small producer was managing to survive in competition with giant capitalist enterprise.[4] In this context, the annihilation of the peasantry (always a touchy issue for Marxists) began to seem not only morally reprehensible but unnecessary in economic terms. The peculiar conjunction of "bourgeois" political opportunity and a non-vanishing peasantry led German Social Democrats like Eduard Bernstein and Georg von Vollmar to argue that Marxists might legitimately appeal to the peasantry not only as petty capitalists but on socialist grounds. In France the revisionist position was exemplified by Jean Jaurès, who claimed that socialism did not require the expropriation of the small landholder. While the views of Jaurès were ideologically unacceptable to the French Socialist Party, his awareness that it was politically dangerous to ignore peasant interests was taken seriously. At the party congress of 1894, a resolution about the differentiation of the peasantry into bourgeois and proletarian elements noted that "it is not up to the socialists to accelerate this development, since their task is not to separate property from labor but to unite these two factors of production in the same person."[5] Such arguments drew the wrath of Engels, who ridiculed the idea of the small proprietor as socialist. As he put it, "We shall never make socialists out of peasants protecting their property any more than [we shall make them] out of artisans hoping to remain entrepreneurs."[6] To prevent such errors from recurring, Engels helped Karl Kautsky to develop a more anti-peasant and theoretically consistent formulation for German Social Democrats to follow. In the Erfurt Program no hope was held out to the peasant as either small producer or potential socialist. The only remedy offered for rural poverty was a system of large-scale social ownership of the means of production, to be established at some future date. It was asserted as well that only the proletariat could establish such a system, because all other social elements had a material stake in the preservation of the existing order.

The revisionists rejected all such arguments. At the Breslau Social Democratic Congress of 1895, Eduard David called for the expropriation of estate owners, the establishment of model farms on state land, and an increase in the amount of property controlled by rural communes and associations.[7] To raise peasant agricultural productivity, Vollmar demanded that Social Democrats support the formation of cooperatives to make capital and machinery available to the peasantry at a minimal cost.[8] Vollmar's arguments were rejected by the congress, as were all the revisionist proposals. Relying upon the most dogmatic pronouncements of Marx and Engels, speaker after orthodox speaker denounced the revisionists. Commitments to the proletariat were reaffirmed, warnings against the dangers of opportunist concession to the petty bourgeoisie were repeated, and all proposals for land reform were rejected as measures which "set before the eyes of the peasantry the improvement of their position, that is, the confirmation of private ownership."[9]

The orthodox Marxist position on the peasant question was spelled out by Karl Kautsky in his immensely influential *Die Agrarfrage* (1897). Politically, the major thrust of Kautsky's argument was that revolutionaries could not promise any protection to the peasant as a small producer. Although Kautsky conceded that small proprietors were *not* disappearing, their survival and their economic successes did not change his prior assessment of their significance and potential. In Kautsky's view, peasants were incapable of rational or constructive action, but they could on occasion appear to disprove the laws of economic development because of their peculiar willingness to engage in "superhuman effort" and to accept a "subhuman" level of existence. In possession of their "pygmy" parcels of land, they retained their backward economic practices, together with the illusion that they could permanently outlast the large-scale entrepreneur.[10] In the long run, wrote Kautsky, the more efficient large-scale capitalist enterprise would inevitably triumph; in the short run, measures for land reform had to be understood as nothing more than "fetters which chain the peasant to his property." Kautsky, whose critics called him "the Torquemada of Marxism," insisted that he was not a heartless promoter of peasant ruin. His strategy was to appeal for the support of peasants as citizens who would benefit from such reforms as progressive taxation, the right of initiative and referendum, and the extension of civil liberties. On economic issues, Kautsky claimed:

> The better the position of the small farmer . . . the sooner he will cease to struggle against industry on a large scale. If he is accustomed to a good living, he will rebel against the privations incident to a protracted struggle and will the *sooner prefer to take his place* with the proletariat. . . . He will pass directly into the ranks of the militant purposeful proletarians and thus hasten the victory of the proletariat.[11]

How or why a peasant earning a decent living on a small plot of land would want to become a militant, landless proletarian was never made clear.

The victory of German orthodoxy over revisionism in the late nineteenth century represented a rejection of reformist socialism. As we shall see, the lessons which Russian Marxists would derive from the experience of the most powerful Marxist political party in Europe was that it was not for principled Marxists to formulate a socialist peasant program.

Lenin

In 1893, Lenin entered the polemical arena which served the Russian intelligentsia as a substitute for political activity. By that time he was twenty-three, and a committed Marxist. Between 1893 and 1900 his writings reflected a fanatic anti-populism and an eager acceptance of the challenges of Marxist revisionism. Although he derived many of his general attitudes from Kautsky, Lenin's economics were more rigid and his politics far more flexible. Denying the validity of all evidence and arguments that the small producer could ever survive in competition with the giant capitalist entrepreneur, he insisted on the inevitability of peasant ruin. But unlike many of his Marxist contemporaries, Lenin's belief in the peasant's dismal fate did not lead him to lose interest in the peasant question. Instead, he polemicized against the populists, formulated programs aimed at gaining peasant support, and made use of his Siberian exile to complete a massive study intended to combat "sentimental" populist arguments on scientific and empirical grounds. From the outset, Lenin's writings reflected an awareness (uncommon among Russian Marxists of his time) that Russian revolutionaries could not very well ignore the peasant majority of the population.

The Errors of the Populists

In their failure to understand the dialectic of historical development and in their defense of the small producer, populists were for Lenin the despicable Russian counterparts of the German revisionists. Content with "small deeds" and "pseudo-scholarly" investigations, they abandoned the heroic, illegal, and violent political struggles of the older generation of revolutionary democrats. In a lengthy pamphlet entitled

"What the 'Friends of the People' Are and How They Fight the Social Democrats" (1894), he ridiculed the "subjectivist" hopes of the populist Mikhailovskii, who had written:

> Our task is not to rear, out of our national depths, a civilization that is positively "original" but neither is it to transplant Western civilization to our own country *in toto*, together with all the contradictions that are tearing it apart; we must take what is good from wherever we can; and whether it be our own or foreign is not a matter of principle but of practical convenience.[12]

"How simple," Lenin commented, as if intellectuals could take from the medieval order "the laborer's ownership of the means of production and from the new capitalist forms . . . liberty, equality, enlightenment and culture." Certain that history proceeded according to discrete and rigidly ordered phases of development, Lenin scornfully observed that progress was not simply a matter of "plucking elements from various social formations,"[13] whatever muddleheaded thinkers like Mikhailovskii might pretend.

Lenin found the populists sensitive to the evils of capitalism, but curiously blind to the "Asiatic abuse of human dignity" which prevailed in pre-capitalist rural life.[14] They somehow failed to notice that bigotry, subservience to authority, barbaric superstition, and a vicious abuse of women flourished within the "peasant idyll." In contrast, Lenin insisted, the brutality of capitalism forced the patriarchal peasantry out of medieval stagnation,

> breaking the chains of enslavement to the local "work-giver" and disclosing the basis of exploitation in general, of class exploitation as distinct from the depredations of a particular viper. . . . [Capitalism drew] the peasant population, cowed and forced down to the level of cattle, *en masse* into the vortex of complex social and political life. . . .[15]

As indifferent as Plekhanov to evidence which suggested that peasants possessed any significant forms of collective life, Lenin avoided any extended discussion of the *mir*. Because peasant families cultivated separate allotments, he considered them "isolated producers."[16] Lenin's Russian countryside was filled with peasants who were like Marx's "sack of potatoes," lacking in social solidarity or historically significant institutions, caught between their former feudal masters and a greedy bourgeoisie. Any Russian of the 1890s who read only Lenin's writings would have been unable to guess that the repartitional land commune still commanded the loyalties of the overwhelming majority of the population. His failure to give any evidence which suggested that a peasant social life existed outside the structures of exploitation imposed by the gentry or the kulaks made the populist claims for the commune cited in his writings appear particularly fanciful—pure assertions rather than judgments based upon the examination of more economic evidence than Lenin was ever to confront. Dismissing the material connection between the majority of the peasantry and the repartitional land commune, Lenin discussed only the social and economic circumstances which made the peasant into a competitive individualist or a ruined proletarian. Refusing to entertain the possibility that the commune might accustom peasants to collectivist political or economic behavior, he denounced the economist N. K. Karyshev as a "liberal cretin" for suggesting that the commune contained equalizing mechanisms which might diffuse the benefits of agricultural improvement among its poorer elements. As Lenin characteristically demanded, "Is this naiveté or is it something worse?"[17] In his view, the only function of the commune was to immobilize the weakest rural elements within a wretched economic situation which forced them into semi-feudal relationships with the gentry.

It should be noted that leading contemporary economists like Karyshev, A. I. Chuprov, N. A. Kablukov, A. A. Manuilov, and A. S. Posnikov were equally aware of the conservative traditions and functions of the commune, but did not consider them rigid or impervious to change. Instead, they took seriously the evidence that communes introduced technological innovations. As proponents of economic development and as consultants to the government on issues of economic policy, they attempted to devise strategies which might make use of the commune to render the process of primitive accumulation less painful for the peasant majority of the population.[18] But for Lenin, any reference whatsoever to constructive commune activity was a sign of the reactionary economic romanticism which, as he put it, "satisfied the narrow need for organization within a patriarchal, immobile society and wanted to apply it to a totally transformed society."[19]

After reading a number of statistical studies which documented inequalities within the commune, Lenin confidently denounced the populists for their superficiality and lack of sophistication and made the ludicrous claim that both urban and rural Russia were essentially capitalist in 1894.[20] Even the apparently uncontroversial populist assertion that most Russians were commune peasants living on inadequate allotments of land came under attack: Lenin claimed that most Russian peasants were "really" proletarians. If either poverty or seasonal or part-time wage labor could be demonstrated, Lenin refused to believe that rights of land use, membership in the repartitional commune, or the ownership of a horse or a cow made peasants less proletarian. In his view, "Capitalism had never anywhere been associated with the complete divorce of workers from the land; yet it was capitalism nevertheless."[21]

To Lenin, the cardinal error of the populists lay in their failure to recognize that the fundamental issue was not unequal distribution of wealth, but a system of production relations which subordinated labor to the owner of capital. Preferring instead to idealize the mythical "average" peasant, they denounced the villainous capitalist as an outsider rather than a central participant in Russian rural life. At the same time, populists who professed to hate the capitalist system were quite willing in practice to maintain and develop petty capitalist, i.e., peasant, economic relationships. Like Marx, Lenin saw the "defenders of the peasantry" as petty bourgeois and utopian socialists whose abstract moral concerns only served to obscure the realities of class struggle. Glorying in denunciations of the "evildoer" and proud of their noble preference for human happiness over human suffering, they denied what was for Lenin the hard truth that historical progress was inevitably costly in human terms. In Lenin's view, peasants had suffered in vain under the feudal system; their sufferings under capitalism would at least culminate in industrial and socialist prosperity for all.[22]

As Lenin pointed out, the populist emphasis upon distribution of wealth rather than control over the means of production led them to categorize impoverished intellectuals, peasants, and urban proletarians all as "working people." Denying the Marxist contention that unalterable conflicts of interest resulted from differing relationships to the means of production, they appealed not only to the poor's hatred of the rich but to motives of honesty, generosity, and fairness. To Lenin, the crucial fact was of course that whatever conscience-stricken individuals might do, capitalists as a class would never meet the needs of the poor by sacrificing the economic system which produced their wealth. Even the "best" of the capitalists (to say nothing of the uncommitted intellectuals) would inevitably deplore the violence of the mob more than the coercive acts of an oppressive government. For Lenin as for Marx, petty bourgeois and utopian denials of the class basis of political and social behavior reflected a fundamental lack of seriousness.

The Revolutionary Peasant

In every mention of the peasant in Lenin's early writings Soviet scholars have attempted to establish Lenin's awareness of the need for a worker–peasant alliance.[23] But in fact, Lenin seldom discussed questions of peasant political strategy during this period. His certainty that peasants were being destroyed by advancing capitalism did not evoke in him any hopes for peasant revolution against their oppressors. In the tradition of the "Communist Manifesto," *The Eighteenth Brumaire of Louis Bonaparte*, and *Capital*, Lenin found in 1895 that the small producer still "stands aloof from the struggle; he is still tied by his tiny enterprise to the old bourgeois system: and although he is oppressed by the capitalist system he is incapable of understanding the true causes of his oppression."[24] When Lenin wrote of the rural proletariat, whose support he considered an "essential" condition for the victory of the working class, his expectations were minimal. Assuming as he did that only the life of the city could generate true revolutionary consciousness, he observed that in rural areas even proletarians were backward, isolated, and fragmented, "capable only of sullen desperation and not of intelligent and persistent protest and struggle."[25]

Given such reservations, it was significant that Lenin nevertheless included an agrarian section in every draft party program which he formulated in the period before 1905. And here as elsewhere one may recognize the tension between his sound political instincts and the demands of his Marxist orthodoxy. Following Plekhanov and Kautsky, Lenin believed that while serfs might rebel against their feudal masters, members of the petty bourgeoisie were incapable of revolutionary political behaviour. For this reason, although his economic analyses had been focused upon the triumph of capitalism, Lenin's political appeals to the peasantry presupposed the existence of a predominantly feudal agrarian economy. In a draft program of 1895, he developed a set of anti-feudal peasant demands which included (1) abolition of redemption payments imposed as part of the emancipation reform process, (2) return of the *otrezki* which kept peasants dependent upon their former masters, (3) abolition of collective responsibility for tax payment, and (4) suspension of all laws which prevented peasants from "doing as they will" with their allotments.[26] At one point, he even suggested that Social Democrats support a bourgeois nationalization of the land.[27] From Lenin's perspective, such demands would be both politically popular and principled, since they would accelerate the transformation of the peasantry into either individualistic, capitalist-oriented proprietors or hired hands. In 1897, Lenin wrote that Social Democrats should no ignore the peasantry, although he conceded that Social Democrats were so few in number that work among the peasantry was "inopportune."[28]

Even this level of concern with a Marxist peasant strategy set Lenin's programs apart from the "Manifesto of the First Congress of the Russian Social Democratic Labor Party" (1898), written by P. B. Struve while Lenin was in exile. This document made no reference to the relationship between proletariat and peasantry, or to the more general issue of securing allies in the political struggles against tsarism. While the "weak and cowardly" Russian bourgeoisie was castigated for failing to play its proper historical role, the peasantry was not singled out for any special notice. Peasants were in fact mentioned only once in the whole document, and then only as one of several exploited groups which participated in the struggle against an oppressive autocracy.[29] As the neo-populist Victor Chernov would observe, there was a fantasylike quality to the manifesto of 1898, which was written as if peasants formed such an insignificant minority within the general population that there was no need for any extended discussion of their political role.[30]

In contrast, Lenin's draft for a party program in 1899 provided somewhat more scope for proletarian cooperation with the peasantry. (It would have been difficult to have provided less.) Claiming that Social Democrats needed peasant support in order to destroy the survivals of feudalism, Lenin went on to argue that to ignore the revolutionary peasant elements was to commit "grave political errors" and break with the basic tenets of Marxism.[31] He contended that the history of peasant revolts had demonstrated that peasants were capable of acting as a positive revolutionary force, and appealed to Russian Marxists to distinguish between conservative and revolutionary peasants just as Marx had done in his "Address" to the German workers of 1850.[32] It should of course be emphasized that for Lenin peasants were revolutionary only in their opposition to feudalism; peasant anti-capitalism remained for him petty bourgeois and reactionary, a form of the peasantry's rejection of economic growth and development. Although he recognized the complex character of peasant dependence on landlords and kulaks, Lenin had not yet developed a strategy for the organization of peasants according to the differing degree of their exploitation. Even more importantly, he did not deal with the mass of commune peasants who neither hired labor nor hired themselves out to others, except to claim that most of them were "really" proletarians. Politically he had not yet confronted the fundamental social realities of Russian rural life.

Russian Rural Capitalism

Lenin's analysis of rural capitalism was greatly influenced by the work of Plekhanov and Kautsky. Like Plekhanov, Lenin incessantly and inaccurately claimed that populists ignored the existence of kulaks and rural proletarians in the Russian countryside. He contrasted the statistician V. Ye. Postnikov's demonstration of economic differences among various types of peasant households with the "usual" populist emphasis upon the income of a mythical average peasant household (without mentioning that Postnikov was himself a populist).[33] In fact, there were few populists of Lenin's time who denied the fact of rural differentiation. Most were agreed, however, that since only a tiny minority were either kulak or proletarian it made sense to concentrate on the majority of subsistence peasants who participated in the operations of the repartitional land commune. It was Lenin who insisted again and again in his writings of the 1890s that the issue most worthy of study was the development of capitalism.

In taking this approach Lenin was following in the footsteps of Plekhanov and Kautsky. And in his enthusiasm for Kautsky's attack upon the revisionists he did not seem to notice that Kautsky had no constructive peasant policy. Although the Kautskian determinism which doomed the peasant and his defenders was clearly at odds with his own interest as a revolutionary activist in a predominantly peasant society, Lenin seemed unable to recognize (much less resolve) this conflict. The German Marxist perspective and his own heartfelt anti-populism drove him to search out all possible indications of a significant proletarian presence in the countryside. At the same time, his Marxism suggested that peasants were revolutionary only in their struggle against the survivals of feudalism. These contradictions were everywhere in evidence in *The Development of Capitalism in Russia* (1899), Lenin's major work of Marxist economics.

Written during his years of exile in Siberia, *The Development of Capitalism in Russia* was Lenin's attempt to demonstrate that within and outside the commune, in the city and in the countryside, Russia was seething with all the contradictions "inherent in every economy and every order of capitalism."[34] Individuals were struggling for economic independence, land and capital were being concentrated in the hands of a minority, and a growing rural proletariat was exploited by the merchant class. Lenin's data suggested that the Russian agricultural economy could no longer be described as a rudimentary network of local markets linking up a scattered group of feudal landlords and serflike peasants. "Money-profit" had begun to dominate the Russian countryside, and the farmers' product was increasingly subject to a national and even an international market. The growth of usury had set in motion a process of economic development which would inevitably result in the triumph of industrial capital and the formation of a predominantly proletarian workforce.[35]

Lenin's analysis contained a number of serious flaws. Like Plekhanov, he treated statistical studies which demonstrated that economic inequality was one of several important elements in Russian rural life as if they proved that rural differentiation was the central factor. Although he was concerned above all to demonstrate the accelerating process of rural differentiation as reflected in statistics on peasant ownership of livestock and agricultural machinery, Lenin never cited contemporary statistics on this topic that dealt with changes in the peasant economy over time. Instead, he tried to demonstrate the *dynamics* of differentiation by using static figures (data, for example, that refer to the level of economic inequality in 1889). Lenin ridiculed the populist P. N. Vikhliaev's study of peasant farming for its emphasis upon egalitarian tendencies within the commune, but did not mention Vikhliaev's statistics on the pattern of peasant ownership of horses, perhaps because these figures did not indicate that rural differentiation was increasing.[36] While he conceded that little precise evidence was available on the rate of the peasantry's separation from the means of production, Lenin claimed nevertheless that what evidence there was indicated not only that the size of the rural proletariat was rapidly growing, but that the peasant bourgeoisie was already the "master" of the Russian countryside.[37]

It was significant that when Lenin used the term "proletarian" he meant not only the farmhand but the peasant who owned a horse, cultivated a small plot of land, and hired himself out to others on a part-time basis. It was typical of Lenin that when he made a problematic argument he was careful to claim that he was saying nothing new. As he put it, "everyone knew" that landholding rural workers abounded in European society (the English cottager being a typical example), while in Russian Courland the fact that capitalist landlords allotted land to farm laborers in order to guarantee a stable labor force did not obscure the essentially proletarian character of landholding farm workers.[38] According to Lenin, Great Russia was filled with proletarians who owned land. He rather foolishly insisted that his definition was perfectly consistent with Marxist theory, although it was not clear how it could be true that an allotment-owning, horse-owning commune peasant who hired himself out on a seasonal or part-time basis was "really" a proletarian. According to Lenin's own description, a landed "proletarian" was obviously more complex in political and economic potential than a rootless proletarian with nothing to lose but his chains.

At the same time, it was doubtful whether the landholding rural worker was the sort of proletarian Lenin had in mind when he attempted to refute the populist Vorontsov's claim that there existed no internal market for Russian industrial development. In the 1890s V. P. Vorontsov had suggested that a destitute, proletarianized peasantry could never afford to purchase the goods produced by Russia's infant industry.[39] In response, Lenin had put forward the argument that farmhands became part of a domestic market regardless of their will or preference, because capitalism forced them to purchase all that they needed in order to live.[40] One did not have to be a populist to see the weakness of Lenin's "unsentimental" position. Peasants with land and a horse who participated in the commune clearly owned more than their labor power. But Lenin insisted nevertheless that the experience of survival on a tiny allotment (no matter how seldom they hired themselves out to work for others) made them proletarians even before their material reality precisely conformed to the Marxist definition of the term.[41]

As we have seen, Lenin's mode of class analysis was extraordinarily flexible. At times he categorized the peasantry according to ownership of land, livestock, tools, or the use of hired labor, but he did not consistently use any one of these indicators as a basis for his division of the peasantry into kulaks or proletarians. As the Polish sociologist Boguslaw Galeski has suggested, there was no category which corresponded strictly either to the peasant stratum as a whole or to any group within it.[42] In 1899, Lenin insisted that peasants on small allotments of land were essentially proletarians in an economy dominated by the bourgeoisie. Later, after the Revolution of 1905, he would put forward with equal confidence the claim that small allotments sustained a system of *feudal* relationships between peasants and the landed gentry. In both cases, economic analysis gave way to the need for a politically constructive peasant policy. In the 1890s a potentially revolutionary rural proletariat could be defined so as to contain almost half the peasant households in Russia. In the 1900s, when Russia regressed in Lenin's writings to a somewhat earlier, predominantly feudal stage of economic development, the bourgeoisie was no longer put forward as the master of the Russian countryside. At that time, Lenin would claim that allotment peasants were engaged in struggle against a predominantly *feudal* economic order.

But even in the 1890s Lenin did not claim that all of Russia's rural poor were proletarians. He recognized the existence of "serflike" peasants, and his research on the survivals of the past was (perhaps unsurprisingly) far more solid and convincing than his assertions on the triumph of the bourgeoisie. According to Lenin, the emancipation of 1861 had created new forms of feudal dependence by imposing onerous financial burdens on the peasantry, diminishing allotment size, and restricting freedom of movement. He pointed out that the system of redemption payments favored the wealthiest peasants, since higher charges were attached to the first unit of a peasant holding; the larger the allotment, the smaller the payment the peasant was required to make per *desiatina* (2.7 acres). Preexisting inequalities were thereby increased, as redemption payments went to support the inefficient as well as the more economically efficient landlords. Lenin agreed with many social critics that the emancipation was unjust and unfair. But its most fundamental defect in his view was its failure to end all financial subsidies to the feudal gentry and establish the conditions for the most rapid and rational development of capitalism.[43]

Before 1861, serfs had worked without compensation on the lord's land with their own tools; but now "free" peasants bound to inadequate allotments of land farmed the gentry estates under the same conditions in return for the right to use the *otrezki* lands taken from them by the terms of the emancipation. The feudal *barshchina* became the *otrabotka* system; the peasant need for the *otrezki* guaranteed the survival of servile dependence. Tied to their communal allotments, peasants were unable either to compete freely with other proprietors or to sell their labor at will as rural proletarians. In this context, Lenin argued that a free labor market would bring increased agricultural productivity and prosperity. In social and cultural terms, proletarian competition would destroy the restrictions of the *otrabotka* system and emancipate peasants once and for all from the isolation and stagnation of the village.

In backward Russia, Lenin believed that free markets were far more educational than any schools which enlightened reformers might devise. In a statement that could have come from Witte, the "state capitalist" finance minister of Nicholas II, Lenin wrote that it was "naive to imagine that a village school can teach people what they can learn from an independent acquaintance with the differing relations and order of things in agriculture and in industry."[44] Peasants would be "civilized" by the experience of poverty in a more stimulating environment. Freed from the patriarchal dependence and mindless routine of rural social life for the presumably varied work to be found in the Russian factory, peasants and their children would achieve the level of class consciousness that only the socialized production process of industrial capitalism could generate. Taking pride in his Marxist humility, Lenin distinguished himself from the supposedly subjective and naive populist intellectuals who claimed to possess the "superhuman power" to choose "more or less favourable paths" for Russia's future development. Lenin argued that Marxists were truly scientific because they could accept evidence demonstrating that the economic laws Marx had discovered applied not only to England but to Russia as well.[45] The conditions of rural proletarian labor were therefore for Lenin both a deplorable necessity and an educational part of the cost of progress.

In general, Lenin's work provided a far more complex and contradictory picture of Russian rural life than Plekhanov's. Stressing always the social element upon which a revolutionary struggle might might be based, Lenin categorized the awkward majority of peasants who neither employed labor nor hired themselves out to others either as serflike peasants who might be induced to do battle with the feudal gentry or as some sort of potentially revolutionary proletariat. And although he criticized "legal Marxists" like P. B. Struve for emphasizing the progressive virtues of capitalism more than the contradictions which generated proletarian revolution,[46] Lenin made no explicit statement about revolution in *The Development of Capitalism in Russia.* Insistent upon the indissoluble connection between capitalist brutality and progress, he put forward no economic alternative to massive peasant ruin in the modernization process.

Like Plekhanov, Lenin saw rural differentiation as the central fact of Russian rural life,[47] and exaggerated the degree of Russia's capitalist development. Looking at the same sort of evidence which had convinced Plekhanov (but not Marx) that populist anti-capitalism was based upon sentimentality and an ignorance of economics, he concluded that Russia was bound by the same laws which governed West European historical development. Lenin argued that capitalism was not to be welcomed and loved or avoided and hated; it was rather the scientifically determined stage which followed feudalism and prepared the way for socialism. Seen dialectically, capitalism caused massive human suffering and created at the same time the social classes and productive forces necessary for the building of a socialist society. Although Lenin sometimes succumbed to the temptation to avoid discussion of the "capitalist injustices" which so concerned the Russian populists, he was far more dialectical in his analysis of capitalism than either Plekhanov or Struve. Concretely, this meant that Lenin would answer Vorontsov's claim that rural prosperity was essential for the development of a domestic market for Russian industry with the assertion that brutal poverty and cutthroat competition could serve the same progressive purpose.[48] For Lenin, the hard truth was that capitalism was at once a cruel and a civilizing process. As a Marxist, he wanted Russia to move as quickly as possible into (and out of) a painful and necessary capitalist stage of historical development.[49]

In his early writings, Lenin dealt with the economic challenges of populism as tough-mindedly as he would later answer the political challenge of revisionism in *What Is To Be Done?*. His stance was always that of a defender of scientific Marxism against muddleheaded, sentimental, and opportunist critics. In his economic analyses, he used carefully selected evidence to support his argument for the triumph of rural capitalism at the turn of the century. But he was wrong, and admitted as much in the years after 1905. To his credit, Lenin's ideas on the politics of the peasant question were far more realistic than the doctrinaire pronouncements of Kautsky and Plekhanov. His use of the term "landed proletarian" in draft programs of the 1890s reflected an awareness that Social Democrats needed to direct their appeals to peasants who were neither serfs, petty capitalists, nor landless wage laborers. This recognition would be expressed even more clearly in his "To the Rural Poor" (1903). But since Lenin prided himself always upon his fidelity to the letter and spirit of *Capital* and to the economics of Kautsky, he did not further explore the economic and social implications of his insights. Then and later, his recognition of a reality far more complex than was permitted by categories of Kautsky would fail to enrich the Marxist tradition. Lenin's overriding ideological concern was to demonstrate that nothing new had been said or done.

II

Peasant Militance and Petty Bourgeois Capitalism, 1901–16

4

Proletarian Theory and Peasant Practice: Lenin, 1901–4

BY THE EARLY TWENTIETH CENTURY most Russian Marxists were content either to ignore the stubborn fact that the majority of the population lived in the countryside or to recognize in the peasantry a feudal survival that might have to be destroyed as peasants in order to be "saved" as proletarians. Both of these positions were fraught with potential for political opportunism. For an exclusive focus on urban social elements in a predominantly peasant society would rule out the possibility of political success for years to come, while an appeal to the peasantry as a class destined for annihilation could scarcely be considered a fruitful or constructive strategy. In "peasant" Russia, at least, the pursuit of power was therefore inescapably linked to the willingness to practice a more or less substantial degree of political deception. Such dilemmas were not uniquely Marxist; they plagued every political movement whose members were dubious about the economic or political capabilities of a peasant majority. While Western Lenin scholars have attributed Lenin's interest in peasants to his awareness of the way in which they could be used to support the revolution he wanted to lead and organize,[1] similar motives were discernible among other political organizations in early twentieth-century Russia.

Political Responses to Peasant Violence

In the early twentieth century, a decade of relative social tranquillity in the Russian countryside came abruptly to an end. A series of famines,

57

combined with a state modernization policy which placed a major share of the financial cost of economic development squarely on the shoulders of the rural populace, sparked the popular violence for which a generation of revolutionaries had striven in vain. In 1902 a "miniature revolution" erupted in the southwestern regions of the empire. Peasants, particularly in commune districts, began to take over private estates; in some cases they even enforced prohibitions on the leasing and sale of landed property. In its efforts to restore order, the government resorted to the forms of reprisal which had so often proven effective in the past, and before long the burning of peasant villages, flogging, "preventive punishment," and Siberian exile reestablished a terror-stricken and resentful calm in the countryside. The usual "revolutionary agitators" were blamed for stirring up the "peaceful peasantry," while students, intellectuals, and wealthy philanthropists who tried to aid the famine-stricken were castigated for "eagerly taking advantage of the famine to pursue their criminal aims under the pretense of helping their neighbors."[2]

But significant changes in government policy were discernible within the familiar pattern of peasant rebellion and state coercion. The fact that the outbreaks of 1902 were most violent in districts where repartitional land tenure prevailed led a steadily increasing number of government investigators to relinquish their belief in the commune as a guarantee of order and stability. Among even the most anti-Western bureaucrats of the tsarist regime the suspicion began to dawn that a European-style property system might do more than the traditional guarantees of the peasant commune to encourage obedience to authority. Such conservatives would eventually come to agree with Finance Minister Witte that the collectivist behavior fostered by the commune was both a cause of peasant poverty and an obstacle to agricultural progress.[3] In this connection, it was especially significant that the decree suspending the system of collective responsibility for tax payment was prepared in the office of V. I. Plehve, the arch-conservative minister of the interior, and took effect after Plehve's intrigues helped to drive the "progressive" Witte from office.[4]

The peasant unrest which convinced the government to forge a link between the individual peasant as proprietor and the autocracy as defender of property rights simultaneously inspired the government's critics with the hope that the countryside might at last have become fertile ground for their efforts. One of the most interesting of the ensuing political shifts took place within the upper ranks of the Socialist

Revolutionary Party. Although SRs were heirs to a populist tradition which committed them to the goal of peasant revolution, by 1901 some had begun to prefer the tactics of political assassination or the organization of urban factory workers to the slow and thankless task of political work among the peasantry. As late as January 1902 many of these neo-populists were content to emphasize that the intelligentsia and the industrial workers were "the chief support of the party."[5] The eruption of violence in the countryside quickly recalled leading SR intellectuals to their original political commitment. In June 1902 the SR Party officially recognized that its organizers were obliged to leave the narrow circles of propaganda among urban workers and intellectuals for the greater task of revolutionizing the peasant masses.[6]

While Russian liberals had no interest in revolutionizing the peasantry in any populist sense, their political instincts were at least as sound as those of SR Party leaders. The specter of peasant "anarchy" in 1901-2 did not prevent a number of liberal landlords from responding in a constructive fashion to the political opportunity which now seemed present in the Russian countryside. In May 1902 the all-Russian Congress of *Zemstvos* moved beyond traditional concerns with *zemstvo* rights and civil liberties to adopt a program which stated, "Since the agricultural question is to a considerable extent the same thing as the peasant question, it is first of all necessary to elevate the person of the Russian peasant and to secure the development of his initiative."[7] An aggrieved landlord's proposal that the *zemstvo* program should emphasize the injustices suffered by landlords as well as peasants was rejected by the congress.[8]

Outside the *zemstvo* movement, scholar-activists like Miliukov were often willing to condemn autocratic violence more vehemently than the violence of the poor,[9] and ex-Marxists like Struve and Bulgakov attempted to develop a program which would explicitly link peasant demands with liberal slogans. In Struve's journal *Osvobozhdenie* ("Liberation") numerous articles emphasized that government concessions came only as a result of peasant unrest,[10] and a number of editorials attempted to awaken enlightened landlords to the moral necessity of social justice for the peasantry.[11] Bulgakov argued that it was necessary to transfer land "to the laboring masses" even if this meant the compulsory alienation of privately owned land by the government,[12] while Miliukov observed that "Russian liberalism was always tinged with democratism, and Russian democratism has been strongly impregnated with socialistic teachings and tendencies ever since socialism made its appearance."[13]

The Union of Liberation's responsiveness to the political significance of peasant unrest was reflected in a resolution voted by its congress of January 1904: " . . . in the realm of social-economic policy, the Union of Liberation will follow the same principle of democracy, making the direct goal of its activity the defense of the interests of the laboring masses."[14] On the other hand, there were limits to the power of moral appeal: the idea of compulsory alienation of privately owned land was explicitly rejected.[15]

It is clear then that the government, the SRs, and the liberals responded to the outbreak of peasant violence by attempting to win peasant support for the very different goals of autocratic order, peasant socialism, and constitutional government. Their political common sense (which members of each group would see as opportunism in the other) was not shared by anyone in the Russian Marxist movement except V. I. Lenin. And unsurprisingly, his position generally appeared opportunistic to non-Marxists and Marxists alike.

Lenin

Lenin's first attempts to construct a Marxist peasant policy had done little to make clear what Social Democrats might legitimately expect from the peasantry, or more important, what the peasants might hope to gain from support of the Social Democrats. In 1901 it had seemed to him "impossible and irrational" to think of sending Social Democratic organizers to the countryside,[16] and he repeatedly invoked Kautsky's *Die Agrarfrage*[17] to prove that Social Democrats could do nothing to preserve the peasant's status as a small proprietor. Such arguments were intended to demolish "utopian" hopes for peasant socialism or agrarian reform expressed by SRs like V. M. Chernov or liberals like Bulgakov.[18] Yet just as in the 1890s, Lenin's suspicion of the populists did not keep him from proposing a series of agrarian programs for the Russian Social Democratic Party. He now suggested that the "best" peasant elements could be stimulated, if not to direct political action, then to support of working-class struggles against the autocracy.[19]

As peasant rioting began to spread in 1901–2, Lenin's writings were filled with quotations from the official press which exposed the government's callousness,[20] and with criticism of private philanthropy as a solution to problems caused by economic backwardness and the survivals of "feudalism."[21] By the end of 1902 Lenin had begun to devote himself in earnest to the peasant question. Like the SRs, the liberals, and the government, his reasons were undoubtedly political, but Lenin never believed that his political insights were in conflict with a serious commitment to the eradication of rural poverty.

"To the Rural Poor" (1903) was Lenin's first full-fledged effort to move beyond emigré doctrinal disputes to a concrete political approach to the "petty bourgeois" majority of the Russian population.[22] In style, the pamphlet provided a striking example of what Lenin had meant by political education in *What Is To Be Done?* (1902). As a specifically Marxist appeal for revolutionary peasant action, "To the Rural Poor" represented a real breakthrough in the history of Marxism, especially Russian Marxism: Lenin had taken on what would be the thankless task of enriching a revolutionary tradition which had consistently placed the peasant majority of the world's population at the periphery of its social and political concerns.

As befitted an honest Marxist who believed in revolutionary consciousness as an awareness of grievances *shared* by exploited social elements, Lenin opened his appeal to the rural poor with a description of urban working-class activities. His brief and unsensational description of contemporary labor struggles ended with the suggestion that peasants consider the ways that their lives would change if they could be assured the medical care, education for their children, and decent wages that urban factory workers were fighting to get.[23]

As he approached the peasant's special grievances, Lenin presented an abundance of evidence to show that the commune collected exorbitant taxes on the government's behalf, while the *otrezki* forced the peasant into a dependence reminiscent of the feudal system.[24] He argued that such practices were part of a system which preserved the traditional rights of landlords and officials over the rural population. Lenin claimed that the abolition of these "feudal" practices was immediately necessary for all peasants, just as the abolition of restrictions on political liberty was essential for all of the Russian people. And to link the facts of peasant poverty with the need for political struggle was the basic and openly admitted goal of "To the Rural Poor."

The political enslavement suffered by the rural poor was not, Lenin pointed out, the work of the tsar or any other individual.[25] It is interesting to note in this connection that the existence of traditional peasant loyalties to the "Little Father" did not produce in Lenin the despair which had once led populists to distribute forged imperial manifestos ordering peasants to rebel (similar manifestos of unknown origin were circulated in 1902). Much of Lenin's analysis of the Russian political system was in fact based upon an aspect of the peasant "monarchist" tradition. The popular belief, repeatedly expressed throughout Russian history, that the tsar was kept from ruling justly by evil advisers of gentry or merchant origins now became part of a Marxist account of a *system* of interdependent landlords, merchants, and officials which operated to prevent the tsar from acting as defender and protector of the people. If peasants understood the system's operation they would presumably be able to organize for the struggle necessary to change their lives. And only under conditions of political and civil liberty would they be able to learn the truth of the Marxist contention that a political order based upon class exploitation was the fundamental cause of their poverty.[26]

In other words, Lenin argued that if pamphlets like "To the Rural Poor" were allowed to circulate freely, there would be an end to the blind and unorganized peasant uprisings which in the past had succeeded only in bringing punitive expeditions to the Russian village. Political consciousness and organization were clearly the only hope for change: "to say that life is hard and to call for revolt, any loudmouth can do that, but it is of little use. The working people must clearly understand why they are living in such poverty and with whom they must unite in order to liberate themselves from want."[27]

Lenin accurately observed what any peasant might see—that poverty existed in the midst of Russian "progress." He presented evidence which indicated that Russian factories were owned by a minority largely exempt from the financial burdens carried by the majority of the peasantry. He pointed out that in 1900, 924 Russian families owned 27 million *desiatiny* of land, i.e., less than a thousand families owned as much as two million peasant families.[28] And he assumed that facts like these would *in themselves* be subversive of traditional attitudes and potentially political in their impact. Lenin stated repeatedly, and in the most unambiguous terms, that once the facts of property ownership were clearly understood, a majority of the rural population would be willing to fight alongside the working class in order to take land from the great landowners, factories from the factory owners, and money from the bankers.[29]

Hired hands and "semi-proletarians" (the rural poor, who owned land and a draft animal but survived only through the sale of labor or the lease of their land to the rich) would in his view be the most quickly receptive to this sort of Marxist economic and political education.[30] The middle peasant was a more difficult case: since his situation was less precarious than most, he was more likely to dream of future prosperity within a private enterprise system. Lenin attempted to prove that the hopes of the middle peasant were groundless, and assured proletarians, semi-proletarians, and middle peasants that a Social Democratic government would "*never*" (Lenin's emphasis) take away the property of the small and middle peasants who did not hire labor.[31]

On the other hand, Lenin emphasized that without free political discussion, open exchange of information, and the right to organize, it would be impossible to make even the majority of the rural poor (to say nothing of the middle peasants) aware of their real interests. In the absence of political and civil liberties, peasants would never understand their real problems well enough to be able to resist the suggestion that they could escape their poverty through diligent private efforts. They would be taken in by government reforms or by "misguided" SR proposals for strengthening the commune, establishing cooperatives, or introducing easy credit terms for the peasantry.[32] Only peasants who were politically "conscious" in Lenin's sense would know that in truth the "opportunities" available for middle peasants were similar to a lottery. One could win and the rest would lose, while the belief that each had an equal chance to succeed functioned to undermine collective efforts to destroy the lottery system.[33] Politically ignorant peasants would never be able to see that piecemeal changes disproportionately improved the lot of the already prosperous peasant while leaving the relationship between rich and poor the same as before.[34]

In "To the Rural Poor," the peasantry was thus being asked to recognize its common interests with urban workers, see the need for political and civil liberty, and resist the reformist plans and ideological appeals which distracted peasants from an awareness of the material reasons for their poverty. With an extremely careful use of statistical evidence and a belief in the potential force of the peasants' hatred of external authority, Lenin attempted to describe the existing political system in terms so vivid and concrete that a peasant would *have* to see the connection between the evils of his personal situation and the requirements of that system. On the basis of this sort of understanding, Lenin believed that peasants would fight for the establishment of peasant committees to abolish feudal survivals; they could fight for a progressive income tax, political rights, and an end to the military training which so brutalized peasant soldiers that they willingly put down the rebellions of their fellow peasants.[35] However, with a scrupulousness not usually associated with his name, Lenin emphasized that the rural poor could not yet hope to fight for the establishment of socialism, i.e., for a social and economic order which would guarantee their welfare.[36] At the current level of Russia's historical development, they had to join forces with the kulaks against the survivals of feudalism.[37]

And here lay the crucial and glaring weakness of Lenin's appeal. When it came to the question of tactics, Lenin had not yet progressed very far past the political foolishness of Kautsky and Engels, who had advised Marxists to appeal to peasants by explaining to them that they would soon become extinct.[38] Despite an awareness of the complexity of the Russian social and economic order with its feudal survivals, agricultural capitalists, semi-proletarians, etc., Lenin seemed unable in 1903 to reject a scheme of historical development which proceeded by neat and abstract stages from feudalism to bourgeois democracy to socialism. Peasants were advised to fight side by side with their kulak exploiters to establish a bourgeois society which would *not* eradicate their poverty, in order that they might later go on to battle the kulak in a future revolutionary struggle for socialism. According to Lenin's arguments, peasants were to become sophisticated and realistic fighters, capable of understanding the need to establish more progressive forms of exploitation. Always more aggressive when he was making a dubious argument, Lenin insisted that anyone who told the peasantry that they could simultaneously take the first step (against feudalism) and the final step (against the bourgeoisie) was a liar and a fraud.[39] It was impossible to tell when the "final step" could be taken,[40] but somehow "all Russian workers and all the rural poor must *fight with both hands and on two sides*: with one hand—fight against all the bourgeois, in alliance with all the workers; and with the other hand—*fight against the rural officials, against the feudal landlords*, in alliance with all the peasants."[41]

In Lenin's view, the uprisings of 1902 had failed because the peasants had not recognized the importance of political power—they had no organization, allies, or political demands. The tsarist regime, through floggings and executions, had therefore been able to demonstrate the effectiveness of legal violence. More concretely, the armed forces had "shown the peasant what state power is." The peasants had above all to learn what Lenin took to be the lesson of 1902: any uprising would fail unless it was organized and directed toward a change in the political order and the establishment of political liberty.[42]

The pamphlet ended with instructions on the proper way to read the enclosed Social Democratic party program.[43]

For the task of raising the peasant from blind anger and frustration to the level of a Marxist understanding of the causes of economic exploitation, "To the Rural Poor" was unequaled in early twentieth-century political literature. It was refreshingly free of the polemical bludgeon which produces such a numbing effect in works like *What Is To Be Done?*. SRs were criticized but not vilified, and even the tsar was to be "understood" rather than blindly hated. Lenin wrote sympathetically of peasant suffering and presented evidence of the ignorance and lack of organization which had doomed the "martyrs" of earlier peasant rebellions. Strikingly different from modern conceptions which separate inevitably dishonest "propaganda" from "education," Lenin's pamphlet was (1) scrupulous in the use of facts to support his analysis of the causes and solution to the problem of rural poverty,[44] (2) emphatic, in the year after *What Is To Be Done?*, in the belief that the peasant had to be *conscious* of the reasons for his exploitation, (3) lacking in rash promises and precise in description of the benefits of political freedom for the poor, and (4) honest in stating that the purpose of the pamphlet was to gain adherents to the Social Democratic cause. In its attempt to link the facts of property ownership in Russia with the need for collective political action in a steadily widening context, "To the Rural Poor" provided what may be a more convincing practical example of Lenin's idea of consciousness-raising than *What Is To Be Done?*.

Nevertheless despite its value as a text for Marxist political education "To the Rural Poor" also reflected the constricting pressures of contemporary Marxist orthodoxy. The repartitional commune, which had provided the institutional framework for so many of the recent peasant outbreaks, was completely ignored; peasants were praised because their willingness to fight the gentry had proven that they were capable of what Lenin called "spontaneity," or "embryonic consciousness." Arguing that peasants were not inevitably conservative, Lenin praised them for being intelligent enough to absorb the insights and follow the leadership of a revolutionary vanguard. Among the "best" peasants, Lenin had discovered a collection of blank slates upon which the RSDLP might eloquently write. "To the Rural Poor" illustrated clearly the emerging tension between Lenin's political insights and the arid dogmatism of his sociology. It is to Lenin's credit as a revolutionary that this tension was deepened not by ideological debate, but by the eruption of peasant violence against the existing socioeconomic order.

Toward a Social Democratic Agrarian Program

Although the "miniature revolution" of 1902 might have underlined the need to develop a specifically Marxist peasant policy, questions of party organization and structure continued to concern Lenin and other Russian Marxists far more deeply than the problem of their political relationship to the peasant majority of the population. And it is perhaps a measure of the sectarian quality of the Russian Marxist movement that at a time when both liberals and SRs recognized the practical need for conspiracy and secrecy,[45] the Russian Marxist movement was being torn apart over the issue of whether to have an "open" or a "closed" political party. Lenin's exaggerated response to the realities of political organization in Russia during this period was attacked as immoral and unorthodox by many of the most prestigious Russian Marxist emigrés.[46]

In this context, Lenin's insights into the peasant question were a burden as well as an asset to him as a revolutionary Marxist. The benefits of a broadened political and social perspective were obvious, but so were the problems involved in the attempt to reconcile his recognition of the peasant's importance with the shared truths of a Marxist tradition which assumed (1) that the peasant was politically weak and barbaric, and (2) that only urban culture and the urban proletariat generated the ideas and movements which could revolutionize the existing order. These are some of the reasons (along with the hypocritical element which is seldom absent from the appeals of educated politicians to their illiterate constituents) why Lenin's references to the peasantry were far less humane in writings directed toward his fellow Marxists than they had been in "To the Rural Poor." In 1902, for example, Lenin warned Plekhanov (whose contempt for the peasantry would have seemed to render such a warning superfluous)[47] that "the proletariat alone is a really revolutionary class."[48] A disciplined political party had to draw a "line of demarcation between ourselves and all this riff-raff, between the proletariat and the petty bourgeoisie." Once the Social Democratic position was clear, it would be possible to call on everyone, "undertake everything, include everything."[49]

Lenin's agrarian proposals of the 1900s reflected a dramatic shift in his economic analysis of rural life. Once the controversy with the populists over the existence of capitalism in Russia had been won, Russia seemed to regress in Lenin's writings to a more feudal stage of economic development. "Now," he argued, "in view of the enduring elements of the feudal system," the Russian peasants were as a whole engaged in a struggle against landlords unwilling to surrender property or privilege except under the pressure of a revolutionary movement.[50] "Inasmuch as this class antagonism between the 'peasantry' and the privileged landowners, so characteristic of a serf-owning society, still survives . . . insomuch a working class party must undoubtedly *urge it on to fight* against all remnants of serf ownership."[51]

These "specific historical circumstances" made Social Democrats into temporary defenders of small-scale property in the struggle against feudalism. In this context, Lenin's idea of a crucial and popular issue for a Social Democratic agrarian program was the "revolutionary" (i.e., forcible) return of the *otrezki* lands to the peasantry. He presented an abundance of statistical evidence to demonstrate that the peasant was forced into a feudal relationship with his former master because he so desperately needed the pasture and the forest lands which the emancipation reform had placed in the hands of the gentry. Only after such relationships had been destroyed by the proletariat and the rural poor would it be possible to go on to the struggle for nationalization (the transfer of land rent to the state). At that future date, Lenin suggested, no sentimental preference would be given to the "working peasant" over the agrarian capitalist. The class struggle in the countryside would develop to its logical conclusion, and under just and democratic bourgeois labor laws the most efficient system of large-scale production would emerge victorious.[52]

At the Second Congress of the Russian Social Democratic Labor Party, which met in the summer of 1903, the Bolshevik and Menshevik positions which emerged in debates on party organization were not clearly differentiated on the peasant question, although Lenin's opponents on that issue were all eventually to become Mensheviks. Everyone was agreed that the survivals of Russian feudalism delayed the progress of capitalist economic development, but in the confused and rancorous debates over the agrarian program it was evident that a substantial number of delegates could not believe that it was the task of proletarian socialists to lead either an anti-feudal struggle by serflike primitives or a pro-capitalist battle on behalf of a peasant bourgeoisie. The delegate Makhov argued that Social Democrats could promise nothing to the hopelessly inefficient and property-hungry small producer. Since the peasant didn't want the *otrezki*, but more land of his own, any support of the "so-called revolutionary peasant movement" was in Makhov's view economically reactionary. Makhov claimed that there should be no RSDLP agrarian program, and although few at the congress were willing to express their views in such simple terms, many future Mensheviks (including Liber, Egorov, and Martynov) raised similar objections in a more sophisticated manner. They criticized what they called the "bourgeois" nature of Lenin's proposals, finding it unthinkable that socialists, who denied in principle that landlords had a right to *any* of the land they possessed before 1861, should now fight for a "return" of the *otrezki* to the peasantry. On a practical level, Liber and Egorov observed that if Social Democrats wanted peasant support, Lenin's meager program would be no match for the SR slogan of land redistribution;[53] while Martynov concluded that in any event it was not for Social Democrats to enter into a competition in which those who promised most to the peasantry would be considered the most revolutionary.[54]

On the other hand, a number of delegates to the congress challenged the exclusively anti-feudal character of Lenin's agrarian program. The Georgian Social Democrat N. Zhordaniia (Kostrov) pointed out that in Georgia the peasant movement was most powerful in areas where feudal survivals were weakest. Zhordaniia demanded that the congress formulate a set of peasant demands which were appropriate for the peasant moving toward socialism as well as for the serflike opponent of feudal survivals. The Georgian Urutadze (Karskii) emphasized that Social Democrats were successful when they appealed to the progressive and revolutionary peasant with urban proletarian demands for lower rent and a shorter work day, while the delegate Gusev made the revealing admission that "we appeal to the peasants *not as peasants* [emphasis added] but as a mass either already proletarianized or in the process of proletarianization."[55]

Lenin denied that his agrarian proposals were superficial or theoretically inconsistent, but he did not really meet the arguments of his critics. He simply asserted that the *otrezki* were feudal survivals which delayed the capitalist development that was necessary at Russia's current economic stage.[56] Plekhanov, Martov, and Axelrod supported Lenin, while Trotsky explained that the Russian peasants had not yet fulfilled their historic, i.e., their bourgeois, role. In an uncharacteristically humane reference to the rural populace, Trotsky noted, "In the coming revolutionary period we must link ourselves with the peasantry—as much in the interests of the poor peasants as in the interests of the proletariat."[57] Lenin claimed that Social Democrats were in fact the only party to fight for the "revolutionary," that is to say violent, abolition of feudal survivals. If peasants went further than this, the party's general platform permitted enthusiastic support to be given to peasant demands for a general redistribution of the land.[58] As Lenin put it, "When we point out to the poor peasant the cause of his poverty, we may count on success. . . . The Social Democrats have now taken up the struggle for the interests of the peasants . . . [and] the peasants will get used to looking upon Social Democracy as the defender of their interests."[59] What seemed crucial to Lenin at this point was to establish the principle of a Social Democratic commitment to look out at the vast non-urban social and political world within which the RSDLP was operating. He was not willing, however, to challenge conventional Marxist wisdom on the question of class struggle in the countryside, nor did he attempt to introduce the "rural poor" as a category to be inserted somewhere between the rural bourgeoisie and proletariat.

After lengthy debate, the congress adopted Lenin's agrarian program. Accordingly, Russian Social Democrats called for the establishment of peasant committees to return *otrezki* land, lower high rents, and invalidate unjust contracts. Redemption payments were to be abolished, and the government was to return to the peasant all money taken from him for payments made in the past. In order to achieve these goals, the party would support all opposition and revolutionary movements against the existing social and political order.[60]

The main body of the party's general platform began with the statement that the position of exploited working people was "hopeless" in a society where capitalism was already the dominant form of production. All who recognized this "fact"—in other words, those who adopted the point of view of the proletariat—were encouraged to join the Social Democratic Party. The agrarian section of the program emphasized the need to abolish all feudal survivals which slowed the development of the class struggle in the countryside. Although Liber had sensibly noted that a predominantly capitalist economy would seem to require an agrarian program which applied to capitalist as well as feudal agricultural relations,[61] he was strangely unable to convince Plekhanov, or Trotsky or Martov, on this rather obvious point. Plekhanov argued that in economically backward areas, the return of the *otrezki* would accelerate the process of modernization. And in the more economically advanced regions, as Plekhanov put it, "We stand with Kautsky" as principled Marxists and opponents of revisionism, and in contrast to "opportunists à la David."[62] In the Russian context, such statements meant that it was not necessary for Marxists to formulate an agrarian program specifically for peasants in a capitalist society. But neither Plekhanov's dogmatism, nor the rhetorical flights of Trotsky,[63] nor Martov's accurate observation that Liber had no constructive suggestions to make[64] could mask the fact that no Russian Marxist was in possession of a policy toward revolutionary peasant action in a capitalist society. Peasant action could thus only be "anti-feudal," and feudal survivals had to be the major concern of the Social Democratic agrarian program.

The Problem of a Leninist Agrarian Program

Lenin's writings after the Second Congress were dominated by the organizational split within the party, and many of his writings on the agrarian question during this period can be best understood as part of an attempt to develop a specifically Bolshevik position. This was an especially difficult task, because Lenin had not yet developed a strategy to deal with a differentiated peasantry within a capitalist society. His conception of the rural poor was perhaps the beginning of a direct confrontation with this problem, but a "rural poor" comprised of proletarians and allotment peasants was not easy to incorporate into a Marxist analysis based upon relationship to the means of production.[65] Lenin was equally hard pressed to answer criticism which came from the SRs, who claimed to represent peasant interests, and from liberals, who accurately noted the similarity between Lenin's agrarian program and their own.

Once peasant violence had renewed SR hopes for peasant socialism, Marxists were again vulnerable to the traditional Populist attacks upon the dogmatism of their insistence that the peasant was petty bourgeois.[66] Pointing out that some of the peasant rebels of 1902 had removed land from the "sphere of arbitrary and private dealings," SRs ridiculed the Marxist position that it was the task of a "progressive" peasant to fight for the individual right to buy and sell his own private property.[67] In rebuttal, Lenin vehemently attacked the SRs for confusing the "primitive peasant idea" of small-scale equality of land tenure with socialist, large-scale management and control of the means of production. According to Lenin, the SRs were foolish to imagine that proletarians and peasants could ever carry on a unified socialist struggle. The concern which SRs expressed for the poor as a whole was, he claimed, only another example of the failure of petty bourgeois socialists to understand the basic issue of class conflict which existed even among social groups which did not prosper in tsarist Russia. While the proletariat and the peasantry had common interests which could sometimes be foolishly disregarded, Lenin insisted that the conventional Marxist analysis was fundamentally valid. Without referring to any concrete evidence from the actual events of 1902, he argued in principle for the superior "political steadfastness" of proletarians in comparison with the "unreliability" of the petty bourgeoisie, whose insecure position generated pathetic fantasies of prosperity on private plots of land.[68] Admitting that peasants were indeed capable of revolutionary action, Lenin argued that it was important to explain to them the limits of their struggle. It was "dishonest and unworthy to treat the muzhik as though he were under tutelage, or to conceal from him the fact that at present he can achieve only the complete eradication of all remnants of the serf-owning system."[69]

In certain respects, the liberal ideological challenge to Russian Social Democrats was far more serious than that of the SRs, because liberals and Marxists shared a common commitment to bourgeois political and civil liberty as immediate goals. It could not have been pleasant for a Russian Marxist revolutionary to read in the columns of the liberal *Osvobozhdenie* that the demands of serious and educated Social Democrats did not go beyond "broad political and economic reforms in the democratic spirit."[70] It was obvious that despite the humane statements of liberals and the silence, evasion, or occasional harshness of the Marxists, both groups were agreed that agricultural progress in Russia meant the development of capitalism. Liberals did not accept, and in this context Russian Marxists were unwilling to emphasize, the fact that agricultural capitalism seemed to be dependent upon the formation of a peasant bourgeoisie made wealthy by the increasingly efficient exploitation of rural wage laborers.

However, Lenin was no more willing to admit agreement with liberals on the question of economic progress than he had been to agree with SRs on the desirability of a socialist revolution. He found a world of difference between the "enthusiastic spirit" of the Social Democrats and the attitude of "half-hearted liberals" who wanted to abolish feudal survivals by means of conciliation and reform. In the context of the historical dependence of Russia's middle class upon financial subsidies granted by the autocracy, Lenin claimed that the liberal bourgeoisie would never sacrifice the state's protection of their private property in order to wage a violent struggle against feudalism.[71] Yet Lenin's insistence on the difference between Marxist and liberal "spirit," "attitude" or "willingness to use force" was not a particularly convincing tack for a materialist to take.

Perhaps the clearest insight into Lenin's attempt to develop a peasant policy during this period may be found in *What Is To Be Done?*, a work which does not deal directly with the problem of peasants, SRs, or liberals. For it was in this handbook for party organizers that Lenin outlined the process by which the acquisition of revolutionary consciousness made a bourgeois intellectual into a "proletarian" who alone could provide (at least initially) reliable leadership in a revolutionary struggle.[72] Defining the difference between Social Democrats and other political groups so as to justify the primacy of Leninists in any future revolution, *What Is To Be Done?* suggested that Social Democratic consciousness always and everywhere legitimated claims to leadership. Even if the revolution was bourgeois, it was impossible for Lenin to conceive of an actual situation in which Marxist theory would require him and his fellow Marxists to carry out the instructions of their petty bourgeois or bourgeois class enemies.

Lenin's recognition of the need to incorporate the peasant into a Marxist revolutionary framework became increasingly explicit in the period before the Revolution of 1905. His arguments were various and not always satisfactory. He claimed that the "best" peasants would support the coming revolution.[73] He contended that the "forcible" return of lands cut off at the time of emancipation would be a revolutionary act,[74] and insisted that only "vulgar Marxists" underestimated the peasantry.[75] But the best Lenin himself could do was to openly admit that it was impossible to say in advance whether the peasantry would appear as a democratic revolutionary force, or as the party of Order. As he wrote in 1904, "We must draft our program so as to be prepared even for the worst, and if the best combinations ensue, then that will facilitate our work, and give it a new stimulus."[76]

Such statements may reflect the stirrings of a rare humility on Lenin's part, or at least a willingness to refrain from doctrinaire and prescriptive statements on the peasant question. Within the context of his own struggle with a Marxist tradition of condescension toward and contempt for the peasantry, and in the face of hostile criticism from inside and outside the RSDLP, it was evident that Lenin was trying very hard to enlarge the Marxist revolutionary perspective. After 1902 there developed what would become a permanent separation between Lenin and those Marxists who were unsure if Marxist theory permitted them to support revolutionary action by such inappropriate actors as the Russian peasantry. For Lenin, the conflict between his acceptance of a rigidified theory and his awareness of complex and fruitful possibilities for change and struggle on the part of the peasant population was strained not so much by emigré polemics as by the outbreak of mass action against the existing social and economic order. It was not until 1905–6 that the renewal of such mass action would enable Lenin to go further. But in the insights and concerns of "To the Rural Poor" we see at least the beginning of Lenin's attempt (never completely successful) to use Marxism not as a dogma which prevented him from confronting the realities of Russian society, but as a guide which could help him to act in accordance with an awareness of the peasant's political importance.

5

The Outbreak of Revolution: The Challenge of Peasant Militance in 1905 and 1906

> Unfortunately, Marx did not know this situation and he did not write of it. Therefore, the analysis of this situation can neither be confirmed nor refuted with simple quotations from Marx.[1]
>
> LENIN

IN 1904, THE RUSSO-JAPANESE WAR, with its revelations of corruption, bureaucratic incompetence, and technological backwardness, pushed the Russian autocracy to the brink of disaster. Whatever hopes there may have been that a "short, victorious war" would unify the country, the humiliating defeats suffered by Russia's army and navy in the course of 1904–5 provided instead a focus for long-standing economic, social and political grievances. As peasant unrest began once more to exceed "normal" levels, factory workers under the influence of radical activists put forward demands for a Constituent Assembly. By December, 1904, solid, respectable citizens were welcoming the assassination of government ministers by Socialist Revolutionary terrorists.[2] The rejection of traditional institutions and authority which forms part of any popular revolution had already begun to make itself felt on every level of Russian society when Father Gapon led the demonstration which precipitated a revolution in January 1905.

Although Gapon and his "Assembly of Russian Factory Workers" took to action in St. Petersburg, their debt to Russian peasant tradition was very much in evidence from the outset. Suspicious of the *intelligenty*, they appealed instead as Christians and as loyal subjects to a patriarchal and benevolent tsar. Like seventeenth-century peasants, Gapon and his followers were certain that malevolent bureaucrats had prevented their tsar from reaching out to his people. In its expressions of humility, then, their 1905 petition represented no departure from the past. But its contents were quite untraditional; in place of the familiar plebeian demands for more generous and charitable treatment by the authorities, the petitioners were humbly requesting revolutionary change, elevating the political need for a Constituent Assembly above all other concerns.[3]

Whether or not the 200,000 icon-bearing men, women, and children who marched unarmed to the Winter Palace on January 9, 1905, understood with any degree of precision what "their" petition contained, they had posed a political challenge which no autocratic government could have met in a conciliatory fashion. A Russian state which laid claim to unlimited political authority could hardly negotiate over the degree to which its power was to be restrained by its subjects. Despite last-minute appeals for restraint by a variety of public-spirited citizens, Gapon's followers were fired on by the army and the police, and well over a hundred were killed. Among the grief-stricken and enraged survivors of this "Bloody Sunday" massacre, there were few who were still willing to absolve the tsar from responsibility for the actions of his troops. Monarchist loyalties had received a mortal blow on January 9, 1905. The liberal newspaper *Osvobozhdenie* was quick to denounce the acts of "Nicholas the Bloody" and proclaimed "Revolution in Russia!" on January 12, 1905. Socialist Revolutionaries and Social Democrats called on workers to construct barricades in the streets of St. Petersburg for defense against the police force and the army. The Revolution of 1905 had indeed begun.

The autocracy's initial responses were a traditional combination of threats and warnings. Fearing that the news of Bloody Sunday might set off a new round of peasant disorders,[4] the government reaffirmed the inviolability of private property and promised that peasants would be held collectively responsible for any damage to land or property. At the same time, it was clear that more constructive initiatives were necessary if public order was to be secured and maintained. As A. S. Ermolov, the minister of agriculture, wrote to the tsar in late January,

What shall we do when disorder spreads from the towns to the villages, when the peasants rise up and when the slaughter starts in the countryside? What forces and what soldiers shall we use then to put down a new peasant revolt which will spread across the whole country? And in the second place, Your Majesty, can we be sure that the troops who have now obeyed their officers and fired into the people, but who came from that very same people, and who are even now in constant contact with the population, who have heard the screams and curses hurled at them by their victims, can we be sure that they will behave the same way if such incidents are repeated?[5]

Still hopeful that the "truly Russian" muzhik would remain loyal to his masters and to the tsar, the autocracy offered to establish a consultative duma, with a franchise limited to the European and rural sector of the population. Petitions of the Bloody Sunday variety remained unwelcome, but on February 18 (the day after Grand Duke Sergei was assassinated by the SR Fighting Organization) an imperial decree invited proposals and petitions for the purpose of "improving the public well-being."[6]

The decree of February 18 brought a rapid, sustained, and enthusiastic response from the Russian countryside. Commune assemblies eagerly discussed peasant grievances and prepared petitions for the tsar. Some sought the "true emancipation" which was rumored to have been hidden by the gentry ever since 1861; others protested the arbitrariness of government officials or the lack of schools or decent medical care. Particularly interesting (although apparently rare) were demands of the sort which came from the village of Chirikovo in Saratov province, where peasants combined a demand for a Constituent Assembly based upon universal suffrage with a pronouncement which had resounded through centuries of Russian folklore: "Land cannot be owned by any man. Like air or water, it can only be used." Chirikovo called for the transfer of all land to the peasantry.[7] By the early spring of 1905, the commonplace view of peasants as passive and resistant to change began to give way, as some 60,000 peasant petitions came in from every corner of the empire.[8] Peasant hopes that a compassionate government would respond to their just demands were at least as striking as the level of peasant violence, which increased steadily from February onwards, radiating southwest and north from the central Black Earth region.

A number of the autocracy's most outspoken critics were quick to offer their leadership to dissident peasants. Russian liberals, eager to represent the interests of the nation as a whole, set out to appeal to the muzhik as well as the landlord. Although their enthusiasm for violent peasant action was short-lived and never very widespread, *zemstvo* men and the liberals to their left made use of the February 18 decree to mobilize support for their political reform programs. Volunteering assistance to would-be peasant petitioners, they attempted to ensure that a call for representative government and civil liberties would accompany the omnipresent demand for land. Liberal concerns were clearly self-interested and political, but not exclusively so. Well before the revolution, many progressive-minded lawyers, economists, and historians had been willing to recognize the need for land reform measures which would involve a massive transfer of gentry land to the peasantry.[9] In March 1905 the Union of Liberation approved a resolution which stated that the peasantry's legitimate needs warranted the confiscation of state, cabinet, and appanage land, and "where necessary" the confiscation of private property at a just price.[10] Inspired by Prince Peter Dolgorukov's dream of a united Russia where private landowners would no longer be threatened either by "external catastrophe or internal pangs of conscience,"[11] a *zemstvo* conference dominated by liberal landowners voted in April 1905 for the compulsory alienation of private land. Within the left wing of the liberal movement, ex-Marxists like P. B. Struve and S. M. Bulgakov even supported the idea of an All-Russian Peasant Union. More enthusiastic about the emergence of peasant activism in the spring than they would be by the autumn of 1905, many liberals considered it possible that the old regime might be replaced without the violence and terror of class war.

In contrast, Socialist Revolutionaries were generally unafraid of direct and violent peasant action against the gentry. Although they did not resemble the Marxist stereotype of the populist as uncritical admirer of the peasant, SRs were certain that the collectivist and democratic aspects of communal peasant tradition were essential to the formation of a successful revolutionary socialist movement.[12] Contemptuous of the Marxist willingness to accept proletarianization of the peasantry for the sake of future progress, they wanted instead some immediate improvements in the peasantry's living standard. V. M. Chernov's plan for socialization, the provision of land on equal terms to all who worked it, was intended to offer relief to the peasantry even before the advent of socialism. It was true that maximalists within the movement were often indiscriminating supporters of peasant violence, but Chernov, L. E. Shishko and P. A. Vikhliaev consistently opposed any "arbitrary" seizure of land by rebellious individual peasants. Instead, they favored a "revolutionary expropriation" by peasant unions which could hold the land until a democratically elected Constituent Assembly decided issues of ownership and use once and for all.[13]

Such hopes were not based simply upon utopian fantasy. In the spring of 1905 peasant organizations were actually participating in large-scale collective seizures of land. In the central Black Earth region, where unions of peasants and rural school teachers had established peasant "brotherhoods" in the 1900s, thousands of peasants refused in May 1905 to meet any government obligations until their demands for land and liberty were met.[14] According to the editorials in the SR newspaper *Revoliutsionnaia Rossiia* in the spring of 1905, if such actions persisted and spread, if peasants fought not only against landlords but in opposition to tax collectors, army recruiters, and policemen, the success of the revolution was assured.

Unconcerned with the ideological distinctions between peasant, petty bourgeois, and proletarian which so fascinated Russian Marxist emigrés, SRs in early 1905 provided a kind of object lesson in the advantages and disadvantages of theoretical and political flexibility. It was obvious from the outset that their demands and goals were easily understood by working people who were new to political action. SRs set no prior limits to the possible scope of the current revolution, and called upon peasants, proletarians, and impoverished intellectuals to fight the rich in order to win at least "socialistic" gains. Emphasizing the common interests which united all who were exploited and persecuted by the tsarist regime, they even invited the Kadet P. N. Miliukov to join the SR Central Committee. Filled with the cooperative spirit, SRs attempted to work with liberals to establish an All-Russian Peasant Union. Nevertheless, with all the good will in the world the conflict between SR and liberal approaches to political action precluded even a short-term alliance. For Miliukov did not want, after all, to join in an anti-capitalist, armed peasant uprising in alliance with the urban factory workers, and the SRs did not believe that fighters for social justice could renounce violence and terror as political tactics. Although SRs were relatively free of the dogmatism which would plague Russian Social Democrats, they would find the goals of unity and clarity of purpose increasingly unattainable in 1905 and in the years to come.

Initial Marxist Responses

Regardless of their differences, liberals and SRs were alike in their desire for political success. Bolsheviks and Mensheviks were in a more difficult position, since they believed that Russia was experiencing a bourgeois-democratic revolution which they as proletarian socialists could not even want to win. Agreed that (1) peasant interests were petty bourgeois, and (2) the peasantry was destined to disappear in the course of a bourgeois social transformation, Russian Marxists welcomed the outbreak of bourgeois-democratic revolution in an "Asiatic" peasant society.

However, despite the similarity in their initial ideological judgments, Bolshevik and Menshevik differences rapidly emerged in the area of political strategy. For while Mensheviks were certain that economic backwardness imposed an absolute limit to the initiatives of principled Marxists, Lenin wrote in March 1905: "The revolutionary Social Democrat . . . will not confine himself on the eve of the revolution to pointing out what will happen 'if the worst comes to the worst.' Rather, he will show the possibility of a better outcome. He will dream—he is obliged to dream if he is not a hopeless philistine."[15] Inspired by the spectacle of peasants attempting to "burn out" the landed gentry, Lenin set out to bridge the gap between the logical Marxist position that the bourgeoisie made bourgeois revolutions, and the political fact that the actions of peasants (rather than industrialists, financiers, or their intellectual spokesmen) were threatening the foundations of the existing social and political order. From his place of exile in Zurich, Lenin avidly studied press accounts of peasant uprisings and government repression as well as the pronouncements of socialist and non-socialist political organizations. And in the spring of 1905 he proposed that a revolutionary-democratic dictatorship of the proletariat and the peasantry establish a provisional government to carry out a bourgeois-democratic revolution.[16] This formulation was so inconsistent with pre-revolutionary Marxist programs that Lenin would be forced to prove again and again in the course of 1905 that he had not sacrificed his Marxist principles upon the altar of the Russian revolution.

As we have seen, Lenin's political thinking had begun to diverge from a rigidly deterministic Marxist mainstream even before 1905. In *What Is To Be Done?* (1902), he claimed that intellectuals of middle-class

origin became proletarian once they acquired proletarian consciousness; no restrictions of a class nature were placed upon the professional
revolutionary's potential for leadership. After 1902, Lenin attempted to
deal constructively with the minority position of Russia's urban
proletariat by constructing a social category called the "rural poor"
with a potential for proletarian consciousness roughly equal to that of
the radical intellectual. In 1903 he appealed to the rural poor to ally
themselves with the kulaks in an anti-feudal struggle against the landed
gentry.[17] In 1905 Lenin adopted still another socioeconomic analysis
to deal with the political challenge of the revolution. Now, he said, the
rural poor were to recognize that their material differences with the
kulaks had become so great that they had far more in common with the
proletariat than with the bourgeoisie "in the real and strict sense of the
word."[18]

This supposed material change had come about with extraordinary
rapidity, and the expediency of Lenin's shifting analysis was obvious. At
the same time, it should be emphasized that in 1905 the rigidity of
traditional Marxist thinking on the stages of historical development
confronted Lenin with a choice between opportunism and an indefinite
wait until "history" had prepared the appropriate economic and
political foundations for socialist revolution. Engaged in a valiant (but
not very successful) attempt to transcend these repellent alternatives,
Lenin emphasized the importance of revolutionary consciousness,
developed through the experience of struggle and increased contact
with Social Democratic organizers. He argued that the rural poor could
learn to fight alongside the proletariat for the abolition of feudal
survivals, land nationalization, and a provisional revolutionary government. Whatever their economic shortcomings as small producers, they
were in Lenin's view capable of becoming politically conscious socialist
revolutionaries.

Within the Marxist movement, such assertions were extremely
controversial, and Lenin would demonstrate his commitment to a more
traditional class analysis by repeatedly putting forward unsubstan-
tiated but apparently sincere arguments for the rural proletariat as the
leading force within the peasant movement.[19] According to Lenin,
urban and rural proletarians had always to be the primary focus of
Bolshevik organizational efforts. At the London Bolshevik "Congress"
of April 1905, when M. K. Vladimirov and V. Vorovskii expressed
skepticism about the supposed revolutionary character of a petty

bourgeois peasantry,[20] Lenin emphasized that the peasantry were not permanent allies of the proletariat. It was scarcely possible, he wrote in April, "for the entire peasantry to remain solid on any issue beyond the demand for the return of the cut-off lands, for when the limits of such an agrarian reform are exceeded, the antagonism between the rural proletarians and the 'enterprising muzhiks' will inevitably assert itself more sharply than ever."[21]

Lenin placed extraordinary weight upon the good sense and superior judgment of politically conscious revolutionaries who would know enough to (1) refrain from the foolish enthusiasm and "revolutionary phrase-mongering" of the Socialist Revolutionaries, (2) put forward their own "sober estimate of the heterogeneous elements within the peasant population," and (3) encourage peasant militance when it was "progressive" and stand aside if it was merely a question of settling accounts between two more or less greedy sections of the landowning class. It was not for revolutionary Marxists to compete with naive or demagogic agitators who were "intent on popular revolutionary slogans calculated for effect and do not understand the great and serious dangers of revolutionary adventurism, particularly in the sphere of the peasant question."[22] At the same time, with such reservations held firmly in mind, he claimed that Social Democrats could conclude fighting agreements with the SRs and grant unconditional support to the peasant movement, and in particular to the actions of revolutionary peasant committees. Lenin's draft resolution on the peasant question, approved by the April Congress, called on Social Democrats to "energetically support all revolutionary measures undertaken by the peasantry to improve their position, including the confiscation of gentry, state, church, monastery and appanage lands."[23]

According to Lenin, political consciousness was not a permanent monopoly of the Social Democrats, or even the urban proletariat. Peasant uprisings were not inevitably blind and spontaneous; political consciousness could be "instilled" into the peasantry by revolutionary propaganda, and above all by a material situation which ensured that they "could not help" but want to go further than the bourgeoisie. Lenin argued that in practice, when peasants were confronted by moderates who asked them to return the land which they had taken or pay out a ruinous compensation, they would come to understand that only a revolutionary government of workers and peasants would sanction their efforts to reclaim the land they worked.[24]

In this context, Lenin was particularly concerned to distinguish the peasantry from the bourgeoisie. He cited the agrarian resolutions passed by the Union of Liberation and by the Moscow *zemstvo* conference of March 1905 as evidence that liberals were eager to make hypocritical promises of land reform to an all-too-credulous peasantry. And although liberals before 1905 had been less fanatic than Marxists about the "historically progressive" rights of property ownership, purchase, and sale,[25] Lenin argued that liberals were "objectively" treacherous. Their intellectual commitment and generosity of sentiment were not linked up with a willingness to engage in unconditional struggle; even the most radical liberals would balk at the use of force to defend the social and political ideals they claimed to hold sacred. "Seeing that their lands are in danger of being taken away for nothing, they magnanimously consent to sell them—at a suitable price, of course."[26] Contrasting them to the rural poor who risked everything in a desperate effort to change their lives, Lenin claimed that liberals passionately urged reform, initially encouraged peasants and workers to fight, and then themselves made deals with the old order if "violence threatened anarchy," i.e., if there were some real threat to the system of private property. He argued that the untutored peasantry's capacity for unconditional struggle made them more likely than educated liberals to act as revolutionary democrats, "great as may be the evidence of non-class-consciousness and of reactionary sentiment in particular instances."[27] For this reason, it made more sense for Social Democrats to fight for the leadership of the peasantry in a bourgeois government than to support liberals who had no intention of creating the best conditions for a future socialist revolution.

To the Mensheviks, who held their own separate conference in Geneva in May 1905, Lenin's enthusiastic preference for one segment of the bourgeoisie over the other seemed both un-Marxist and politically irresponsible. It seemed to them that Lenin, with his assertions that "history" and a "correct" understanding of objective conditions would somehow enable Social Democrats to lead a bourgeois government, was abandoning the principles of economic determinism. In their speeches to the conference, both Plekhanov and Martynov lashed out against the dangers of peasant activism, arguing that if enterprising petty capitalists and land-hungry primitives took to action, they could only succeed in fragmenting the large-scale capitalist enterprises which created the material basis for socialist revolution.

Mensheviks found the specter of political success as demoralizing as the reality of peasant land seizure. As Martov pointed out, if Social Democrats came to power in a society just emerging out of feudalism, the historical requirements of bourgeois development would force them to enact bourgeois measures which would alienate their proletarian supporters.[28] Impressed by the twin dangers of peasant backwardness and opportunist submission to the temptations of revolutionary leadership, Martynov and F. I. Dan argued that in Russia, the proletariat and its political representatives had to force the middle class to perform its proper historical role.[29] In March and April, the Menshevik *Iskra* had suggested that if the current revolution should somehow bring Social Democrats to power, they would have to abdicate rather than attempt to rule a bourgeois social order.

But it would prove increasingly difficult for Mensheviks to maintain such iron consistency in the spring of 1905, when peasants under the influence of Social Democrats organized powerful centers of political resistance to tsarist authority in the Caucasus. Reluctantly, the delegates to the Geneva conference came to recognize "the expediency of partial, episodic" seizures of power for the sole purpose of weakening the tsarist regime. In an editorial of May 1905 the Menshevik *Iskra* conceded that "if we should finally be swept into power against our will by the inner dialectics of the revolution at a time when the national conditions for the establishment of socialism are not yet mature, we would not back out."[30]

Although Lenin's brand of initiative attracted little support, Trotsky's theory of "permanent revolution" posed a more appealing challenge to Menshevik caution. Rejecting both peasants and liberals as fundamentally unreliable allies for the working class, Trotsky wanted to rely upon the actions of a revolutionary West European proletariat to aid in the transformation of backward Russia into a socialist society.[31] In political terms he was as enthusiastic an activist as Lenin, and equally prone to simplify problems of revolutionary leadership. For Trotsky, there could be no revolutionary situation or phase of economic development in which Marxists were less fit to govern than non-Marxists. At the same time, he was as eager as Lenin to assume that Marxists (whatever their own class origins) could lead proletarians, semi-proletarians, or peasants without fear of class antagonism. Trotsky's political vision was far more utopian than Lenin's, since it was rooted in the hope that a nonexistent European revolution would guarantee the success of Russia's urban proletarian minority. Yet it was significant that his views were less "morally" offensive to Russian Mensheviks, who preferred the idea of proletarians leading an at least potentially socialist revolution to the prospect of dragging a primitive petty bourgeoisie into a futile struggle to establish Marxists as leaders of a bourgeois capitalist regime. At Geneva, the Mensheviks adopted a resolution which allowed for the possibility of a socialist revolution in Russia if the Russian revolution were to "leap over" into the advanced countries of Western Europe.[32]

Criticism of Lenin's policy of unconditional support for peasant land seizure was widespread among Marxist and non-Marxist socialists. Within the RSDLP, emigré leaders and provincial Social Democrats were equally fearful that land seizure might delay the necessary advance of progressive, large-scale capitalist enterprise.[33] It was ironic that the Socialist Revolutionaries were the most eager to criticize Lenin's program for being insufficiently socialist. According to V. M. Chernov, Lenin was a demagogue whose desire for short-term political gain made him indifferent to the possibility that in the course of land seizure, the richer peasants might seize the most land and deny the claims of the poor.[34] In the opinion of the SR A. R. Gotz, socialists had to fight to prevent this from happening; they could not simply encourage action and hope to profit from its consequences. As Gotz put it, socialists had to exert themselves to ensure that land seizure became a step toward socialism rather than the consolidation of kulak power in the countryside.[35]

Undaunted by such criticism, Lenin wrote his "Two Tactics of Social Democracy in the Democratic Revolution" (July 1905), a work filled with realistic political insights and tortuous theoretical justifications of his peasant strategy. With numerous citations from Marx and references to the traditional dependence of Russian industrialists upon the autocracy's protection and support, he argued that it was hopeless to expect the Russian bourgeoisie to function as a revolutionary class. But as he went on to paint a picture of bourgeois revolution in which the bourgeoisie were somehow "not good enough" to play a leading role, it was obvious that the materialist conception of history was being strained to the utmost to accommodate Lenin's political suspicions of the Russian liberal movement. "In a certain sense," he wrote, bourgeois revolution was "more advantageous to the proletariat than to the bourgeoisie," because the bourgeoisie would refuse to enact measures like the eight-hour day or nationalization of the land once they realized that such measures would strengthen the social classes which were most hostile to capitalist economic domination.[36] In contrast, Lenin argued that politically conscious revolutionaries, guided by a superior level of revolutionary consciousness and supported by the proletariat and the peasantry, could promote capitalism in such a way that it would rapidly create the material foundations for socialism.

Such arguments for capitalist economic domination politically controlled by Marxian socialists had little to do with conventional Marxist analysis of the state as a representative of the ruling class. But when freed of their ideological trappings, Lenin's arguments made eminent sense. Any political activist could understand why a revolutionary might fight to win a political struggle and attempt to introduce changes which would lead toward the realization of the revolution's future goals. The SRs, for example, were quite hopeful that the militance of the laboring poor might enable them to lead Russia from economic backwardness to an at least "socialistic" organization of production and distribution.[37] It was only Marxism which left its adherents with the dismal choice between patient preparation for action at some future date, or a proletarian socialist effort to establish in Russia a capitalist economic and social order notable for the superior efficiency of its exploitation of proletarian labor.

Lenin was both optimistic and unsentimental in appraising the two components of his potential constituency. Recognizing that both the proletariat and the peasantry were disunited, backward, and ignorant, he admitted as well that Social Democrats had a "very, very inadequate" influence on the proletariat and a "quite insignificant" influence on the peasantry. His hopes for the future were not based upon any simple faith in the virtues of the "people," whether peasant or proletarian. As he wrote in July, "In classifying the big social groups according to their political tendencies we can, without danger of serious error, identify revolutionary and republican democracy with the mass of the peasants—of course, in the same sense and *with the same reservations and implied conditions* that we can identify the working class with Social Democracy [*emphasis added*]."[38]

At the same time, Lenin argued that it was equally important that Marxists faced by a revolutionary peasant movement not use class analysis as a device for isolating the working class, or dividing "the 'people' into 'classes' so that the advanced class will become locked up within itself, will confine itself within narrow limits, and emasculate its activity."[39]

The Deepening of the Revolution

In practice, both Lenin's Marxist critics and his supporters found it extremely difficult to figure out how to use either class analysis or a materialist conception of history to extend and deepen their awareness of the potential for agreement as well as hostility between workers and peasants. With the emergence and growth of an All-Russian Peasant Union in the summer of 1905, the irrelevance of traditional Marxism to peasant demands became more and more obvious. At,the first congress of the Peasant Union, in July 1905, most participants were "middle" peasants, a group notoriously difficult for Marxists to deal with. In general although the delegates failed to see any particular contradiction between loyalty to the tsar and the calling of a Constituent Assembly, many did seem nevertheless to understand that there was some connection between the need for land and the Constituent Assembly that the *intelligenty* talked so much about.[40] One peasant representative from Vladimir, identifying himself as a descendant of a serf of the Decembrist Pestel,[41] called for the abolition of autocracy and the establishment of a democratic republic, but his view was not widely accepted. Most delegates considered themselves supporters of the monarchy, and saw no contradiction between monarchism and their deeply held conviction that land should not be anyone's private property.

Clearly aware that it was enlightened of him to be present, the Social Democrat A. V. Shestakov came before the assembled peasants to announce that seizure of the large estates might fragment the more efficient, large-scale economic enterprise which formed the basis for progressive capitalist development in the countryside. He went on to explain that without the factory worker, all peasant revolutionary efforts were doomed to failure. Infuriated by his condescension, the angry delegates retorted, "Without the peasantry a handful of factory workers would get nowhere."[42] But Shestakov remained true to his principles, and presented Marxism to the assembled peasants as an ideology alien to what they conceived to be their own interests. The Peasant Union delegates for their part rejected Marxist pro-capitalism, and finally voted to demand a Constituent Assembly and the confiscation of the landed estates.

Rural unrest steadily escalated in the summer and fall of 1905. By September the All-Russian Peasant Union had grown to an estimated 100,000 members and supporters in forty-two provinces of the empire. Local members tended to be more sympathetic to appeals for direct action than the liberal-oriented Central Committee, which had advised peasants to participate in elections to a consultative assembly in August 1905.[43] The meager harvest of 1905 made previously law-abiding peasants more willing to listen to the dissatisfied war veterans and rural school teachers who urged violent and "illegal" action to avert the danger of famine. Despite the Marxist emphasis on class differentiation within the village, peasant violence was primarily directed against the landed gentry (in the form of arson). There was little in the autumn of 1905 that resembled class war between kulaks and proletarians, and many land seizures were undertaken by peasants acting as members of the traditional, repartitional land commune (the *mir*, or *obshchina*). Lenin, attempting to appropriate peasant violence for the constructive use of revolutionary Marxists, went so far as to suggest in late September that in economically advanced regions of the empire, where "agricultural laborers" were willing to fight, an "uninterrupted revolution" might continue until socialism was established.[44]

The explosion of peasant violence in September and October provoked increased government repression and elicited unprecedented concessions. As loyal Cossack troops carried out public floggings and burned peasant villages, the tsar issued a manifesto on October 17, 1905, which promised civil liberties and a legislative duma, as well as a reduction and eventual cancellation of all peasant redemption payments. A substantial amount of appanage land was sold to the Peasant Bank for resale on easy terms; this move was accompanied by the general warning that the needs of the peasantry would not be satisfied at the expense of other landowners. But by October even these measures were insufficient to check the mounting popular resistance to traditional authority and property relationships. Provincial officials complained that peasants took the October promises of civil liberty as an invitation to seize forest and pasture land.[45] A wave of pogroms followed the release of the manifesto, and by November the Russian countryside was ablaze with the most widespread rioting of the revolutionary year. Mutinies erupted in St. Petersburg, Kronstadt, Kiev, and Sevastopol. Soldiers' councils (*soviets*) voiced political demands in Krasnoyarsk and Vladivostok, where unrest among the predominantly peasant troops demobilized after the conclusion of the

Russo-Japanese War became so serious that it threatened state control over the Trans-Siberian Railway.

Of more conventional interest to Marxists but outside the scope of our discussion was the factory unrest which culminated in an October general strike and the formation of soviets in St. Petersburg, Moscow, and elsewhere. Suffice it to say that in the autumn of 1905 the workers thoroughly vindicated Lenin's faith in them; in his view it was not the peasantry but the plebeian architects of the soviet who had "wrested from the tsarist regime a recognition of liberty in a paper manifesto."[46] Finding more political potential in the factory workers' soviets than in the All-Russian Peasant Union, he argued in October that the revolution could only succeed if the urban and rural petty bourgeoisie could be brought to *imitate* the factory workers' heroic examples of resistance to traditional authority. The proletariat would never triumph alone; in Lenin's words, "revolutionary war differs from other wars in that it draws its main reserves from the camp of its enemy's erstwhile allies, erstwhile supporters of tsarism, or people who blindly obeyed tsarism."[47] But only the proletariat was reliable as a revolutionary social class.

After Lenin returned to Russia in November 1905, the scope of his political appeals continued to expand. With the experience of popular dissidence closer at hand, he enthusiastically suggested that the "fair-minded and alert and politically conscious elements in every class of the population" might constitute the basis for a successful revolutionary army. Characteristically, he refused to judge the state's repressive violence and peasant violence by the same standard, although the peasant pogroms which had followed the October Manifesto put this approach to a rather severe test. While he warned against any idealizing of the peasantry, Lenin emphasized the role of the police and the "Union of the Russian People" as instigators of the pogroms. Inspired by the successes of the soviet-directed general strike, he praised the St. Petersburg soviet as the embryo of a provisional revolutionary government,[48] and braved the criticism of Bolsheviks as well as Mensheviks. (Many fellow Leninists were fearful of the spontaneity and lack of discipline of soviet leaders, who they considered in no sense committed to the ideals of "democratic centralism." The editors of the Bolshevik-oriented *Novaia Zhizn* were so deeply opposed to Lenin's position that they refused to publish his articles on the soviet's revolutionary potential.)[49]

The brutality of the government's punitive measures and the continuation of peasant resistance increased the intransigence of the All-Russian Peasant Union, which voted on November 6 to regard those who participated in the "fraudulent" state-sponsored duma as "enemies of the people." Demanding a Constituent Assembly, the transfer of all landed property to the state, and the abolition of hired labor in agriculture, the Peasant Union threatened a nationwide agricultural strike or, if necessary, an armed insurrection based upon the joint action of peasants and industrial workers. In December 1905 its leaders signed a "Financial Manifesto" together with other members of the socialist opposition, which called for (1) a mass refusal to pay taxes, (2) a withdrawal of all bank deposits, and (3) a demand by depositors for payment in gold. The autocracy, engaged at that very moment in delicate negotiations for a much-needed loan from France, responded by arresting 230 soviet delegates. Those who managed to remain free called for a new general strike and an armed insurrection. Shortly afterward, an uprising organized by the Peasant Union and the SR Party briefly held out against government forces.[50]

Although Lenin continued to ridicule SR tactics and misstate their goals, there was in late 1905 a marked similarity between the political analyses put forward by Lenin and by the SRs. Like Lenin, SRs believed that the revolution would continue. They shared both his scorn for the October Manifesto and his hope that the coming year would bring a final end to the autocracy. But Lenin, intent on proving to his fellow Social Democrats that he remained as suspicious as ever of the petty bourgeois intellectual, brought out and repeated all of the anti-populist polemics of the 1890s. As a result, at the very time that SRs were demanding a Constituent Assembly and Chernov was gaining support within the SR Party for his theory of a two-stage revolution with a long transition period before socialism could be established, Lenin was busy denouncing "populist romantics" for ignoring politics and dreaming of an immediate socialist revolution.[51] Insisting that Marxists and SRs could do no more than conclude "temporary fighting agreements," he contrasted the petty bourgeois SRs with the "real" peasants of the All-Russian Peasant Union, who were "coming forward as the conscious maker[s] of a new way of life in Russia."[52]

While the spread of land seizures, strikes, and mutinies brought joy to the hearts of radical agitators, revolutionary militance had begun by the year's end to lose its attractiveness for many individuals associated with the liberal movement. The continued outbreaks of popular violence gradually undermined the fragile efforts of leftist liberals to maintain their ties with Social Democrats and SRs. Instead, leading representatives of the Kadet Party and the *zemstvo* entered into negotiations with the tsarist regime. As the Peasant Union issued its bitter and militant call to resistance, a Congress of Zemstvo and Town Duma Representatives convened in Moscow to discuss the restoration of order, and submitted proposals for agrarian and legal reform to the government. Although a pardon was requested for political prisoners, no mention was made of amnesty for peasants arrested for participating in agrarian disturbances.[53] Critical of the government's repressive measures as a *"Pugachevshchina* from above," leading Kadets had nevertheless become increasingly reluctant to participate further in illegal popular activities. Peter Struve argued that after the October Manifesto, further revolutionary action was useless, even harmful. A. A. Kaufman suggested that the party withdraw from active political struggle until things were calmer.[54] A suggestion that the Kadet Central Committee take up a collection on behalf of the Petersburg strikers was rejected as "untimely." And while the left wing of the Kadet party officially continued to support the radical peasants and workers, no positive action in support of revolutionary activity was forthcoming. The widespread recognition that the duma was itself the product of the revolutionary unrest which had begun in January 1905 did not shake the conviction of liberal party leaders that further upheaval was dangerous and futile. In many respects, the Kadets seemed to be fulfilling many of Lenin's earlier predictions. As he had suggested, they preferred the rather dubious concessions of the tsarist regime to the prospect of peasant "anarchy." Obeying the government's new decrees, they hoped that the new duma could be transformed by their efforts into a truly parliamentary institution. In contrast to the Kadet willingness to compromise, Lenin claimed in December that the peasant and proletarian revolution was reaching new heights and that government repressive efforts were bound to fail.[55]

Duma or Revolution

Despite the government's promise of civil liberties and a legislative duma, the revolutionary peasant movement did not subside in 1906. The level of urban unrest diminished, but collective attacks on gentry estates and resistance to government authority continued to prevent the reestablishment of any semblance of normal, i.e., pre-revolutionary, village life. Propaganda directed against the rights of property owners even made headway within the army, and many landlords began to fear that peasant soldiers might soon declare themselves unwilling to suppress the repeated outbursts of violence which were taking place in the Caucasus, the lower Volga region, Siberia, Poland, and the Baltic provinces. In January, for example, a frightened landlord from Kursk reported overhearing a soldier in his district announce to his comrades, "If they don't let a single *dvorianin* out of Petersburg, then there will be land for all."[56]

In 1906 the persistence of rural unrest would destroy all semblance of unity among the autocracy's political opponents. Once the specter of peasant anarchy began to haunt the progressive intellectuals who had called for a revolution against the tsar in early 1905, many hastened to disassociate themselves from the "firebrands" of the left. Within the Kadet Party, it was agreed to revise the official agrarian program in order to permit a more thoroughing defense of private property rights and a search for constructive and legal opportunities within the state duma. *Zemstvo* groups, finding the Kadets too radical, formed separate organizations of landowners and nobles to defend their own interests against the peasantry.[57]

The general expectation of a massive peasant uprising in the spring of 1906 was shared by Finance Minister Witte, by the SRs and the All-Russian Peasant Union, and by the Bolsheviks. The latter groups accordingly boycotted the duma election campaign and rested their political hopes upon the continued growth of violent revolution. Lenin called for the organization of guerrilla operations in order to merge workers, peasants, and soldiers into a single victorious "stream of insurrection." As he wrote in March 1906:

> We must say to the peasants: after taking the land, you should go further; otherwise you will be beaten and hurled back by the landlords and the big bourgeoisie. You cannot take the land and retain it without achieving new political gains, without striking another and even stronger blow at private ownership of the land in general. In politics, as in all the life of society, if you do not push forward, you will be hurled back. Either the bourgeoisie, strengthened after the democratic revolution . . . will rob both the workers and the peasant masses of all their gains, or the proletariat and the peasant masses will fight their way further forward.[58]

In contrast, the Mensheviks, who were dismayed by the effectiveness of the government's repressive action against the St. Petersburg and Moscow soviets and quite unwilling to rely upon the peasant movement, left the question of participation in the duma campaign up to local Social Democratic committees.

The Stockholm "Unity" Congress of the RSDLP

It was thus in an atmosphere charged with conflicting assessments of peasant violence and parliamentary opportunity that Social Democratic delegates met in Stockholm in April 1906. Although the Stockholm "Unity" Congress was intended to reconcile Bolshevik and Menshevik differences, it was immediately evident that Lenin would concede nothing to his critics. Contemptuous of their "parliamentary illusions" about the duma, he called for the formation of revolutionary peasant committees to confiscate the gentry estates and nationalize all landed property.[59] His proposals aroused a storm of controversy, particularly among the many Social Democrats who were still convinced that the revolution currently taking place was essentially not "theirs" because it was neither proletarian nor socialist in character. F. I. Dan was at great pains to make clear that a Social Democratic agrarian program was not designed for the peasantry; its purpose was to define the proper relationship of the proletariat to the land question.[60] Economic determinists all, the Mensheviks dealt with the political challenge posed by peasant land seizure as an aspect of the deeper issue of Russian backwardness. Their overriding fear was that revolutionary peasant action might fragment already existing large-scale capitalist property and delay the development of the material foundations for a socialist revolution.[61] Lenin would reverse the Menshevik priorities, in recognition that peasant political action was currently threatening the very survival of the tsarist regime (and, cynics might point out, in recognition of the fact that he had no real answer to the economic questions raised by the Mensheviks).

The Menshevik agrarian program developed by Peter Maslov was intended to combine agricultural progress with the level of social justice which Mensheviks considered realizable, given Russia's level of historical development. The Maslov plan provided for "municipalization," or the transfer of large landed estates to local democratic organizations representing both rural and urban proletarian elements.[62] Although no one suggested that it was likely that urban proletarians would be invited to join village committees, F. I. Dan was able to convince a majority of the Stockholm delegates that in principle, reliable local decisions on the land question could only be made with the participation of the more "advanced" social classes.[63] Under urban proletarian guidance, estates which had formerly hired labor on a capitalist basis were to function as before, on condition that they paid rent to the new and democratic municipal organizations. Maslov believed that any encroachment upon the traditional allotment would turn even the poorest peasants against the revolution. He reminded Lenin of his statement in "To the Rural Poor" that Social Democrats would never take away the land of small and middle peasants and demanded to know if peasants were to believe the Lenin of 1903 or the Lenin of 1906.[64] According to the terms of Maslov's plan, peasant allotments were to be left untouched, and any land which had not previously been managed in capitalist fashion was to be leased out to the peasantry.[65]

On political grounds, Plekhanov denounced Lenin's "utopia of the seizure of power by the revolutionaries," pointing out that such an event would depend upon a combination of such unlikely circumstances as (1) a steadfast revolutionary peasantry, (2) a proletariat able to exercise power wholly out of proportion to its numbers, and (3) a proletarian party capable of carrying out bourgeois policies without betraying its socialist principles. As for Lenin's program for nationalization of the land, Plekhanov argued that if the revolution failed, the transfer of land to the state would leave the autocracy in possession of more landed property than ever before. In contrast, municipalization would confront any Russian government with a situation in which land was controlled by local democratic organizations which could serve at the same time as centers of resistance to reaction. Referring contemptuously to Lenin's "populist" notion of "popular creativity," he argued that Lenin tried to substitute enthusiasm for stubborn material facts. Plekhanov insisted that however sympathetic to the proletariat any peasants might become in the course of political struggle, Russia remained economically backward, and backwardness imposed limits which could not be transcended at will by Marxist revolutionaries.[66]

Delegates to the congress who were confused by the intricacies of a debate over what would happen to land which had after all not yet been taken by the peasantry preferred simpler formulations. Stalin proposed, for example, a straightforwardly expedient program. On what many Marxists would consider practical grounds, he argued that it was impossible to ignore the peasantry's desire to divide up the land and claim it as their own private property. Ignoring the economic issues raised by Plekhanov as well as the prevalence of popular demands for the abolition of private property, Stalin flatly asserted that division of the land by the peasantry would neither delay economic development nor check the progress of the revolution. In his view, it was only political common sense to reject the proposals of Lenin and Maslov and to support the petty bourgeois demand for confiscation and division of the land.[67]

As Lenin attempted to defend himself against such attacks, the strain imposed by his effort to keep political optimism and distrust of the petty bourgeoisie in some sort of balance was clearly discernible. Striving to provide a material basis for his nationalization program, he cited passages from *Capital* which supported the idea that the transfer of land to the state was a bourgeois measure which would create in Russia the sort of capitalist competition among free farmers which prevailed in the American West. An "American-style," radical, bourgeois economic transformation would, he claimed, provide the best possible basis for the future establishment of socialism.[68] In one of his rare arguments against the advantages of scale, Lenin emphasized that large estates were no more rationally cultivated than the peasant allotments and did not therefore have to be preserved at all costs.[69]

In general, however, Lenin focused upon issues of political strategy. He recognized quite frankly that the danger of counterrevolution was real, and even likely, regardless of the agrarian policy which Social Democrats might adopt. As certain as Plekhanov that "under each and every form of possession and property the small proprietor will always be a bulwark of restoration,"[70] he admitted as well that if the revolution failed, it would be realistic for Social Democrats to encourage peasants to divide the land among themselves as Stalin had proposed. Such a process would not be as "politically educational" for peasants as a nationalization carried out by revolutionary peasant committees. But "land division" would confront the state with the unenviable political task of compelling each peasant to return newly seized land to its former owners. In contrast, Lenin argued that a resurgent autocracy could easily smash any local democratic organizations of the sort envisioned in Maslov's municipalization plan.[71]

As dubious as Trotsky that a Russian revolution could triumph in isolation, Lenin predicted that if the agrarian movement were successful, it might set off a Western socialist revolution which was the only *absolute* guarantee against tsarist restoration.[72] But whatever happened in the West, Russian revolutionaries had to continue their efforts to incite the peasantry to action which would break traditional habits of subservience to the gentry and the state. They were obliged to discover within economically unsound or meaningless beliefs about "the land being God's, nobody's, or the state's" a sound basis for the building of peasant political consciousness.[73] In Lenin's view, Social Democratic propaganda, accompanied by the experience of participating in peasant committees which could settle accounts with the officials and landlords "in a plebeian manner," would develop in peasants the "popular creativity" reflected in the formation of peasant conferences, unions, and soviets in the course of 1905. In April 1906 he claimed that the time was ripe for an armed worker and peasant insurrection.[74] The possibility that land seizure by peasant committees could be manipulated by kulak elements or perpetuate backward economic practices was not as important to him as the immediate need to take seriously, encourage, and organize the peasant actions which were currently shaking the foundations of the tsarist regime. In this context, Lenin argued that "municipalization" was in political terms an appeal to the most conservative elements within the rural population. Because it focused only upon peasants who were obsessed with holding on to their tiny plots of land and excluded those who were at that very moment demanding the abolition of private property, municipalization did not allow for the possibility of a successful revolutionary peasant movement.[75] (In an aside clearly intended for fellow Marxists rather than peasants, he admitted that after the success of a bourgeois-democratic revolution Social Democrats would not need to concern themselves with proprietors, whether large or small. At that time, they would be free to concentrate upon the rural proletarians who would soon become the majority of the agricultural population.[76]

Lenin was unable to convince a majority of delegates at the "Unity" Congress that his tortuous arguments were sensible and valid. Maslov's plan was overwhelmingly approved, and despite Lenin's insistence upon the difference between the fighting SRs and the cowardly Kadets, equal condemnation was given to "utopian petty bourgeois socialist SRs" and to Kadets who appealed to the peasants' property instincts.

Over Bolshevik opposition, the congress voted to abandon any further boycott of the state duma, and to run candidates for office in areas where duma elections had not yet been held.[77] Lenin took defeat with his usual bad grace, attacking the party program and especially the decision to participate in the duma as a "deal with reaction, a Kadet program."[78]

The First State Duma

While Lenin hoped that revolutionary action would sweep away the autocracy as well as the duma, there were indications even in the spring of 1906 that the government might survive with its prerogatives essentially unchanged. Tsarist officials found that many formerly dissident landlords were ready by 1906 to support the restoration of order by whatever means necessary. An immense foreign loan obtained by Finance Minister Witte even before the duma opened provided the government with the resources to financially secure the army's loyalty and to resist any duma challenge to its authority. And among those who still believed that peasants were the natural supporters of a conservative traditional order, the numerical strength of peasant delegates in the new duma gave real (though brief) satisfaction. For the peasants had not observed the boycott advocated by most of the revolutionary left. Instead, they had participated in the elections and voted into office a Kadet majority and more than a hundred peasant deputies as delegates to the new, presumably legislative assembly.

Lenin's attitude toward the duma was determined by his jaundiced view of the Kadets who dominated it. As self-proclaimed moderates prepared to mediate between the extremists of the left and right, the Kadets represented for Lenin a particularly sinister threat to the growth of the revolution. In his view, liberals cynically appealed for "reasonable" solutions, as if justice could emerge out of compromise between exploiter and victim. By supporting the transfer of private land to the peasantry on condition that a "just price" be paid to the former landowner, liberals attempted to demonstrate to the politically naive that they were concerned with the welfare of society as a whole. Lenin's ready contempt for Russian liberals was reinforced by the "revelation" that Kadets intended the question of a just price for confiscated land to be decided by committees made up of equal numbers of peasants and landlords. To Lenin, a settlement based upon the assumption that a poor peasant and a rich landlord were equal in their power to negotiate agreements was typical of "shoddy" liberal conceptions of justice.[79] The willingness of Kadet delegates to fully discuss the question of land reform in the duma seemed to him part of an overall strategy aimed at bribing the peasant to accept a deal between the bourgeoisie and the supposedly "more honest" representatives of the old order.

Lenin looked instead for support from the 107 peasant delegates who made up the so-called Trudovik group in the duma.[80] While Kadets complained that Trudoviks treated the first duma as a place for polemics and demonstrations rather than lawmaking,[81] Lenin's faith in revolutionary peasant attitudes was sustained by Trudovik denunciations of greedy landlords who cheated the poor, violated peasant women, and called in the army to burn down rebellious villages. Although he emphasized that the Trudoviks were as naive in their socialist claims as the SRs,[82] Lenin praised them nevertheless as non-liberal representatives of the rural poor who were willing to do battle against gentry power and privilege. He did not consider the Trudoviks socialist for demanding that land be transferred to the "whole people," with rights of use reserved for those who worked it with their own hands. In Lenin's view such slogans meant nothing. But he insisted as well that the peasantry's "trivial dreams" could not be allowed to "obscure the genuinely revolutionary action of this class in the present revolution." The petty bourgeois fantasy of land for all was worth supporting because it could only be realized by means of a revolutionary struggle which took place outside the confines of the duma.[83]

Unlike the Mensheviks, Lenin took peasant "dreams" seriously as a stimulus to action. But as a Marxist he insisted nevertheless that most peasants, like their SR defenders, could only be fighters for some form of capitalism. Whether they demanded social control over landed property or, like the SR Chernov, argued that land socialization was only the first step in the building of socialism,[84] they could never for Lenin be anything but petty bourgeois. And although Trudoviks in the duma proved to be more consistent defenders of political amnesty and the right to freedom of assembly than the Kadets,[85] Lenin continued to insist that the Trudoviks embodied the simple, radical petty bourgeois belief that if peasants got land, all of their problems would be solved.[86] While they claimed to be socialists —and unlike the liberals they were in Lenin's sense willing to fight—Trudoviks and SRs could only be incorporated into his Marxist analysis if it was asserted that what they "really" wanted was petty capitalist development on free land, unencumbered by feudal restrictions. The substance of the numerous peasant demands for a transfer of all land to the *mir* without compensation to former owners was never taken seriously by Lenin or by any other Russian Marxist during this period.

Despite the distinctions that Lenin attempted to draw between Kadets and Trudoviks, by the spring of 1906 these two groups had managed to agree on the need for substantial limitations on the rights of property. And in late June, forty Trudoviks and twenty-three non-aligned peasants had formed a new party intended to act in close tactical alliance with the Kadets. To Lenin, this news provided a depressing indication that "petty bourgeois" compromise had come to the fore.[87] But the tsarist regime viewed the prospect of Kadet – Trudovik cooperation with deep misgiving, since it coincided with eruptions of rural violence so serious that the Emperor of Austria had been queried on the possibility of Austrian intervention in Russia to restore order.[88] Unwilling to risk the possibility that nationally elected peasant and liberal delegates might join in a call for the confiscation of the gentry estates, Premier P. A. Stolypin ordered the duma dissolved in July 1906.

In response to the dissolution decree, a number of duma deputies withdrew to Vyborg, where they issued a manifesto calling for a mass refusal to pay taxes or to perform military service. In contrast, Social Democrats, SRs, and Trudoviks appealed for an armed peasant uprising to expel the landlords and seize their land. It is significant that here as earlier Lenin wholeheartedly supported the appeal for peasant land seizure. Conceding that excessive damage to land, tools, and livestock might occur in the process, he insisted nevertheless that "only pedants or traitors to the people can bewail the fact that peasants always resort to such methods."[89] In his view, the outbreak of a violent upheaval aimed at preventing any resurgence of autocratic power took precedence over every other consideration.

But by July 1906 the prospect of continuing revolution was no longer sure. Although strikes and mutinies took place after the duma's dissolution, and peasant disturbances between May and August 1906 were as widespread as they had been during the last four months of 1905, the government was able to sustain its repressive violence longer than peasants could persist in their attacks upon land and property. No official limits were placed on the methods considered acceptable for the restoration of order, as was demonstrated by Minister of the Interior Durnovo's notorious telegram to a provincial governor: "Take the sternest measures to bring the disorders to an end; it is a useful thing to wipe the rebellious village off the face of the earth, and to exterminate the rebels themselves without mercy, by force of arms."[90]

The army generally remained loyal to the government, and the huge loan obtained before the duma opened allowed the government to maintain and even strengthen its forces in 1906. In order to broaden its base of political support, the government launched a full-scale effort to break the unanimity of peasant demands for the abolition of private property. Appealing to the property interest of the potential entrepreneur, in July 1906, the Stolypin regime launched a program intended to replace the peasant commune with a class of sturdy individual proprietors devoted to the improvement of their land and loyal to the government which established them as property owners.

In this context, Lenin began to place more emphasis upon peasant backwardness. Although it might have been argued, given the explosion of rural violence in 1906, that the peasants were in fact the *last* social element to abandon the revolutionary struggle, Lenin's Marxist analysis led him to insist that the peasantry had proven to be less steadfast than the proletariat. Once proletarian unrest had begun to decline, Lenin began to fear that "the traditional peasant prejudices, fostered by all sorts of opportunists, will be sufficient to outweigh the good sense of the poor peasantry awakened in the flames of the revolution."[91] While peasant unrest encouraged the SRs to continue their boycott of the duma, Marxist intellectuals feared that Stolypin's effort to appeal to the peasant as a petty bourgeois was bound to succeed. Lenin shifted his policy of duma boycott and called on party workers to participate in the election campaign for the new duma in cooperation with the Trudoviks. He now argued that the duma might be a useful forum for inflammatory political agitation.

Conclusion

Having recognized in 1905 that the peasant majority of the population was the crucial factor in any Russian revolution, Lenin argued that the experience of opposition to traditional authority might bring them to support a "revolutionary-democratic movement" led by Social Democrats. Unlike the Mensheviks, he was unafraid of the possibility of defeat, and pointed out with unassailable political realism: "Real support in a general struggle is given to those who strive for the maximum . . . and not to those who opportunistically curtail the aims of the struggle before the fight."[92] On the other hand, Lenin's "principled" rejection of the possibility that peasants might be anti-capitalist (much less socialist) prevented him from making a convincing case that peasants were an appropriate political constituency for revolutionary socialists. Despite his repeated and baseless claim that rural proletarians were the leading revolutionary force in the country-side, he was unable to convince his critics on the left that he was anything but an opportunist par excellence.

Lenin provided a reasonably accurate summary of his position in July, 1906, when he wrote:

> We support the peasantry to the extent that it is revolutionary-democratic. We are making ready (doing so now, at once) to fight it when and to the extent that it becomes reactionary and anti-proletarian. The essence of Marxism lies in that double task, which only those who do not understand Marxism can vulgarize or compress into a single or simple task.[93]

Lenin's formulation left most Russian Marxists in the camp of "those who do not understand Marxism." Despite the extraordinary incisive-ness of his political insight into the problems of his adversaries, the deficiencies of Lenin's economics and sociology continued to render the concept of Marxist peasant revolution a contradiction in terms.

6

A Strategy for Marxist Bourgeois Revolution, 1907–16

By 1907 MARTIAL LAW was in force in every corner of the Russian Empire. The influx of generous amounts of foreign aid, the continued loyalty of the armed forces to a government which ruled by decree, and the emergence of a politically active segment of the gentry class purged of its pre-revolutionary attachment to liberal programs and principles enabled the tsarist regime to survive the revolutionary challenges of 1905 and 1906 with most of its prerogatives intact.[1] In this situation, Premier Stolypin was able to freely ignore the liberties granted in the heat of revolution. The twin policies of political retrenchment and obliteration of the traditional peasant commune were accordingly pursued without effective opposition either from his revolutionary or his law-abiding critics.

The Economic Challenge

The anti-communal policy associated above all with the name of Stolypin was the culmination of decades of debate between those who had defended the commune as a guarantee of stability and order, and the politically conservative proponents of economic individualism. Like the architects of Prussian economic reform in the 1820s, Russian bureaucrats of the 1900s had become increasingly convinced that peasant property owners were the most reliable defenders of law and order.[2] After 1906 they moved to establish the security of Russia's more privileged social elements upon a new foundation. The collective character of peasant attacks upon gentry property in the course of 1905 and 1906 had finally destroyed the case for the commune as a politically stabilizing force.

The shift away from the commune was not sudden, but it entailed nevertheless a rejection of the bulk of available evidence as well as the judgments advanced by most contemporary economists and statisticians. The prevailing scholarly view that communes could at least in the short run provide a measure of security to the social elements most heavily burdened by the process of primitive accumulation was dismissed. By 1906 fears of backwardness and admiration for the achievements of Western European entrepreneurs had combined with perceptions of the commune as a hotbed of revolution to bring the Russian autocracy to the point of irrevocable commitment to private enterprise in every sector of the economy. At a time when commune peasants were seizing land and burning landed estates, Stolypin and his supporters were able to argue with increasing persuasiveness and a certain amount of evidence that the commune protected only the "needy and the drunken" and perpetuated Russian economic stagnation. Traditional government claims to benevolent paternalism were abandoned; instead, it was hoped that a new class of politically conservative rural entrepreneurs would become the promoters of economic prosperity and social stability. In order to create a *Vendée* for any Russian revolution, government decrees issued between 1906 and 1911 made it progressively easier for peasant families to claim their communal allotments as private property.[3]

The Stolypin reforms placed Russian Marxists in a cruel dilemma. As Stolypin acted to aid the entrepreneur and allow the rest of the population to become free proletarians, the logic of the Marxist position seemed to require that Stolypin's policies be accepted as a brutal yet rational response to the requirements of Russian historical development. With impeccable consistency, the Menshevik P. P. Maslov suggested in early 1907 that Marxists would have to choose between a brutal capitalist strategy which would destroy the peasantry or a futile struggle to help the small producer resist the course of economic progress.[4] Given the conventional Marxist assumption that revolution and economic progress were indissolubly linked with the growth of class struggle and large-scale enterprise, the peasantry's poignant demands for equal access to the land could only be judged economically reactionary. The Menshevik Iu. O. Martov went so far as to hope that peasants could be emancipated from their anarchist and utopian traditions of "leveling" and brought into line with "the interests of the urban bourgeois-democratic revolution."[5] From the Menshevik point of view, the egalitarian demands of revolutionary peasants in 1905 and 1906 were hopelessly at odds with the capitalist requirements of economic development.

While Mensheviks had something of a gift for perceiving tragic and ultimately paralyzing alternatives, both tragedy and inaction were alien to Lenin, who proposed instead an audacious Marxist rural modernization program. In search of a strategy which would allow for meaningful initiatives by Bolshevik revolutionaries, Lenin suggested that the choice was not between Stolypinist progress and peasant stagnation but between "Prussian" and "American" modes of capitalist development. Judging the Russian bourgeoisie to be as unfit to build capitalism as it was to establish a democratic political order, he attempted to establish small producers in the role of chief supporters of bourgeois democracy.[6]

In order to be able to argue that it was for Marxists to further the development of capitalism in Russia, Lenin had first to abandon once and for all his earlier claims that Russia was already capitalist. Aggressive even in his admission of error, Lenin argued that he and his fellow Marxists had not been mistaken about the general trend toward capitalism in nineteenth-century Russia, but merely wrong in their assessment of the particular level which Russian agricultural development had reached. Although he conceded that Marxist "exaggerations" had made it more difficult to formulate an effective peasant strategy, Lenin made no effort whatsoever to explain why he and other Marxist writers had insisted upon the preeminence of the Russian rural capitalist in the face of overwhelming evidence to the contrary in the economic literature of the 1890s. If Marxists had been wrong, the statisticians and economists who had been right were nevertheless in Lenin's view subjective and naive; it was the Revolution of 1905 which had "exposed" the Marxist error. Furthermore, he argued, the current Marxist position was overwhelmingly correct. The revolution had somehow "confirmed the trend of development as we had defined it. The Marxist analysis of the classes in Russian society has been so brilliantly confirmed by the first two dumas in particular, that non-Marxist socialism has been shattered completely."[7]

Lenin argued in 1907 that feudal privileges and property systems were the most serious obstacles to economic progress. He criticized the Stolypin reforms for failing to create the conditions for a full-scale mobilization of the land and the peasantry for the battle against economic backwardness. In Lenin's view, the Russian government resembled the Prussian "Junker" monarchy of the early nineteenth century, which modernized by retaining feudal estates and abolishing only the communal traditions and practices of the peasantry. Lenin considered such policies unacceptable not only because of their gentry bias; he claimed as well that the "Prussian-Stolypin" reforms were inadequate because they failed to completely clear the land for capitalist development. According to Lenin, the "medieval" system of peasant allotments which attached the worker to the land was a central feature of the feudal system, just as the liberation of the worker from the land was a distinguishing feature of capitalism. As a Marxist, he considered both systems exploitative because they depended upon the appropriation of the worker's surplus labor by a master or employer. Within the feudal system, the gentry retained their power by means of state-enforced restrictions on the right of workers to move freely and to dispose of their "wretched" allotments. In contrast, capitalism's property owners and proletarians were bound by economically rational contracts transacted under free market conditions.[8]

In Lenin's view, the Stolypin reforms encouraged the rich, socially prominent, and economically incompetent landlord to become a Prussian-style "bourgeois" Junker, and invited the "enterprising" farmer to share in the exploitation of his weaker neighbors. Lenin claimed that if such a strategy were fully implemented, most peasants, unable to compete with the kulaks and the gentry, would be driven from the land, their failure to prosper attributed to ignorance or lack of initiative. But in fact, he contended, the decisive factor would *not* be intelligence or strength of character, but the ownership of capital. A clever and industrious peasant without the capital necessary to improve his newly purchased land would fail just as surely as his more conservative neighbor.[9]

Lenin's solution to the problem of Russian rural development was what he called a "relatively humane" and far more efficient "American" capitalist revolution which eliminated the feudal estates, put an end to the *otrabotka* system which kept the peasant in a serflike relation to his master, and checked the endless fragmentation of land which kept agricultural prosperity from rising. According to Lenin, farmers in the American West prospered because land belonged to the state and investments of labor and capital could be carried on without "superfluous" expenditures for rent or purchase. He claimed that if such a system were introduced in Russia, where the obstacles to free competition and investment were so much more powerful, immense benefits would result. Nationalization would at once destroy the survivals of feudal obligation and clear the land for an American-style prosperity through free competition.[10]

Although in Lenin's view the transfer of landed property to the state served the purely economic interests of the capitalist, he did not believe that Russian capitalists would support it. Instead, they would oppose the abolition of landed estates, fearing that the political consequences of an attack upon one form of property might threaten the general security of all private property rights. According to Lenin, only peasants who were *not yet* property owners could be thoroughgoing opponents of all forms of feudal property. And in their willingness to struggle for a complete renovation of existing systems of landownership, these small proprietors were in his view more economically rational than the liberal bourgeoisie.[11]

According to Lenin, his theory of "American" capitalism simply followed from the writings of Marx and the conclusions of a number of leading American economists. Yet with all of his careful citations from the third volume of *Capital* and from *Theories of Surplus Value*, it was difficult for him to make the case that Marx had ever really taken pride in the economic virtues of the small farmer. Even Lenin's argument for the petty bourgeoisie did not reflect any weakening of his faith in the ultimate superiority of large-scale capitalist efforts. His was a tactical response that reflected the strain which the complex reality of the Russian situation placed upon his Western-centered ideology. Lenin argued that Russia was a backward society still faced with the task of eliminating its feudal estates. In such a context, he claimed, "capitalism *begins* with a more 'equalized' land ownership, and out of *that* creates large-scale farming on a new basis, on the basis of the wage labor, machinery, and superior agricultural technique and not on the basis of *otrabotka* and bondage."[12]

As in 1903, when he had described the "rural poor" as a category of potentially revolutionary peasants, Lenin insisted in 1907 that his economic strategy was completely unoriginal.[13] His writings on American capitalism always included a denunciation of his critics as "un-Marxist." And although Marx had himself recognized that his writings could not be taken as prescriptions for Russian economic development, Lenin was never satisfied until his views could be validated by a reference to the pages of *Capital*.

Lenin's belief in the peasants' capitalist mission was not based upon any generalized commitment to satisfying the small producer's desire for more land. He considered peasant demands progressive in the Russian context, because the rural economy was so backward that a choice still existed between more and less efficient paths of capitalist development. Russia was not like Germany, where capitalism was already consolidated in the hands of a Junker bourgeoisie and the support of peasant demands had become a reactionary policy.[14] In Russia, Lenin claimed, concrete historical developments had placed the peasant in conflict with the landlord who prevented him from becoming a "free," bourgeois citizen:

> In the present epoch the mass of Russian peasants are not displaying the fanaticism of private property owners (a fanaticism which is fostered by all the ruling classes, by all the liberal-bourgeois politicians) . . . [this] is due to the fact that the real conditions of life of the small culti-vator . . . confront him with the economic problem of clearing the ground for the creation of a new agriculture . . . upon "free," i.e., nationalized, land.[15]

Although liberal landlords, dreaming of new redemption payments, might propose to satisfy the peasantry with an additional allotment of land, Lenin argued that the allotment was in fact a "ghetto" from which the peasantry was trying to escape. Instead of providing security, the allotment bound peasants to the land and ensured that they would be too poor to survive without engaging themselves to work on feudal terms for their traditional masters.

After 1905, the peasants' demand for the transfer of all land to the state was proof to Lenin of their desire to break their feudal ties to the allotment and arrange peasant affairs in a rational, capitalist manner. In 1906, when a Trudovik peasant delegation to the first duma presented a "Petition of the 104" calling for a "socialist" abolition of private property in land, Lenin insisted that the Trudoviks wanted a clearing of the land for capitalist development. As proof that the Trudoviks were true capitalist peasants, unconcerned with guarantee-ing equal rights to the land for all, he cited a clause in the petition which stated that in granting land for use by the "people," first priority would be given to local inhabitants, and second to the agricultural over the non-agricultural population. Although this was a quite strained interpretation of the Trudovik document, it fit in well with Lenin's eagerness to dismiss as meaningless the Trudovik promise that the poor would be granted the means to acquire agricultural equipment so that they would not be at the mercy of the richer peasants.[16] Although Trudoviks considered themselves socialist, Lenin supported them as petty capitalists. And while he believed that a revolutionary upheaval led by the proletariat would bring a far superior achievement than the Trudovik proposal both in economic and political terms, Lenin claimed that both the Trudovik and the Bolshevik agrarian programs held out the hope that Russia's rural development need not be as brutal as the Stolypin reforms. Under a system of American-style capitalism, the masses would achieve the best living standard possible within the framework of commodity production. With characteristically uninflated enthusiasm, Lenin argued in 1907 that nationalization provided the peasant with the chance to live a "more or less human life."[17]

The commune played no role in Lenin's plans and strategies. He continued as before to ridicule the suggestion that the "medieval" commune retained any of its traditional equalizing functions. The social relations of peasant communal production were of interest to him only as they could be made to resemble a capitalist class struggle between kulak and proletarian. In 1907 and 1908 Lenin repeated his earlier claim that an accelerating process of rural differentiation had already destroyed the commune in all but name. Yet the statistics cited in his writings during this period do not bear out this contention. It was as easy for Lenin as it had been for Orlov and Vorontsov long before him to show that economic inequalities existed among the peasantry; it was harder to demonstrate that inequalities were becoming more pronounced. In 1908, for example, Lenin admitted that (1) the peasantry as a whole owned fewer horses in 1896 than in 1888, and (2) the poorest group of peasants continued to own almost exactly the same percentage of horses in 1888 as in 1896, while the richest 20 percent owned 52.6 percent of the total number in 1888 and 53.2 percent in 1896. Although Lenin argued that such figures had to be understood in connection with the structure of relationships between horse ownership, renting of land, and use of tools and hired labor,[18] it was nevertheless true that none of Lenin's statistics suggested that the rate of differentiation was increasing. The possibility that the commune might still function as a stabilizing and unifying force remained inconceivable to Lenin. And in place of empirical evidence to demonstrate the growth of rural differentiation we find numerous assertions of Lenin's dogmatic faith in the commune's inevitable disappearance.

It should be evident at this point that the difficulties of Lenin's position were neither accidental nor temporary. As in 1921, when he devised the New Economic Policy, Lenin insisted that Marxists had to make their peace with the peasant majority of the population. In need of peasant support, yet convinced that peasants as members of the petty bourgeoisie were neither reliable as allies nor likely to survive in the modern world, Lenin's solution in 1907 as in 1921 was to rely on petty capitalist initiative to revolutionize Russian agriculture. Certain that once the peasantry was freed of all feudal restrictions agricultural productivity would inevitably rise, Lenin argued that "if we do not believe in the possibility of achieving a wider and more rapid increase in the productivity of labor on small farms after they have been freed from the yoke of serfdom, then all the talk about 'supporting the revolutionary actions of the peasantry' . . . is meaningless."[19] It seemed possible to Lenin that with the guidance of Social Democrats, the experience of most small farmers in competition on "free" land might eventually teach them that only large-scale socialist enterprise would guarantee their security and prosperity. As on other occasions, Lenin relied in the last analysis on consciousness-raising as a solution to the contraditions into which a straightforward class analysis had driven him. It was, after all, not out of character for the author of *What Is To Be Done?* and "To the Rural Poor" to claim that small producers would come to understand the virtues of large-scale economic effort, just as revolutionary socialists would understand how to carry out a principled capitalist strategy for economic development.[20]

To many Marxists and non-Marxists Lenin was a simple opportunist, who appealed to peasants on the basis of short-term political considerations. But at least during the Stolypin era, his writings for peasants and for his fellow Social Democrats contained far too many scruples and conditions for the term "opportunist" to adequately explain his position. Lenin argued in 1908 that it was necessary to

> clearly demonstrate to the people the price paid for such a [Stolypinist] success, and to fight with all our strength for another, shorter, and more rapid road of capitalist development through a peasant revolution. A peasant revolution under the leadership of the proletariat in a capitalist country is difficult, very difficult, but it is possible and we must fight for it.[21]

Lenin provided no timetables, guarantees, or absolute promises in reference to the future. When a radical agrarian revolution was fought and won, he wrote, "we shall see whether such a revolution is only the basis for a development of productive forces under capitalism at an American speed, or whether it will become the prologue to a socialist revolution in the West."[22]

Even in his most simply written propaganda efforts, Lenin insisted on the limits of peasant revolution. Emphasizing always that Social Democrats were not asking peasants to fight for liberty and prosperity, he wrote in 1909 of the "more or less human life" attainable under capitalism.[23] The recurrence of such formulations suggested that, for better or for worse, many of Lenin's Marxist principles remained intact during the Stolypin period. He seemed to want to win the peasantry by an honest appeal to their capitalist interest in truly free and equal competition. Insistent that capitalism would bring them a "relatively human life," Lenin nevertheless refused to hold out the hope that capitalism was compatible with social justice. His statements on this subject at least are extremely difficult to reconcile with the charge of opportunism.

Lenin's analysis of the peasant question remained nevertheless quite contradictory. His writings reflected the continuing conflict between a realistic perception of the peasantry's political significance and the unrealistic assumptions of a typical nineteenth-century modernizer whose Marxism rendered him insensitive to evidence that non-capitalist peasant cultivators could survive and even prosper. If peasants were "backward," he focused upon their economic obligations to a feudal landlord and state. If they were "modern," he defined them according to the degree of their participation in class conflict over the issues of wages, property, and profit. Although Lenin conceded that land was distributed far more unevenly on private property than it was within the commune,[24] he refused to attribute this phenomenon to the survival of any persistently egalitarian tendencies. Certain that the peasantry lacked historically significant forms of social organization, he inaccurately referred to commune peasants as proprietors and to the commune itself as only a tool of the village kulak. Lenin tried to expose the universally "bourgeois" character of peasant interests, and found in his strategy for "American" capitalism a plausible explanation as to why a peasantry supposedly imbued with the instincts of property owners nevertheless came forward as socialists and demanded the abolition of private property in land. Unlike the Mensheviks, Lenin did not use his Western-centered assumptions as a justification for turning his back on the "would-be" capitalist majority of the population, but attempted instead to bring peasant demands into some sort of constructive relationship to a Marxist economic analysis. Whatever the inadequacies of his approach, he had in this respect at least moved far closer to some sort of realistic position than any other member of the RSDLP.

The Political Challenge: Marxist Debate

In 1905 popular violence and the formation of mass political organizations had convinced Lenin that the proletariat and the peasantry would be responsible for whatever gains the revolution might achieve. He argued at that time that Social Democrats should lay claim to both the right to and the responsibility for leadership in a bourgeois-democratic struggle. As revolutionary socialists in the midst of a revolution, they had to fight to win; Marxists could not ask the poor to risk their lives in order that political power might pass into the hands of an exploitative bourgeoisie. While Lenin followed out the implications of his perception that peasants, fought for change with far greater persistence than liberals, the Mensheviks sought in vain for a revolutionary bourgeoisie which could extend urban patterns of industrial organization, social behaviour, and culture to the Russian village. They found support in *Capital* for their belief that Russian backwardness rendered bourgeois leadership a regrettable necessity.[25]

In the political repression which followed after the dissolution of the Duma in June 1906, both Mensheviks and Bolsheviks attempted to see what could be salvaged from the failure of revolution. Their differences were striking. Plekhanov, intent on drawing lessons from the mistakes committed in 1905, suggested that "[perhaps] we should not have taken up arms,"[26] while Martov argued that Russian Marxists should model themselves on the German Social Democrats, who survived the period of Bismarck's anti-socialist laws by focusing their efforts on peaceful legal activities in the Reichstag and elsewhere.[27] In contrast to the Mensheviks, Lenin argued that the workers and peasants who had "stormed heaven" in 1905 were like the Communards of 1871. Their defeat had proven "not that the immediate aims were 'utopian,' not that the methods and means were mistaken, but that the forces were insufficiently prepared, that the revolutionary crisis was insufficiently wide and deep."[28]

Lenin insisted that when peasants fought violently to change the conditions under which they lived, they gained more even in defeat than they could have won from the legal or constitutional promises made by duma parliamentarians. According to Lenin, peasants learned painful and salutary lessons every time they refused to act like "cattle" to be herded about according to the interests of their exploiters. The violence with which "society" responded to actions which unconditionally asserted the right of peasants and workers to live free of hunger provided invaluable lessons about the nature of upper class benevolence. Above all, Lenin insisted that defeat in revolutionary action was not an argument for the superiority of legal duma activity.[29]

Lenin paid tribute as well to the SRs and Trudoviks who with all of their failings nevertheless represented a powerful and revolutionary peasant movement for the abolition of the feudal estates. Although he found them petty bourgeois in their inability to see that a triumph over feudalism could only lead to the establishment of capitalism, Lenin regarded SRs and Trudoviks as revolutionary in their willingness to fight the gentry and in their distrust of legal and parliamentary procedure.[30] Militant populist groups were thus to be distinguished from the Kadets, who eagerly compromised with a tsarist regime which had defended their property against the attacks of peasants and workers in 1905 and 1906. As Lenin noted, "When the people appeared in the streets, the Kadets appeared in the offices of the tsarist ministers."[31]

Although the state duma provided a platform from which popular grievances might be voiced, Lenin was suspicious of the eagerness with which educated revolutionaries took to parliamentarism as a more "rational" form of activity than popular violence. Mensheviks in particular had to beware, he said, of preferring "a little drab, beggarly, but peaceful legality" to the "stormy alterations of revolutionary outbursts and counter revolutionary frenzy."[32] As materialists, Marxists were after all supposed to understand that parliamentary decisions were only effective when they reflected the realities of class domination which existed within the society at large. A case in point was the *otrabotka*, or "labor service," performed by peasants upon gentry estates. According to Lenin, the *otrabotka* was neither created nor maintained by the law. It was a product of the peasant's economic dependence upon the gentry, and it survived because the army protected the gentry's disproportionate share of Russian agricultural land. In the same way, the state's armed might would protect the gentry and the kulaks who ruined the peasants in accord with the dictates of

Prussian capitalism and the Stolypin reforms. It therefore followed that agrarian proposals which conformed to this social and political reality would have the force of law; others would be ignored. The will of wealthy landlords and bourgeois proprietors would be carried out and defended by the armed forces.[33] It seemed to Lenin that the temptations of "civilized" legal procedure had blinded Mensheviks to the obvious fact that revolutionaries could not rely either upon the bourgeoisie or upon the legal methods associated with the bourgeois triumph in Western Europe.

At the London Congress of the RSDLP in May 1907 the Mensheviks Dan and Martynov expressed regret for the unfortunate weakness of the Russian bourgeoisie,[34] while Martov attacked what he called the "one-sidedness" of the Bolsheviks and admitted that fighting petty bourgeois illusions seemed to him as important as any struggle against liberal halfheartedness. In his view, peasants were not any less bourgeois or unreliable simply because they happened to act in a revolutionary manner during a bourgeois-democratic revolution.[35] Speaking in support of a united Kadet–Social Democrat–SR–Trudovik opposition to the Stolypin regime in the state duma, Plekhanov argued that Mensheviks were only following the example of Marx when they offered conditional support to the bourgeoisie. It was folly, after all, to deny the bourgeoisie a leading role in what all Marxists agreed was a bourgeois revolution.[36] In arguing for cooperation with the Kadets, Tsereteli quoted Bebel's statement that he would "go to the devil and his grandmother to help the cause of the proletariat."[37] But it was significant that despite their claim to regard peasants and Kadets with equal degrees of suspicion, Tsereteli and Cherevanin referred frequently to instances of progressive Kadet behavior in 1905[38] but made no mention of constructive action by peasants or by any of the political groups which claimed to represent them. After a year of demands by peasant congresses, unions, and Trudovik delegates for the abolition of private property in land, Mensheviks held to a municipalization program which preserved the peasant allotments. Perhaps the essence of the Menshevik position was revealed when Abramovich argued that whatever its failings, the Kadet bourgeoisie was nevertheless culturally and politically much closer to Russian Social Democrats than the "spontaneous-revolutionary, dark peasantry."[39]

The political strategy of Trotsky was distinct from both Lenin and the Mensheviks. Far more evenhanded in his criticism of the big and petty bourgeoisie, he agreed completely with Lenin's assessment of Menshevik politics. What Lenin called a Menshevik inability to recognize the historical initiative of the workers and peasants, Trotsky designated "revolutionary pessimism." Like Lenin, Trotsky pointed out how inappropriate it was for Marxists to regret the weakness of an exploitative bourgeois class.[40] From his perspective, the liberal was treacherous and the peasant dull-witted, capable of struggle but incapable of leadership. He argued that the urban proletariat could, like the sansculottes of 1793, sweep away the rubbish of medieval privilege—the liberal would not, and the peasant alone could not, accomplish this task. For Trotsky, the inconsistencies and contradictions involved in a proletarian development of capitalism were resolved away in a theory of permanent revolution which did not require Marxists to moderate their criticism of the bourgeoisie or to restrict themselves to a struggle for the establishment of a radical capitalist order.[41]

Trotsky's view of peasants and permanent revolution was not accepted by the congress, and despite the prestige of Lenin's critics, most of Lenin's proposals were supported. His effort to transfer the historic functions of the bourgeoisie to a peasantry led by the proletariat found wide support among congress delegates who had not yet accepted the idea that the period of revolutionary upheaval was over by the spring of 1907. With the spectacle of Kadet denunciations of Social Democrats in the duma still fresh in their minds, they responded enthusiastically to the speech of Rosa Luxemburg, who compared the timid Russian bourgeoisie to its "cowardly" German counterpart. Although leading Mensheviks found her analogy simplistic, many delegates applauded Luxemburg's assertion that the bourgeoisie seemed always to triumph at the cost of its own liberal values, by supporting a repressive state against the working class and zealously guarding its own narrow economic interests.[42] The delegates to the London Congress voted to rule out political cooperation with the Kadets, to support the revolutionary demands of the peasantry, the Trudoviks, and the SRs, and above all to fight for Social Democratic hegemony in the bourgeois-democratic revolutions.[43]

The Agents of Russian Progress: Liberals or Peasants

While hopes for lawful change were common among pious and obedient peasants, unenlightened workers, and Mensheviks, the principle of legal and non-violent reform was the *raison d'être* of Russian liberals who were for Lenin the most dangerous purveyors of what he called constitutional illusions. The proceedings of the second duma provided him with abundant evidence to support his prior belief that parliamentary agreements, debates, and reform proposals did not bring significant change, but functioned instead to divert the attention of workers, peasants, and radical intellectuals from the serious task of building a revolutionary movement. When the second duma opened, Kadets and Social Democrats agreed to refrain from polemical attacks upon each other on the subject of the agrarian question, in order that they might put forward a joint demand for confiscation of the large estates. The agreement was immediately broken by N. N. Kutler, the first Kadet speaker in the duma agrarian debates. Kutler launched a tirade against the propagandistic "excesses" of Trudoviks and Social Democrats. Tsereteli, the Menshevik chairman of the Social Democratic delegation, furious at the Kadet betrayal, allowed the Bolshevik Alexinskii to respond with a blistering attack on Kutler. At the same time that these initial clashes were taking place, members of the Kadet Party entered into secret talks with Premier Stolypin. In the duma, they proposed an agrarian reform which would grant state and private land to the peasantry, with private land to be purchased with government funds at a cost to be determined by the landlords and peasants concerned. In contrast to their proposals of 1906, where peasants were to comprise half of the membership in the committees which were to establish the "just price," in 1907 landlords and officials were to form the majority and peasants were to pay half of the interest charges on the price of land they received.

As in 1906, Lenin denounced the Kadets for engaging in "orderly" delibrations on the land question while assuming that peasants would continue in the interim to pay exorbitant rents to their landlords. Careful to establish their dominance on the committees which would shape the land reform and equally careful to ignore the difference between the material resources of the poor peasant and the wealthy landlord, they sought a middle ground between Russia's ten million poor peasant families and its 28,000 rich landlords. According to Lenin, only the bourgeoisie would be capable of equating the grievous burden imposed upon peasants by the requirement that they pay interest with the "sacrifice" required of wealthy landlords "forced" to sell some of their land.[44] Class interest determined for Lenin not only the Kadet approach to land reform, but the conditions and limits which Kadets placed upon their own political activities. Since liberal landlords, lawyers, and professors of the Kadet Party would derive no material benefit from the violent abolition of old forms of landownership, they would in Lenin's view be far more likely than the rural poor to see the advantages of gradual, non-violent change.[45] Russian liberals were quick to place conditions on their support of the peasantry; their moral reservations operated in practice to protect landlords from coercion, but not to undermine the sacred, state-imposed obligation of the peasant to pay his rent. Lenin pointed out that while liberal principles of law and constitutionalism repeatedly gave way to compromise with the arbitrary policy of the autocracy, liberal parliamentarians maintained a "principled" opposition to the "lawless" actions of the peasantry.

As early as 1905 Lenin had drawn a distinction between the bourgeois liberals, who preferred autocratic order to popular "anarchy," and the peasants, whose desperate situation made them eager to destroy existing forms of economic exploitation. He ignored, as a Marxist had to do, the communal framework for much of the peasants' revolutionary activity in 1905 and 1906. Instead, he focused upon the burgeoning conflict between "serflike" peasants and "semi-feudal" nobles which heralded the rise of the individualistic, competitive, capitalist peasant proprietor. The bourgeois limitations of the peasantry's historical role did not in Lenin's view nullify their power or the significance of their insights. Although the "untamed" muzhiks knew nothing of the Western European constitutions with which better educated Russians were intimately acquainted, their deep and narrow understanding was linked with a plebeian readiness to fight for what they believed. Peasant delegates did not pretend to represent the "nation" in any abstract "liberal" sense of the term. According to the non-party peasant Semyonov,

> the people asked me to demand that the church, monastery, state and crown lands, and the land compulsorily alienated from the landlords should be handed over to the working people who will till the land; and it should be handed over locally; they will know what to do. I tell you that the people sent me here to demand land and freedom and all civil liberties; and we shall live, and we shall not point and say, these are gentry and those are peasants; we shall all be human, and each will be a gentleman in his place.[46]

Even the duma speeches of conservative peasants seemed to Lenin permeated with the knowledge that they represented the ten and a half million peasant families who held seventy-five million *desiatiny* of land.[47] When the right-wing peasant Storchak observed in the duma that "if his Majesty said that there should be justice and order, then of course, if I am sitting on three *desiatiny* of land, and next to me there are 30,000 *desiatiny*, that is not order and justice," Lenin argued that he was taking a potentially revolutionary position.[48] Unlike the liberals, Storchak conceived of order in concrete terms; he had not learned to believe in order as an abstract principle to be defended regardless of its social content or its consequences for his life or the lives of his neighbors.

Although Lenin observed that the speeches of peasants in the second duma were filled with a far more spontaneous revolutionary spirit than were those of the worker delegates, he nevertheless insisted that only the proletariat (by which he meant the Bolsheviks) could lead the bourgeois peasant struggle. In a rhetorical flight to heights where it must have been difficult for many Marxists to live and breathe, Lenin asserted that "only the proletariat can be a consistent (in the strict sense of the word) supporter of the bourgeois revolution, because the class of small proprietors must inevitably vacillate between the proprietary urge and the revolutionary urge."[49]

While Lenin insisted that the duma was a forum for the call to revolution, Mensheviks, Kadets, and parties of the right debated the question of a ministry "responsible" to the duma, and engaged in rancorous exchanges on the agrarian question. But from the government's perspective, all of the proposals for land reform made by duma opposition groups were equally "impermissible" and dangerous because they encroached on the rights of private property. On June 3, 1907, the second duma was dissolved on Stolypin's orders. Electoral laws were rewritten in order to provide the government with a duma in which wealthy Great Russians would predominate. The third duma fulfilled Stolypin's immediate requirements. Dominated by conservatives, more or less anti-Semitic groups, and the liberals who were most willing to accept the Stolypin reforms, this duma was the only one to complete its full term of office (November 1907 to June 1912).

Hoping for constructive political action from the Kadets in the third duma, Mensheviks continued to insist that an exclusive reliance on the peasantry would contradict the whole direction of Russian economic development. In his criticism of Lenin's position, P. P. Maslov asserted:

Not only has the strength and importance of the bourgeoisie been underestimated, but the historical role of this class has been viewed out of historical perspective: the participation of the middle and petty bourgeoisie in the revolutionary movement and the sympathy towards it by the big bourgeoisie in the first stage of the movement have been ignored, while it is taken as a foregone conclusion that in the future, too, the bourgeoisie will play a reactionary role. . . .[50]

Maslov held to this position even while the Kadet Party steadily shifted to the right and Kadet duma delegates revealed an increasing sensitivity to the reservations of the landed gentry. Accused by a conservative speaker of a bias toward the peasantry, the Kadet delegate Berezlovskii spoke in the following manner in support of the Kadet Land Bill:

I am profoundly convinced that this bill is far more advantageous for the landowners as well . . . [If the bill were passed, the result] . . . would undoubtedly have been the genuine satisfaction of the real needs of the population, and linked with this, pacification and preservation of cultured estates, which the party of people's freedom never wished to destroy, except in case of extreme necessity.[51]

Lenin referred to Berezlovskii's remarks as an honest statement of the Kadet position, and in contrast to those Marxists who decried Stolypin's emasculation of the duma and Kadet "betrayals" of trust, he put forward the provocative argument that the third duma was in fact less fraudulent than the first two. The new "Black Hundred" duma reflected the realities of class domination in 1909: "Representative institutions, even the most 'progressive,' are doomed to remain pasteboard institutions so long as the classes represented in them do not possess real state power. . . . The essence of a constitution is that the fundamental laws of the state in general . . . express the actual relation of forces in the class struggle."[52] Earlier dumas had raised and spread constitutional illusions; the third duma had the advantage that it did not. Lenin believed that the lessons of the third duma would not be lost on Russian peasants and workers.

Most of Lenin's contemporaries were comfortable with simpler enthusiasms. The complexity of Lenin's position was evident in a brilliant series of articles written between 1908 and 1911 on the subject of the novelist Tolstoy. Lenin wrote of Tolstoy as he wrote of the peasantry, with enthusiasm for his virtues and hatred for his failings.

According to Lenin, the miraculous power of genius had transformed Tolstoy, a cultured aristocrat, into the voice of the Russian peasantry with all of its strengths and weaknesses. With relentless clarity and truth, Tolstoy had in Lenin's view been able to express the peasant's instinctive hatred and distrust for liberalism, the rights of property, and the legal principles of the bourgeois state. At the same time, his despairing lament for modern Russia, his concern with the peasant at the moment he was being crushed by the bourgeoisie, was for Lenin an attitude typical of the backward, petty bourgeois "classes which are perishing." Tolstoy had what Lenin called the peasant's characteristically moralistic and shallow understanding of the reasons for poverty and exploitation. Like the peasant, Tolstoy passed judgment on the evil landlord or moneylender but failed to understand that spiritual transformations, humility, and non-resistance would never fundamentally improve the lives of the peasantry. Lenin argued that human dignity and material security did not result from the attainment of elevated feelings, but from a social revolution which destroyed the existing structure of class relations.[53]

It was significant that Lenin's love of Tolstoy (he had re-read Tolstoy's novels many times during his years in exile) did not prevent him from denouncing the aspects of Tolstoy's life and work which he considered questionable from a revolutionary point of view. In the same way, Lenin's enthusiasm for the peasant's revolutionary activity did not prevent him from seeing that peasants were often unreliable, bigoted, and ignorant. In his view, peasants demanded equality and thought themselves socialists without ever understanding the class structure of which they were a part. Their "socialism" was for Lenin simply the dream of small producers chained to their allotments and forced into "feudal" dependence by the impossibility of earning a living by cultivating their scattered strips of land. According to Lenin, peasants imagined that social justice was equivalent to the right to farm a decent-sized plot of land, because they did not understand that an equal distribution of land could never be maintained within an economic system which distributed money, machines, and livestock so unevenly. The peasant demand for the abolition of private property (nationalization) thus had nothing to do with socialism. Rather, it expressed in the most consistent manner the interests of capitalism, "which the radical peasant in his simplicity tried to ward off by making the sign of the cross." The peasant's just anger at his oppressors was inextricably bound up with his illusions and ignorance, because "the whole past life of the peasant taught him to hate the landowner and the official, but did not, and could not, teach him where to seek an answer to all these questions."[54] The "idiocy of rural life" could not provide the answers to be gleaned from the more dynamic forms of exploitation existing in urban factory centers.

While the peasant might perceive the concrete wretchedness of his situation, intelligent principles and ideological sophistication could not in general be expected from him or from the groups which claimed to represent his interests. For Lenin, the Trudoviks were opportunist and unreliable, all too willing to cooperate with the Kadets in preparing compromise proposals to the duma. SRs on the other hand periodically "lost faith in the people" when circumstances altered or became particularly difficult. Incapable of "steady, stubborn work," they succumbed to reformism with the typical logic of the "keyed-up intellectual," or issued ultimatums to the conservative duma and engaged in sporadic acts of terrorism. Lenin argued that the dejection of the opportunist and the desperation of the terrorist were alike products of the petty bourgeois incapacity for systematic, realistic, and principled action.

SRs and Trudoviks were in Lenin's view as illiterate as the peasantry on the subject of economics. Such ill-founded charges were common in Lenin's writings. They formed part of his substantial contribution to the myth that Marxists were realistic and empirical while SRs were abstract and naive. In fact Lenin had been quite dogmatic and inaccurate in his own assessment of the Russian rural economy at the turn of the century, while SR theorists were far more flexible than he was ever willing to admit. The SRs V. M. Chernov, P. A. Vikhliaev, and A. A. Karelin explicitly denied that the abolition of private property or the establishment of equal access to the land were equivalent to socialism. Chernov would argue that such measures were steps in that direction, just as Lenin would claim in 1917 that the transfer of land to the state was "not only the 'last word' of the bourgeois revolution but also a step toward socialism."[55] Yet for Lenin in 1908, SRs and Trudoviks were irretrievably petty bourgeois. Their merit lay in the fact that on balance, they were nowhere near as afraid of mass struggle as the liberals. The "foolish" socialist claims they put forward did not obscure the "objective rationality" of their commitment to the specific historical task of abolishing traditional forms of wealth and privilege.[56]

Although radical intellectuals and Social Democratic "philistines" might lose patience with the exaggerations of the peasant and his spokesmen, Lenin pointed out that any social revolution included fighters at different levels of political consciousness. Primitive consciousness embodied in a willingness to act was better than stagnation, and Social Democrats had to set themselves the task of making the peasant understand the merits of a solution which went deeper than nationalization and equal opportunity.[57] The utopian slogans of the populists promised the peasants "a million blessings in the event of victory; while victory will in fact yield them only a hundred blessings. But is it not natural that the millions who for ages have lived in unheard-of ignorance, want, poverty, abandonment, and downtroddenness should magnify tenfold the fruits of eventual victory?"[58]

Lenin, unlike the Mensheviks, took peasant "dreams" seriously. At the same time, he shared with them the Marxist faith that most peasants could only be fighters for some form of capitalism. Trudoviks and SRs were therefore not socialists, regardless of what they called themselves. Whether they demanded social control over the land or, like the SR Chernov, argued that land socialization was only the first step in the building of socialism, for Lenin they could not be anything but petty bourgeois. Despite their socialist claims and their willingness to fight, Trudoviks and SRs could only be incorporated into a Marxist analysis by an insistence that what they "really" wanted was a petty capitalist development on free land, unencumbered by feudal restrictions.

The Impact of "Prussian" Capitalism

The consequences of the Stolypin reforms were complex, and they have been variously interpreted. Of the one-third of the Russian peasantry that left the communes between 1906 and 1917, only 20 percent seem to have done so on their own initiative.[59] Many observers testified that the reforms were enacted by force and were violently resisted. In 1909 and 1910 the village of Bolotovo in Tambov province illustrated almost every aspect of the difficulties the government faced in its anti-commune efforts. Bolotovo was a village of 3,100, where the average peasant allotment was less than six *desiatiny*. In 1909 some of the wealthier peasants in the commune decided to claim their allotments as private land. Despite the commune assembly's opposition, local government authorities allowed the "separators" to claim some of the commune's best land as their private property. When the commune complained to the provincial governor he failed to respond, and the peasants of Bolotovo pulled up the boundary posts which marked off newly established private property. Armed with scythes and axes they broke into the houses of the *otrubshchiki*, the owners of enclosed farms.[60] The district police officer who attempted to arrest the more active peasants was driven away, and when the commune assembly met again, a peasant declared, "If there is a law which permits them to take our land for *otrubs*, then peasants have their own law for not giving it!" More police were sent in and arrests were made, as jeering peasants cried, "Kill the bloodsuckers!" The police opened fire on the peasants, killing eight and seriously wounding thirteen. Cossacks were subsequently called in by the provincial governor to conduct a three-day search of the village, with the result that seventy-seven peasants were arrested. "Order" was restored, but throughout 1910 mysterious fires broke out at the homes of "separators," and boundary signs continued to disappear.[61] Such responses escalated as government pressure for separation from the commune increased.

In 1911 rumors spread throughout the empire that there would be a new uprising on the anniversary of the emancipation. Famine struck in that same year, and official attempts to prevent the organization of famine relief recalled the notorious efforts of tsarist ministers to guard the peasantry from private and unauthorized philanthropic activities in 1902.[62] Of the peasants sent to settle in Siberia, 60 percent had returned to European Russia by 1911,[63] while peasants who borrowed money from the Peasant Land Bank were soon bent beneath a burden of debt reminiscent of the redemption payments imposed after 1861.[64] Between 1910 and 1914, the 17,000 recorded agrarian disturbances in European Russia indicated the degree of violence present in what were generally agreed to be non-revolutionary times.[65]

Writing in increasing isolation from other leading party intellectuals, Lenin claimed that it was now more than ever the task of Russian Marxists to use all legal and illegal methods to popularize the idea of radical bourgeois revolution led by the proletariat in alliance with the peasantry. But after five years of the Stolypin regime, he was less able than in 1907 to convince his fellow Marxists of the correctness of his position. By 1912 Lenin had come to see himself as beset on all sides by the hypocrisy, ignorance, and dishonesty of various "opportunist" Social Democratic factions. He viciously denounced "liquidationist"

Mensheviks like Martov and Axel'rod who wanted to abandon clandestine political work for open union activity, "doctrinaire boycott-ists" opposed to participation in the "Black Hundred" duma, and Menshevik proponents of municipalization who he charged with encouraging "private property fanaticism" among the peasantry.[66] Unable to build a disciplined Bolshevik organization capable of dominating the Russian Marxist movement, he convened a tiny Bolshevik conference in Prague in 1912. With stubborn enthusiasm, he argued that peasant life had become so wretched that "democratic feelings" were springing up with an "elusive and spontaneous inevita-bility." Social Democrats had to build political consciousness among the peasantry by explaining "the connection between the famine and tsarism and its entire policy; to distribute in the villages for agitational purposes the duma speeches not only of the Social Democrats and the Trudoviks, but even of such friends of the tsar as Markov the Second."[67] As an increasing number of small farmers sold their newly purchased lands to those with the money to exploit it profitably, Lenin claimed that the would-be proprietor was "trapped both by the old bondage and by the system of allotting scattered strips of land that has resulted from the notorious landowners' solution to the land problem."[68]

In the context of Stolypin's "failure," Lenin hoped that the strikes and mutinies of 1912 might be the beginning of the long-awaited radical bourgeois revolution. Even within the anti-semitic Black Hundred movement, he insisted, it was important to look for elements of "ignorant peasant democracy, democracy of the crudest sort, but also extremely deep-seated."[69] He quoted from a peasant's letter to the reactionary Bishop Nikon as an example of the revolutionary potential of the "conservative" peasant:

> The land, bread, and other important questions of our Russian life and of the region do not appear to reach either the hands or the hearts of the authorities or the Duma. These questions and such solution of them as is possible are regarded as "utopian," "hazardous," untimely. Why do you keep silent, what are you waiting for? For moods and revolts for which those same "undernourished," hungry, unfortunate peasants will be shot down?[70]

Nevertheless, despite Lenin's hopes and arguments, the failure of popular unrest to shake the foundations of the tsarist order began at last to raise the specter of the success, rather than the failure, of "Prussian" capitalism. Although he insisted that agrarian capitalism was developing slowly within a predominantly feudal system of productive relationships, Lenin's writings during this period reflected a growing fear that the Stolypin reforms had created a situation in which "the peasant is more entangled in the net of capitalist dependence than is the wage worker. He thinks that he can 'make good,' but to survive he must work (for capital) harder than the wage worker."[71] Lenin feared that many years of disillusionment with the deceptive bourgeois ideology of hard work and competition might be necessary before the peasant would come to understand the realities of his situation.[72]

The Stolypin legislation aroused a great deal of resistance among commune peasants, and the most recent scholarship on the subject has emphasized the ephemeral character of the reforms' impact. While there were some success stories of peasants able to make it on their own, most were reluctant to become private proprietors, and many who left the commune in the early reform years made their way back to its protection in the period shortly before the war. Due to population increase, the number of households in communes in forty provinces of Russia in 1915 was actually higher than the number in fifty provinces in 1905.[73] By 1916 peasant violence against the "separators" and against local administrators had become so serious that further efforts to break up the commune were suspended.[74] Even the modernizing mission of the Stolypin reforms proved unsatisfactory in many respects. Although agricultural productivity increased and the land area under cultivation rose by 10 percent between 1906 and 1916, peasants who separated from the commune did not necessarily improve their methods of cultivation. In 1915, for example, two-thirds of the "new proprietors" were still plowing on scattered strips which were intermingled with the land of their commune neighbors.[75] At the same time rents increased, grain prices rose, and a substantial amount of land came into the hands of the peasantry through purchase and rent.[76]

It may well be that between 1906 and 1916 the Stolypin reforms scored their most overwhelming and unquestioned triumph in the minds of educated Russians. The rhapsodizing of tsarist bureaucrats about the miracles wrought by the liberation of the peasant entrepreneur from the fetters of the commune has an obvious ring of sincerity. At the other end of the ideological spectrum, leading SRs like Zenzinov and Gotz, and even the old populist Vorontsov, became convinced that primitive peasants, dreaming of "making good," were deserting the commune eagerly and en masse. N. N. Sukhanov, an SR

turned Menshevik, took for granted the victory of Stolypinist capitalism, and suggested a joint Marxist–populist effort to form a truly united
socialist left. According to Sukhanov, the SRs had abandoned their
romantic faith in the commune, recognizing at last the indisputable
necessity for bourgeois-democratic revolution. They now appealed to
the peasantry on the same grounds and for the same immediate purpose
as the Marxists. SRs and orthodox, i.e., Menshevik, Marxists had
become so similar in their views that Sukhanov found it "impossible to
establish where Marxism ends and populism begins."[77]

Increasingly fearful of peasant anarchy, greed, and prejudice,
moderate SRs had come to believe that a long civilizing process had
to take place before the backward common people would be capable of
participating in the creation of a socialist society, while Mensheviks
remained convinced that the bourgeoisie was the historically designated agent of economic and political progress.[78] As pessimism and
ideological principle turned non-Bolshevik socialists reluctantly toward
the liberals, the Kadets began to discover an increasing number of
redeeming qualities in more traditional forms of order. As we shall see,
the perceived dangers of peasant backwardness and peasant suscep-
tibility to the appeal of the Stolypin program would in fact lead SRs and
Mensheviks to cooperate in 1917 along precisely the lines which
Sukhanov had suggested, and both parties would find themselves
equally constrained to join forces at that time with the Kadets.

Although Lenin shared the Menshevik view that the Stolypin
reforms could not help but appeal to the instincts of the petty
proprietor, he dealt with such fears (as he had earlier dealt with the issue
of failure)[79] in a strikingly un-Menshevik fashion. Lenin denounced
Sukhanov's analysis of the current political situation on the left as the
kind of "philistine realism" which flourished during politically difficult
times, when "rational" people recognized the need to pursue "limited
goals." Lenin insisted that the similarity between SR and Menshevik
aims had nothing to do with Sukhanov's parallels between the new
Populism and "Orthodox" Marxism. Although Menshevik revisionists
and liquidators might at any time come to resemble petty bourgeois SR
reformists, Lenin maintained that real Marxists resisted the temptation
to settle for peaceful means to achieve limited ends. In Lenin's view, the
revolutionary Marxist was committed to a radical democratic revolution which did not depend on the good will of liberals or the reform
measures of parliaments.[80]

Although the Russian peasant revolution on which Lenin had built his hopes seemed distant in 1911, outbreaks of revolutionary activity in China and Ireland continued to sustain his analysis of petty bourgeois and liberal political action. He saw many parallels between backward, "Asiatic" Russia and the Empire of the Manchus. Sun Yat-sen was for Lenin a typical petty bourgeois democrat whose "Trudovik" dreams of socialism were expressed in appeals for nationalization of the land. Lenin emphasized that progressive Chinese who supported Sun were not socialists, but bourgeois comrades of France's "great men of the Enlightenment." And if Sun Yat-sen succeeded, hundreds of millions of people would enjoy the benefits of the bourgeois ideals which the West already possessed.[81] According to Lenin, the Chinese revolution was a great victory in the historic struggle against the feudal order, but since Sun Yat-sen had won with the aid of Chinese liberals, Lenin was doubtful of his ability to stay in power: "Whether the peasants, who are not led by a proletarian party, will be able to retain their democratic positions *against* the liberals, who are only waiting for an opportunity to shift to the right, will be seen in the near future."[82]

While the Chinese Revolution of 1911 represented the victory of a revolutionary petty bourgeoisie, the action of the British in Ireland epitomized for Lenin the triumph of a liberal, constitutional "big bourgeoisie." In the spring of 1914, Lenin described the "appalling destitution and suffering of the Irish peasantry" as "an instructive example of the lengths to which the landowners and the liberal bourgeoisie of a 'dominant' nation will go."[83] When patriotism, poverty, war, and religion set off the Rebellion of 1916, Lenin enthusiastically supported what he called the Irish petty bourgeois cause. Without denying that the rebels were frequently bigoted and superstitious, he preferred to emphasize the more politically salient fact that whoever expected "a 'pure' social revolution would never live to see it."[84] While oppression might give rise to poverty, despair or violent opposition, it did not ever in Lenin's view create perfectly rational and morally unassailable rebels.

Lenin claimed that in Russia, prejudiced peasants, speculators, and chauvinist intellectuals had participated in the events of October 1905 for their own often far from admirable reasons—but he argued that "objectively" the mass movement of that year was engaged in the task of "breaking the back of tsarism." In 1916 Lenin suggested that in the coming European socialist revolution, the working class might have all sorts of prejudices, fantasies, and weaknesses, but "objectively" it found itself in a specific historical situation: Labor was in opposition to Capital, and would smash it.

> To imagine that social revolution is conceivable without revolutionary outbursts by a section of the petty bourgeoisie *with all its prejudices*, without the movement of the politically non-conscious proletarian and semi-proletarian masses against oppression by the landowners, the church, and the monarchy, against national oppression, etc.—to imagine all this is to repudiate social revolution.[85]

On the Eve of Revolution

The outbreak of World War I did not change Lenin's view that Social Democrats were to lead a revolution to establish a democratic republic, nationalize the land, and grant an eight-hour day to the factory worker. However, as his views developed in the course of the war, he came to hope that the imperialist war had "linked up" the Russian revolution with the developing proletarian socialist revolution in the West. It was no longer, it seemed, a question of revolutionary problems in Russia or Germany or France: "The Russian bourgeois-democratic revolution is now not only a prologue to, but an integral part of the socialist revolution in the West."[86] With renewed optimism, Lenin predicted that if the petty bourgeois peasants shifted to the left at the decisive moment, it would be possible to conquer Russia for the revolution. Economic distress arising especially from the burdens of war would combine with military and political crises to lead the peasants in the direction of Bolshevism. Although the government, aided by the press and the clergy, had been successful in raising "chauvinist sentiments" among the poor, "with the return of the soldiers from the field of slaughter . . . sentiment in the rural areas will undoubtedly turn against the tsarist monarchy."[87]

Lenin's hopes were well founded and his prediction of the course of peasant action was proven accurate in 1917. He was inaccurate only about the Marxist classification which it would prove necessary to place upon the Bolshevik revolution. Certain that Russia's revolution would be bourgeois, given the level of Russia's economic development, he ridiculed Trotsky's argument that the impact of imperialism had transformed the proletarian struggle into a movement which would destroy the capitalist order. As he wrote in 1916, "Trotsky has not realized that if the proletariat induces the non-proletarian masses to confiscate the landed estates and overthrow the monarchy, then that will be the consummation of the 'national bourgeois revolution' in Russia; it will be a revolutionary democratic dictatorship of the proletariat and the peasantry."[88]

In emigré squabbles and in isolation, Lenin had completed his peasant policy before the uprisings which began the Revolution of 1917. Although the effort to reconcile the belief that peasant interests were petty bourgeois with the aims of a socialist state would tear Russian society apart in the years after the Bolsheviks won power, Lenin would not face this issue until he was forced to do so during the period of "war communism." Before then, he would put to good use both his recognition of the peasantry's revolutionary potential, and his awareness of the overwhelming burden of government coercion and ideological persuasion which functioned to restrain it. Having defined the leadership of the rural population as a basic party task, he was determined that the Bolsheviks should seize power under any political or economic conditions, and he promised that land would be transferred to the peasant by any Bolshevik-led revolutionary government. Lenin was supremely confident that once the Bolsheviks were in power, "they would know what to do."

III

1917:
Peasant Revolution
in Theory and Practice

7

Problems of Order and Revolution:
February–April 1917

> Disorder is the absence of the order
> that you were looking for.
>
> JEAN-PAUL SARTRE

IN A SOCIAL REVOLUTION, ordinary people claim the right to decide matters which are traditionally considered to be beyond their competence. Rules and habits of obedience ordinarily taken for granted become issues to be debated and decided by individuals and groups unused to the exercise of significant political power. Peasants judge whether land should be privately or communally held; factory workers consider how the product of their labor should be distributed; soldiers and policemen decide whether or not to obey orders to arrest people who are taking food or other property which does not legally belong to them.

In February 1917, under the pressure of strikes, lockouts, and a steadily worsening food shortage, angry housewives, strikers, and unemployed workmen in increasing numbers began to seize bread, threaten violence, and damage private and state property. By the end of the month, General Khabalov, the commander of the Petrograd garrison, was forced to send out troops to put an end to activities which were paralyzing the normal life of the city. And when soldiers refused to fire upon the unruly crowds, that is, when they ceased to uphold the law against those who were disobeying it, the strikes and food riots of the "February days" became a revolution.

The spectacle of massive lawbreaking was accompanied by the

formation of innumerable unauthorized groups which set themselves to
deliberate on matters usually dealt with by industrialists, landlords, and
government officials. To an English gentleman like Bernard Pares, the
popular enthusiasm evident in the streets of revolutionary Petrograd in
early 1917 was ludicrous:

> There were numerous little cliques which took high-sounding titles and
> regarded themselves as the saviours of the country. They indulged *ad
> infinitum* in the deplorable Russian habit of putting on paper schemes for
> the government of the whole world. One placard announced the United
> States of the World, to which was appended the statement "Original
> subscribers become life members." All sorts of inappropriate bodies, such
> as the crew of a ship, formed what they called "universities," really
> centres of university extension. Amidst the orgy of fancies I remember
> coming across a placard, "The Land of the Happy Peasantry"; this on
> examination, proved to come from an organization for propagating in
> Russia the excellent agricultural methods of Denmark. The illiterate
> were begged to learn to read and write as soon as possible. . . .[1]

But to the various political leaders who aspired to lead the "people," it
was not easy to arrive at an appropriate response to such rudimentary
cultural and political efforts. The proliferation of schools and councils
where kitchen maids and privates debated questions of war and peace
forced radical activists to consider more seriously then ever before
whether they really wanted to rely upon the intelligence, the judgment,
or the ability of the masses. As they attempted to distinguish between
rational and irrational popular initiatives, left-wing political leaders
were particularly hard put to define the boundaries of legitimate
behavior for a "primitive" peasantry. As we shall see, Lenin's reaction
to unauthorized peasant "decision-making" on the land question
would emerge in sharp contrast to Menshevik, SR, and even Bolshevik
fears of popular action which they did not control.

Given the Marxist assumption that peasants were petty bourgeois,
any Marxist with a revolutionary peasant policy was quite vulnerable
to accusations of cynicism. And when Lenin claimed that there was
order and rationality in peasant attacks on private property and
established authority, he was clearly aware that such arguments would
have immediate appeal for dissident rural elements. The opportunism
which forms part of the behavior of any political activist clearly
determined many of his actions. At the same time, the disintegration of
traditional order and the increase in popular initiatives in time of

revolution posed a number of objective political challenges. When peasants formed committees to claim their ancient "rights" to land which legally belonged to others, it was significant that most of the Russian left was decisive in seeking to check illegal land seizures and cautious on the issue of land reform. In the revolution's early months, Lenin would reverse these priorities, well aware of the political gains to be made and unwilling to check the violation of property rights before the triumph of a socialist revolution.

Petrograd without Lenin

In February and March 1917 most of the spokesmen for the pre-revolutionary opposition to the autocracy found it difficult to believe in the completeness of the old regime's collapse. Fearing that the autocracy would somehow manage to survive just as it had in 1905, even the Bolsheviks behaved as if they had no enemies on the Left. A self-appointed duma committee, which chose a Provisional Government dominated by Kadets and Octobrists, was therefore able to win the support of a Petrograd Soviet created by the confused and enthusiastic workers, soldiers, and socialist intellectuals in the vicinity of the Tauride Palace on February 28. The Soviet's Executive Committee voted not to participate in the Provisional Government, but approved its program and its right to rule Russia until a Constituent Assembly could be convened.

The Provisional Government. The new government was headed by Prince G. E. L'vov, an opponent of compulsory expropriation of gentry land ever since 1906. L'vov also served as minister of the interior, while the Kadet A. I. Shingarev was minister of agriculture. Although Kadets were not numerically dominant within the Provisional Government, its policies generally reflected the position of the Kadet Party leadership. Viewed by the Russian Left as leaders of the liberal bourgeoisie, the Provisional Government's first program did in fact reflect the priorities of European political liberalism. Democracy, freedom, and justice were key concepts in its first declaration; previous restrictions on civil and political liberty were unconditionally abolished. Above all, it was promised that the form of Russia's future government would be decided by a Constituent Assembly on the basis of universal suffrage. No date was set for the convocation of the Constituent Assembly, and the

Provisional Government's guarantee that elections would not be held without the participation of the soldiers at the front suggested that it would be some time before Russian citizens would be given the opportunity to vote for the national political leaders of their choice. The holding of elections was clearly not one of the new government's most pressing concerns. A Special Council created to draft election statutes on March 25 was not called into session until May 25.

Social reform was also not a high priority on the new government's agenda during the revolution's early months. More effort was made to enact measures for the improvement of food production and supply than to satisfy any peasant demand for land. Even the nationalization of imperial, appanage, and cabinet lands on March 9 brought few direct popular benefits, since it was subsequently decreed that no crown territory would be transferred to the peasantry. The peasantry's immediate gains were thus restricted, but no limits were imposed upon the pre-revolutionary property rights of the landed gentry. The reasons put forward to justify such priorities and preferences were various. It was pointed out that precise information on rural needs and demands was lacking (and a system of land committees was proposed for the purpose of obtaining it). Many liberal economists argued as well that production would fall if there were any sudden, large-scale transfer of property from one social group to another. Premier L'vov argued that a decrease in the available supply of food to the cities or to the front would create intolerable material hardship and render the poorest and most primitive rural elements more vulnerable to demagogic appeals. On the basis of democratic principle, Minister of Agriculture Shingarev claimed that only a Constituent Assembly which represented the whole population had the right to fundamentally alter pre-revolutionary property relationships. And in mid-March the Kadet Central Committee, claiming that only a country at peace could make rational decisions on fundamental issues, proposed that the final solution of the land question be delayed until the end of the war.[2]

Since the Provisional Government's authority was not based upon law, tradition, or a popular vote, such claims were plausible enough. Yet the arguments for caution which were applied to questions of land reform did not extend to other areas of government policy. Liberal ministers did not intend, for example, to forego the right to use force to defend pre-revolutionary property relationships. In March criminal proceedings were instituted against peasants in Kazan who threatened gentry property rights, while punitive detachments were sent out to deal with peasant-gentry conflicts over land in the provinces of Kursk, Mogilev, and Perm.[3] By April 13 it was felt that the incidence of "arbitrary acts" which deprived landowners of the right to "perform their duty toward the country" made it "indispensable to suppress all manifestations of violence or plunder [using] all the forces of the law."[4] As the Kadet *Russkiia Vedomosti* put it, "various anarchistic forces had emerged, and they were threatening to lead the country to new losses of sown areas, and . . . new national disasters."[5] While the Provisional Government, like any government, was quite justified in fearing that chaos would ensue if violence went unchecked, its response to peasant attacks on private property seemed to establish in peasant eyes the connecting links between liberal and tsarist policy: the establishment of order (and, for that matter, the winning of the war and the raising of productivity) would precede any hasty transformation of pre-revolutionary economic relationships. According to an angry peasant resolution from the province of Tver, "The land is being consolidated under the old laws."[6]

The Petrograd Soviet: Menshevik leadership of the SR majority. In March, Kadet Foreign Minister P. N. Miliukov claimed that it was the Petrograd Soviet's obligation to help restore and maintain civil order,[7] and in matters related to the agrarian question the Soviet fulfilled his expectations. The Soviet placed definite limits on what would be considered appropriate revolutionary activity on the peasant's behalf. The narrowness of these limits was evident on March 2, when an enthusiastic group of SRs and Bolsheviks issued a manifesto which asserted that since "already two days had passed" without official word from Rodzianko or Miliukov, the soldiers of Petrograd had a right to an immediate response to their demand that all land be transferred to the people. This manifesto was immediately confiscated by order of the Petrograd Soviet,[8] and denounced by the Socialist Revolutionary Petrograd City Conference as a document tending to "destroy the unity of the people."[9] But the issue raised by such incendiary claims could not easily be laid to rest. In the weeks to come peasant petitions poured into the Soviet, filled with demands for immediate land reform or requests for official approval for various violations of pre-revolutionary property rights. Within the Soviet Executive Committee the warm-hearted and impulsive Alexandrovich created a sensation when he admitted that he had given Soviet authorization to a village request to make use of a landlord's private land. Alexandrovich was sharply reprimanded for taking unilateral action,[10] and in the Executive Committee debates of March and April the Mensheviks Tsereteli, Skobelev, and Chkheidze spoke in opposition to any Soviet incitement or sanction of land seizure.

The policy of support for the Provisional Government reflected the political dominance of Mensheviks within the Soviet's Executive Committee. It should be noted that the Mensheviks were not a monolithic political organization; since the outbreak of World War I, divisions on a number of foreign policy issues had become particularly sharp and bitter, with Martov on the internationalist left and Plekhanov at the extreme, pro-war right. But as we have seen earlier, on economic issues Mensheviks were in general thoroughgoing determinists, certain that advanced industrial capitalism and a numerous, class-conscious proletariat were absolute prerequisites for any attempt to build a socialist society. Despite peasant demands for the abolition of private landed property in 1905 and afterward, they continued to insist upon the limits which economic backwardness and a predominantly peasant population imposed upon the political aspirations of revolutionary Marxists. Driven by their fear of peasants they considered primitive, "Asiatic" and capable at best of bourgeois-democratic behavior, Mensheviks felt bound to aid and encourage a weak Russian bourgeoisie to carry out its designated historical task.[11] Such iron consistency placed them in a cruelly difficult political position. Unable to fight for victory and repelled by the idea of defending the proletariat's bourgeois class enemy, Mensheviks like I. G. Tsereteli and N. S. Chkheidze were left to hope that the Soviet could exercise a sort of "right to dictate" policy to the Provisional Government. According to the scenario they envisioned, Soviet pressure would force the bourgeoisie to act more quickly to establish the capitalist economic and political foundations for a future socialist revolution. In this process, a primitive peasantry would be replaced by a massive and (as a result of Menshevik efforts) class-conscious proletariat. But "at present," as Tsereteli quite unconvincingly explained it, the proletariat and the revolutionary army "understood that the time has not yet come for achieving the ultimate aims of the proletariat."[12]

The Menshevik view of the peasant's revolutionary role was solidly based upon Marx's criticism of the petty bourgeoisie in the

"Communist Manifesto," *Class Struggles in France*, and *The Eighteenth Brumaire of Louis Bonaparte*. Despite the acceptance of Maslov's agrarian program in 1906, and the general recognition of the peasant's unavoidable importance as a food producer, the peasant remained the Menshevik revolutionary's burden.[13] The embodiment of Russian political, economic, and social backwardness, the peasant represented to the Mensheviks the dark forces of superstition, bigotry, senseless violence, and animal greed. In 1917 the Menshevik newspaper *Rabochaia Gazeta* frequently emphasized the danger that the countryside would be the *Vendée* of the Russian revolution.[14] A fear of anarchy within Russia's primitive peasant army led Chkheidze, the president of the Petrograd Soviet, to kneel and kiss the flag carried by the first army regiment to march under its old officers to affirm its loyalty to the pre-revolutionary duma.[15] Sukhanov (a former SR) regretted that the army's role in the collapse of the tsarist regime had given peasant soldiers the idea that they were the heroes of the revolution. If they could not be kept from "intervening" in the revolutionary process, it seemed likely to Sukhanov that peasants would proceed in "typical" peasant fashion, from patriotism to looting to "beating up the Yids." If, on the other hand, peasants managed to get land, they would quickly subside into "rural idiocy."[16] In the context of such arguments, the peasant majority of the population was not only a negligible socialist asset; peasant violence and ignorance made them unreliable even as allies in a bourgeois-democratic revolution.

While such moderate revolutionary expectations were consistent with the belief that a historically necessary bourgeois revolution was taking place, the moderation of the SR Party had little to do with consistency. As inheritors of the Populist tradition, committed in their party programs to a revolutionary socialization of the land, they could not easily justify even temporary support for a "bourgeois" liberal government. Their inconsistency can only be understood if we take into account the political demoralization which followed the Revolution of 1905–7 and the growth of a widespread conviction that the Stolypin reforms had successfully created a capitalist peasantry[17] (as well as the absence of hotheads like Alexandra Spiridonova from the capital when the revolution broke out). Like the Kadets and the RSDLP, leading SR moderates like V. M. Zenzinov and A. R. Gotz had come to believe that Russia could no longer avoid the bourgeois stage of economic development.[18] Like the Mensheviks whose leaders they followed

SRs accepted the necessity for bourgeois-democratic leadership of the revolution and were therefore willing to refrain from appeals for immediate land reform. Therefore, despite the numerical predominance of SRs within the Petrograd Soviet, SR agitators in Saratov and Tambov were confronted in March 1917 with the spectacle of a "party of the peasantry" whose Petrograd leadership was as absorbed as the Mensheviks in developing an honorable position on the war and in rallying peaceful and orderly peasant support for the Provisional Government. It was over a month before the SR Party officially turned its attention to the land question. At their April conference, SRs passed resolutions demanding a suspension of land transactions and all laws which might delay a final solution of the land question in the future Constituent Assembly.[19]

In many ways SR and Menshevik leaders seemed to be acting out the role of the petty bourgeois intellectual as portrayed in the writings of Marx and Lenin. Although SR indecisiveness was all their own, they tended to share with dogmatic Mensheviks a fatal willingness to let other political groups define the limits of their own political behavior. For the SRs, the limits were set by the Mensheviks; the limits of Menshevik behavior were ultimately dictated by liberals of the Kadet Party. This was of course typical petty bourgeois behavior according to the standard Marxist analysis.

Petrograd Bolsheviks. Petrograd Bolsheviks were not quite as determined to be moderate as were the leading Mensheviks and SRs, although they bore no resemblance to the model of a unified and disciplined party set out in *What Is To Be Done?*. V. M. Molotov, one of the young Bolshevik editors of *Pravda*, had worked with the SR Alexandrovich on the inflammatory manifesto which had been confiscated by the Soviet on March 2, while M. I. Kalinin stressed the dangers of spontaneous unorganized action. The tone of *Pravda* was both hopeful and inconsistent in early March. Appeals for Provisional Government action to establish temporary laws for the confiscation of monastic, gentry, and allotment land appeared alongside editorials urging the peasants to organize and take power in their own hands. In the articles of V. Muranov and P. Stuchka (who signed himself "Veteran") there were frequent references to "our allies, the peasant soldiers" who could expect "nothing" from the bourgeoisie and "everything" in the way of support and future prosperity if they followed the leadership of the Bolsheviks.[20] In an interesting series of articles which appeared in March, M. I. Kalinin (one of the few Bolshevik leaders of peasant origin) attempted to spell out the basis for a Bolshevik peasant strategy. Arguing that peasants need not inevitably follow the path of bigotry and greed sketched out by Mensheviks like Sukhanov, Kalinin called for peasant participation in the revolution through land committees which would organize the confiscation of land, prevent pogroms, and "smooth out excesses." Although he claimed that the peasant struggle for land would never be won without the proletariat, it was significant that Kalinin not only ignored the classic Marxist issue of class differences between rural proletarians and kulaks but also failed to refer to Lenin's pre-revolutionary contention that Bolsheviks could claim the right to leadership of the peasant movement.[21]

In mid-March, when Stalin and Kamenev returned from exile to take charge of *Pravda*, its editorials and articles began to reflect a more coherent and Menshevik-oriented approach to the issue of peasants and political power. In their writings for *Pravda*, Kamenev and Stalin assumed that rule by a "bourgeois" Provisional Government was both legitimate and necessary. Like the Menshevik N. S. Chkheidze, Kamenev feared "disorganization within the army."[22] Although Stalin was less cautious, he appealed for demonstrations which would exert pressure on the Provisional Government rather than challenge its authority. During the first months of the revolution, Stalin and Kamenev were no more able than Tsereteli to imagine that actions being taken by workers, soldiers, and peasants could result in the creation of a society which transcended the limits of bourgeois democracy. As Stalin put it, revolutionaries should "decisively" support the Provisional Government as long as it "really" fought against the survivals of the old regime.[23] With Stalin and Kamenev as editors, *Pravda* neither published nor acknowledged the letters which Lenin sent in early March from Zurich to Petrograd. By the end of the month Lenin was writing to ask if his "Letters from Afar" had been lost in the mail.[24] When his contributions were finally published, it was significant that Lenin's strongest attacks on SRs, Mensheviks, and the Provisional Government were deleted. At this point Petrograd Bolsheviks clearly did not constitute a "Leninist" party in any sense of the word. At the same time, their actions indicated that without Lenin it was not clear what distinguished the Bolsheviks from any other socialist organization operating in the capital.

Lenin

> Millions and tens of millions of people who had been politically dormant for ten years and politically crushed by the terrible oppression of tsarism and by inhuman toil for the landowners and capitalists *have awakened* and taken eagerly to politics. And who are these millions and tens of millions? For the most part small proprietors, petty bourgeoisie, people standing midway between the capitalists and the wage workers. Russia is the most petty bourgeois of all European countries.[25]

Unlike the socialist intellectuals of Petrograd, Lenin greeted the February Revolution with an attack upon the newly formed Provisional Government as a reactionary institution, one which would be unwilling and unable to deal with the material problems facing the majority of Russian peasants and workers.[26] Given the appearance of the mass action for which Russian revolutionaries had hoped in vain for the last decade, he imposed few theoretical limits to the scope of the current revolution. Discarding his earlier claim that Bolsheviks were to lead a bourgeois-democratic revolution, Lenin claimed that the events of February had made it possible to go far beyond the guarantee of capitalist-style progress for workers and peasants. Lenin argued in April that once the victory of the peasant over the landlord was complete, the proletariat would be able to establish socialism in Russia.[27] The building of socialism no longer seemed a distant dream, but a real possibility arising out of concrete situations such as the peasant's illegal and violent attacks on private property.

Lenin's optimism was not based upon any idealization of the peasantry. He still operated within a tradition of aversion for peasant initiative which led him to foolishly insist that peasant land seizure was in fact peasant "support for the workers" in the confiscation of the gentry estates.[28] But by 1917 Lenin had come to believe that the war and the Witte–Stolypin policies of "state capitalism" had created a situation in which peasant attacks upon the property of the rich could do more than destroy the material basis for the gentry's political power. Now he was willing to argue that if landed estates were confiscated, a proletarian-led government could institute a system of universal labor service and controlled distribution of basic products which would prepare the way for socialism.[29] Lenin never claimed that socialism could be achieved by such measures alone. His hopes were related to the arguments set out in *Imperialism: The Highest Stage of Capitalism* (1916) and in some of the writings of N. I. Bukharin, who had discovered in such large-scale institutions as banks, trusts and cartels a vast potential for socialist transformation. But Lenin's analysis of the economic preconditions for the transition to socialism remained rather flimsy and superficial.

In contrast, the logic of his political stance was powerful and compelling. In 1917 Lenin clearly found it impossible and in a sense immoral to claim that revolutionary socialists should force peasant discontent to serve the purpose of establishing bourgeois civil liberty and a rule of law defended by a traditional police force and army. He argued that Bolsheviks could not fight to strengthen the institutions which before had sustained the tsarist regime and were now functioning to support a bourgeois political order. Instead, they had to appeal to peasants and workers to resist any reestablishment of the police, the old bureaucracy, or the standing army. Such a policy would encourage the development of truly popular, soviet-type institutions, and as the realistic Lenin recognized as well, it would appeal to peasants and workers who "could not help but hate" their traditional oppressors.[30] If Bolsheviks worked to establish village soviets, giving special attention to the formation of separate organizations of hired agricultural workers, if they made it clear that they supported all of the struggles for land which so frightened "statesmenlike" radicals, a new social and political order might well emerge out of the popular actions which Mensheviks and SRs called "illegal" and "arbitrary."[31]

In March and April 1917, Lenin argued that rural soviets had already shown far greater creative social imagination than the Provisional Government. And while their local actions might be ill-planned or ill-judged, he claimed that Bolshevik organizing efforts could make them conscious and effective in a wider social and political sense. This would be a difficult task because, Lenin insisted, the development of truly conscious peasant action required that Bolsheviks refrain from imposing ideas or policies which the "rural proletarians had not yet fully realized, thought out and digested for *themselves*."[32] Although mistakes were inevitable when inexperienced people tried to participate directly in the political process, Lenin argued that it was better for the masses to make mistakes and go forward than to wait until "Prince L'vov's law professors" drafted laws which would fix Russia within the limits of a parliamentary bourgeois republic.[33] While Bolshevik organizing efforts were extremely important, Lenin insisted in April that the only real guarantee of popular welfare lay in the actions initiated by "the masses themselves, through their effective participation in all fields of state activity, without supervision from above."[34]

Throughout 1917 Lenin supported the Petrograd Soviet as an institution which fostered popular initiative, although he was opposed to its actual policies on the land question, the war, and the Provisional Government. As has been noted, members of the Soviet Executive Committee had not yet acted as uncompromising proponents of land reform. Instead, Soviet resolutions were intended to further the idea that the revolution had brought law and order to the cities and to the countryside. When a peasant committee from Tambov asked the Soviet to authorize action against a rich landlord so that they would not be "forced to take it upon themselves to shed blood,"[35] their request was refused. The Executive Committee scrupulously proposed that no land reform be enacted before the Constituent Assembly, so that the land question could be decided in a legal and democratic manner.[36] But the Soviet did not delay passage of a special resolution directed against individuals and groups who tried to "hide behind the authority of the Soviet" while engaging in seizures which were sometimes "indistinguishable from criminal acts."[37] The Soviet was thus willing to use its authority to maintain pre-revolutionary property relationships, while the Provisional Government on its side was increasingly ready to use force for the suppression of agrarian disorders stirred up, as Shingarev put it, by "Leninist" propaganda.[38] It was this pattern of response which Lenin was at great pains to expose.

Lenin praised the Soviet not for its policies but for its political, social, and economic potential. Created, like the Paris Commune, by the masses themselves, it was in his view superior in principle to any bourgeois institution. A Soviet government could, like the Commune, rely upon the force of a popular militia whose officials were elected or recalled at will by the people's decision. It was not forced to depend upon the alien and bureaucratic controls ordinarily exercised by a traditional army or police force.[39] Arguing that the Soviet embodied a successful "revolutionary-democratic dictatorship of the proletariat and the peasantry," Lenin denounced all those who refused to agree that socialism was a realistic Russian goal as traitors and deserters to the side of the petty bourgeoisie.

Critical as well of those who hesitated because they hoped that revolution would soon break out in Western Europe, Lenin warned against delaying Bolshevik action in the midst of a Russian revolution in deference to events which had not yet taken place in Europe. Peasants in Russia were expressing and acting upon their feelings of discontent, and in Lenin's view, if the peasants "take the land, be sure that they will not return it to you, nor will they ask you for your consent. . . . If the revolution is not settled by the Russian peasant, it will not be settled by the German worker. . . ."[40] Claiming that his opponents were excessively abstract in their understanding of actual political events, Lenin put forward the disarming argument that Bolshevik ideas had "in general" been confirmed by history, "but as to the concrete situation, things have turned out to be more original, more unique, more multicolored than could have been anticipated by anyone."[41]

Lenin had made such claims before 1917. As early as 1903 he had argued that when peasant action threatened the foundations of an exploitative social order, responsible revolutionaries had to encourage it in the hope that they would be able to raise the level of political consciousness of the peasants and workers concerned. And while he had conceded in 1906 that a Western socialist revolution was the only absolute guarantee of Russian revolutionary success, Lenin had nevertheless claimed for Russian Social Democracy a right to revolutionary leadership which did not depend upon the outcome of events taking place elsewhere. When Lenin argued in 1906 for nationalization of the land by peasant committees, Plekhanov had ridiculed what he called Lenin's dangerously "populist" notion of "popular creativity." But then and afterward, Lenin denied that there was anything at all populist in his approach. Generous in praise of the spontaneous action (or as he referred to it in *What Is To Be Done?* the "embryonic consciousness") of the rural masses,[42] he was before 1917 consistently skeptical about the enthusiasm of non-Bolsheviks for spontaneous popular action. It was Lenin's belief that most revolutionary optimists failed to recognize that popular creativity was only the beginning of conscious political action.

When Lenin returned to Petrograd on April 3, his famous speech at the Finland Station was applauded by many workers and soldiers, and by some of the Bolsheviks who came to greet him. But as Sukhanov observed, "the educated, while applauding long and warmly, were staring strangely into space with unseeing eyes—demonstrating their complete confusion."[43] Lenin's arguments for a transition to socialism through peasant revolution seemed cynical to some, and to others like a new form of Bakuninist anarchism.[44] How could Lenin, the centralizer par excellence, call for peasant action without supervision by a revolutionary political organization? How, asked Sukhanov, were the soviets, which represented a small minority of the country, to "construct Socialism?"[45] The Bolshevik Kamenev made it quite clear that Lenin's "Theses" were simply Lenin's incorrect opinions; decisive steps toward socialism seemed to him inconceivable before the bourgeois-democratic revolution had even been completed.[46] Zinoviev temporized, suggesting that Lenin was perhaps insufficiently acquainted with conditions in Russia.[47]

Conceding nothing to his critics, Lenin set himself to prove to members of the Bolshevik party that Sukhanov, Zinoviev, Stalin, and Kamenev were wrong. He insisted that Bolsheviks reject the admiration for legal order and formal equality which characterized the Kadets and the current Soviet leadership.[48] They were obliged to teach peasants to reject the plausible-sounding recommendations which came from Shingarev, who urged individual peasants to conclude voluntary agreements with their landlords. Lenin argued that a politically sophisticated peasant could understand that he was never as free to negotiate as a rich landlord. He could understand that the collective mass action undertaken by local peasant soviets which ignored Petrograd and requisitioned uncultivated land was not leading Russia toward economic chaos, as SRs, Mensheviks and Kadets continually asserted. With the help of a little consciousness-raising, peasants (and even Bolshevik critics of Lenin's policies) were quite capable of understanding that peasant organizations were more able to deal with the food problem than the Provisional Government was.[49]

Outside the Bolshevik Party, Lenin's emergence as a spokesman for Marxist peasant revolution was due at least as much to the ineptitude of the Soviet leadership as to the effectiveness of his appeals for peasant action. Neither before nor immediately after Lenin's return to the capital did the Bolsheviks pose a serious threat to the SRs and Mensheviks who dominated the Petrograd Soviet. In the spring and early summer of 1917, the response of the Soviet's Executive Committee to pressures from above and below would help his cause immeasurably in the months to come.

8

The Burden of Political Opportunity: April–July 1917

> The worst thing that can befall a leader of an extreme party is to be compelled to take over a government in an epoch when the movement is not yet ripe for the realization of the measures which that domination would imply. . . . What he *can* do is in contrast to all his principles, and to the present interest of his party; what he *ought* to do cannot be achieved . . . he is compelled to defend the interests of an alien class, and to feed his own class with phrases and promises. Whoever puts himself in this awkward position is irrevocably lost.
>
> FRIEDRICH ENGELS[1]

The Political Crisis

During the Revolution of 1905–7, Mensheviks frequently cited Engels's statement on the dangers of premature revolutionary leadership in support of their contention that Marxists could not lead a revolution in a backward peasant society. But ironically enough, it was they who would act to fulfil Engels's predictions in 1917, as they drew the more moderate members of the Socialist Revolutionary Party into the pursuit of their resolutely humble political goals. Fearing primitive and irrational behavior by the peasant majority of the population, they placed the responsibility for civilizing and developing Russian society squarely upon the historically appropriate shoulders of the bourgeoisie. At the same time, they insisted that the bourgeois "exploiters," once in power, should refrain from undue exploitation. In plain terms, this meant that Mensheviks expected the Provisional Government to undertake the tasks of national defense, economic reconstruction, and democratic political development which were to prepare the way for socialism. As the Menshevik Tsereteli put it, "All the aims of the Russian Revolution, and even its very fate, are dependent on whether the propertied classes will understand that this is a national platform. . . . Will the propertied classes be able to renounce their narrow group interests and take their stand on the common national democratic platform?"[2] Like the proletariat and the "revolutionary army," the bourgeoisie had to understand that its aspirations would not be realized by the current revolution.

As we shall see, "understanding" of Tsereteli's sort was rarely to be met with. On April 18 the Kadet foreign minister P. N. Miliukov issued a note to the Allies which broke faith with the Soviet by reaffirming many of the imperialist war aims of the tsarist regime[3]. Soviet leaders, while dismayed at Miliukov's action, were equally terrified when thousands of workers and soldiers took to the streets either to protest Miliukov's note or to take up his defense. They listened apprehensively to reports of violent clashes among the demonstrators, aware that the protests might be quelled at any moment by the forces of Kornilov, the commander in chief of the Petrograd garrison. Attempting to arrive at a principled and politically prudent response of their own, Menshevik moderates were unwilling either to sanction the mass protests which might endanger a historically necessary "bourgeois" regime or to strengthen such a government by participating in it themselves. The Menshevik solution was to propose that their Socialist Revolutionary allies join the government. As Chkheidze pointed out, Russia was after all a peasant country, and peasants deserved to be represented by "their" party in the currently existing government.[4] Although Chkheidze did not spell out the rather insulting reason why Mensheviks and SRs had such different options open to them (namely that Mensheviks were socialists while SRs, regardless of what they called themselves, were only petty bourgeois), SRs were nevertheless unwilling to accept the Menshevik plan. Refusing to be compromised unless the rest of the Soviet leadership followed suit, the SR Abram Gotz responded, "We can accept responsibility for participating in the government only if you share it with us."[5] Neither SRs nor Mensheviks were eager to accept political responsibility for the making of government policy.

As Sukhanov had predicted in 1915,[6] SRs and Mensheviks had come to recognize a common interest in the triumph of the bourgeois-democratic revolution. Attempting in 1917 to check the extremism of the left and the right, they wanted to prevent the outbreak of soldier–peasant pogroms or any attempts at a right-wing military coup which might destroy the prospects for moderate bourgeois government. On April 20, on the orders of the Soviet Executive Committee, politically volatile military units in surrounding districts were instructed to stay out of Petrograd, and a halt was called to all demonstrations within the city. The committee demanded as well that the Provisional Government issue a clarifying statement which would repudiate Miliukov's note and explicitly reject any commitment to tsarist imperial goals. Despite its reluctance to seize power, the Soviet's political authority was indicated by the speed with which its orders were obeyed. Demonstrations ended on the day of the Soviet's order, and the government quickly issued a note which met the Soviet's demands.

The Bolsheviks were not particularly successful during the "April Days"; in fact, soldiers and workers beat up demonstrators who carried placards with Bolshevik slogans on them. Nevertheless, Bolsheviks remained less fearful about the consequences of popular initiative than their Menshevik and SR opponents in the Soviet Executive Committee.[7] Lenin continued to ridicule the Menshevik "delusion" that a Provisional Government closely linked with foreign and Russian capital could be tempted by rational persuasion to renounce imperialist war aims. As he put it, it was understandable that an illiterate muzhik might rely on appeals to the conscience of the middle class, but it was "shameful" for a Marxist to believe that "icons and phrases" like "democracy" and "national interest" could win out in the struggle against the material forces of "cannons and capital." Cooperation with the bourgeoisie could in his view lead only to betrayal of the revolution.[8] Menshevik hopes for the bourgeoisie were proof to Lenin of Menshevik unfitness for leadership of the Russian Marxist movement. They had forgotten that "the task of a proletarian leader is to clarify the difference in interests and persuade certain sections of the petty bourgeoisie (namely the poor peasants) to choose between the workers and the capitalists, to take the side of the workers." In effect, Lenin claimed, Tsereteli was asking workers and peasants to confine themselves to the achievement of goals which satisfied the interests of landlords and capitalists.[9]

In Lenin's view, the undemocratic inclinations of the Russian bourgeoisie were exposed by the Provisional Government's policy on the establishment of land committees. On April 21, 1917, a decree established a network of committees to prepare material for future land reform and to make proposals to the Ministry of Agriculture for the suspension of existing agrarian legislation. The committees were to operate under the jurisdiction of a Main Land Committee in Petrograd. It was only at the *volost* level that delegates were to be elected by the rural population. At higher levels and in the Main Land Committee, one-third to almost one-half of the committee members were to be administrative, technical, or legal experts, while in the proposed consultative committees, equal representation was to be given to peasants and landlords.[10]

Reactions to the formation of this sort of organizational structure to deal with the land question were varied in the extreme. Right-wing Kadets like N. A. Maklakov feared that the committees envisioned by the government's decree provided too many opportunities for participation by non-specialists, illiterates, and firebrands unconcerned with constructive and orderly work. But among peasants who learned of the new law on land committees, there was suspicion that beyond the *volost* level, all power would in fact gravitate into the hands of the landlords.[11] To Lenin, it was characteristic of the cynicism of the Provisional Government and the naiveté of many in the Soviet to believe that land committees dominated by middle-class experts and "men of good will" would be able to resolve the problems created by class conflict. His class analysis provided him with what he held to be an objective explanation of the reasons why government land committees would be mistaken in their predictions and proposals. It was obvious to Lenin that on land committees and elsewhere, middle-class intellectuals and philanthropists would categorize popular action which endangered existing patterns of landownership as "anarchic disorder," and view immediate land reform as a regrettable concession to the pressure of mob violence.[12]

The April Conference (April 25–April 29, 1917)

At the April Conference, Lenin's enthusiasm was tempered by a frank recognition that Bolshevik political influence was relatively insignificant. In his words, "So far we are in the minority: the masses do not believe us."[13] The peasants were "to a certain extent 'consciously' on the side of the capitalists," and even the proletarians and semi-proletarians were currently supporting Menshevik, SR, and even Kadet policies.[14] Neither class-conscious nor socialist, Russia's working people had to be organized into independent groups; Lenin insisted that Marxists were not to be confused with populist agitators who claimed to represent the people "in general." In his view, no one was exploited in general—farmhands, small peasants, and middle peasants were exploited in concrete and specific ways. Only as members of separate organizations could they begin to become aware of the class interests which distinguished them from the rest of the population. Only when they understood their own situation could they begin to think concretely about their common interests with other social elements.[15]

Despite Lenin's class analysis of the distinction between farmhands and proprietors, it was significant that at the April Conference he spoke of "preaching socialism" not only to proletarians and semi-proletarians, but to the small peasant proprietor.[16] While recognizing that both the proletariat and the peasantry lacked political experience, he did not precisely or consistently set limits to the potential development of either group. His enthusiasm placed him at the opposite end of the political spectrum from the Bolshevik A. I. Rykov, who argued with paralyzing ideological consistency that it was as impossible to win petty bourgeois peasants to the socialist cause as it was to think that Bolsheviks could "make the working masses join this [bourgeois] revolution."[17] In contrast to Rykov, Lenin found his inspiration in the reports which came from the province of Penza, where peasants were not only converting gentry land and tools into common property but establishing rules for cultivation intended to raise agricultural productivity. Lenin argued that such actions gave Bolsheviks the right to hope that when the peasant took action and became confident that he understood his own situation, "he will himself come to the conclusion that it is essential to utilize agricultural implements, not only in the small farms, but for the cultivation of all the land. How they do this is unimportant."[18]

Just as in the pre-revolutionary period, Lenin's optimism was not linked to any recognition that the constructive economic activity he noted was taking place in commune districts. In Lenin's writings, the actions of the "cooperators" from Penza had no historical roots in peasant tradition or custom. The very existence of the commune was ignored, and no suggestion was ever made that its collectivist practices might have predisposed its members toward cooperative solutions to local problems. When Lenin singled out any rural element as praiseworthy, it was always the rural poor, the landless peasants and hired laborers. Although this group was everywhere insignificant as an independent political factor, and nowhere distinguished by the practice of cooperative cultivation of the land,[19] insistence on the leading role of the rural poor was *de rigeur* for a Marxist believer in class analysis.

But Lenin's orthodoxies were not what distinguished him from his comrades. Far more interesting and original was his concern with consciousness-raising for all peasants, regardless of his belief in the importance of the class distinctions which could be made between them. Untroubled by the attacks which came from Kamenev and others at the conference who were impatient with his "exaggerated" emphasis upon teaching, preaching, and propaganda,[20] Lenin concerned himself above all with the vital need to politicize the masses. In the absence of widespread popular support for Bolshevik policy, he argued that it was all the more important that Bolsheviks exercise caution in their own revolutionary initiatives, patiently explain the Bolshevik position to proletarians, semi-proletarians, and peasants, and wholeheartedly support the creative local initiative of peasants who seized land, livestock, and tools from the rich.[21]

The Bolshevik commitment to a potentially revolutionary peasantry was as controversial at the April Conference as it had been at successive Marxist gatherings since 1906. As in earlier debates, fears of peasant anarchy, backwardness, and bigotry were brought forward and re-examined. When Lenin called for nationalization of the land, arguing that Russian peasants were traditionally hostile to the idea of private property, the Bolshevik Angarskii expressed the sentiments of many delegates at the conference when he answered that "what the peasants really wanted" would come as an unpleasant surprise to Russia's revolutionary optimists.[22]

Implying that one did not look to the peasantry for sophisticated intellectual formulations, Lenin argued that "objective" historical developments had made them supporters of land nationalization. In order to convince doubting fellow Bolsheviks that peasants were relevant to a specifically Marxist revolutionary theory and practice, he attempted to provide a material basis for his position. Lenin argued that economic conditions in Russia and in the international market were concretely expressed in the high prices and poor living conditions which small producers connected with the old forms of landownership. And while Lenin believed (as a Marxist had to do) that peasants really wanted nothing more than to be petty bourgeois proprietors, he emphasized that (1) they wanted a fundamental redistribution of land and (2) this demand required a radical break with existing forms of landholding. It was in this context, Lenin claimed, that nationalization was an appropriate and principled political slogan. While satisfying the peasant's "bourgeois desire" for the confiscation and redistribution of gentry land, nationalization would also ease the transition to socialism by destroying traditional property relationships.[23]

Regardless of the doubtful orthodoxy of Lenin's argument for a Marxist-led peasant revolution, the hope that Bolsheviks could work for more than the establishment of a democratic capitalist order proved irresistible to those who had for various reasons become identified with the Bolshevik Party in the spring of 1917. While a programmatic distinction between the peasant bourgeoisie and the revolutionary rural proletarians and semi-proletarians reflected a continuing commitment to Marxist class distinctions, the Leninist resolution accepted by the April Conference called for the immediate transfer of all land to the peasantry "organized in Soviets of Peasants' Deputies, or in other organs of self-government, elected in a really democratic way. . . ."[24]

The Bourgeois-Socialist Coalition

Despite their earlier misgivings about the difficulties of coalition with the "bourgeoisie," when Minister of War Guchkov resigned on May 1 the majority of the Soviet's Executive Committee voted to support a coalition with the Kadets. In a series of maneuvers singularly lacking in revolutionary idealism, Mensheviks and SRs each tried to send the least possible number of their own people into the government. But since the SR Chernov firmly refused to join without his friend the Menshevik Tsereteli,[25] the upshot was that the most prominent representatives of each party agreed to become part of a socialist minority in a government they considered anti-socialist and bourgeois. As conditions for their entry, they demanded official government support for peace without annexations, democratization of the army, increased state control of industry, and the regulation of agriculture in the interests of the peasantry.

In fact, despite the Soviet "conditions" the priorities set out in the coalition's first declaration would have found substantial support even among the pre-revolutionary ministers of the tsarist regime. The needs of the "nation" were placed first on the agenda; no efforts were to be spared to guarantee a high level of grain production. And since fundamental changes in the system of landownership might disrupt the attempt to increase productivity, the new SR and Menshevik ministers indicated that they were ready to defer any transfer of land to the peasantry until a Constituent Assembly could be convened at some unspecified later date. Their compromises only just begun, Soviet leaders had agreed from the outset to define the needs of the nation as something distinct from the immediate material well-being or satisfaction of the majority of the population.

Although Chernov and his fellow socialist ministers had entered the coalition in order to strengthen the forces of bourgeois moderation, they were dismayed to find that the progressives upon whom they hoped to rely had moved steadily to the right in the spring of 1917. In the debates on the agrarian question which took place at the Kadet Party congress in May, even the left-wing Kadet N. N. Chernenkov agreed that in the interests of maintaining agricultural productivity, land reform should be delayed until after the war. The proposal that the party at least reaffirm its traditional support for the forcible expropriation of land from large landowners was rejected, while the enactment of land reform which encroached upon the property of great landowners was described by leading Kadets as a "political luxury."[26] Concentrating instead upon the dangers of mob rule and the growing popular contempt for legal order, the Kadets Maklakov, Shingarev, and Miliukov denounced the irresponsibility of leftist agitators and peasant groups who used the Provisional Government decree of April 21 or the resolutions of the SR Party to justify land seizures. Such concerns were not uniquely liberal; pre-revolutionary bureaucrats had often responded in similar fashion to violent popular demands for immediate improvement in the material situation of the poor.

Peasant hopes for government land reform before the Constituent

Assembly came to rest almost exclusively with Victor Chernov, the new minister of agriculture. As chief theoretician of the SR Party, Chernov had far more ambitious plans for the coalition than those outlined in its first declaration. In early May he proposed that land disputes be decided by land committees according to the principle which he believed would guide the future Constituent Assembly—the transfer of all land to the "toiling masses."[27] In addition, Chernov proposed a suspension of all land transactions in order to allay peasant fears that wealthy landlords were evading the possibility of future restrictions on property rights by engaging in speculation and sales to foreign and fictitious buyers.[28] On May 17 the SR minister of justice, Pereverzev, sent out a telegraph order to provincial officials suspending land transactions. But the order was officially withdrawn only a week later, just as the All-Russian Peasant Congress passed a resolution in favor of it.[29]

The difficulties of coalition rule were evident at the first meeting of the Main Land Committee on May 19. The Kadet chairman, A. S. Posnikov, claimed that his party was in "general agreement" with other democratic and peasant parties in support of the principle of land-ownership by the "laboring population,"[30] but warned in the same speech that the government expected the populace to calmly await the Constituent Assembly's future decision. In Posnikov's words, there were to be no "deplorable excesses" or "inadmissible seizures of land."[31] In reply, the SR N. Ia. Bykhovskii argued that peasant "excesses" were few in number and had moreover been condemned by all peasant conferences and committees. Despite the frequent rumors of peasant land seizure, Bykhovskii claimed that available evidence indicated instead that the gentry were taking land away from the peasants by means of speculation and fictitious land sales. In his view, the only way to guarantee that peasants would obey the law was to issue a declaration which stated that future land reforms would be based upon the principle of the ownership of all land by the entire people.[32]

The conflicting concerns of Posnikov and Bykhovskii epitomized the difficulties which would prevent the Main Land Committee from ever reaching any constructive solution to the problems which faced it, even though a majority of its members were able to agree to oppose land seizure. The Kadets emphasized the danger to life and property which threatened those who already owned the land, while the SRs focused their attention upon the continuing exploitation suffered by the peasants who wanted to get hold of it. Even within the socialist contingent there was disagreement. When the Bolshevik Smil'ga suggested that organized land seizure directed by local land committees was the only safeguard against the economic ruin of the peasantry, Chernov answered that the phrase "organized seizure" was a contradiction in terms—"seizure" could not be "organized" and would only create further difficulties in the Russian countryside.[33]

After long debate, a majority of the Main Land Committee approved resolutions in favor of the regulation of rental payments, the suspension of land transactions, and even the management of all land by the land committees. The passage of these resolutions was a triumph for Chernov, who repeatedly tried to demonstrate that SRs were not the "prisoners" of the bourgeois Provisional Government, as the Bolsheviks had claimed. He pointed out, for example, that the SR minority had been able to prevent the Main Land Committee from deleting the word "all" from its final resolution on the transfer of land to the land committees.[34] But since no government action was taken to turn the committee's decisions into law, it is understandable that many of Chernov's more vocal critics on the left found his victories less than impressive.

In the late spring of 1917, as peasant unrest escalated and spread, it became evident that the popularity of the SR Party was no guarantee that peasants would confine their activities to the selection of delegates to committees intended to prepare for future land reform. Although Chernov was elected president of the All-Russian Peasant Congress in May 1917 and SR moderates won general approval for the policies of the Soviet leadership, it was significant that congress participants were initially unwilling even to listen to the agrarian report of the Kadets with whom the SRs were joined in a coalition government. Although every speaker who defended the rights of property was shouted down, the enthusiasm expressed for the goals defined in the SR agrarian program blinded party leaders to the possibility that peasant allegiance might not be unconditional. Even when some of the peasant delegates openly declared themselves "fed up" with promises rather than action on the land question, SR moderates refused to recognize the political implications of the fact that their prime constituents were unwilling to peacefully await the granting of benefits at some later date.[35]

Peasant hostility to the Kadets did not (at least in May 1917) mean that the peasantry was willing to support the Bolshevik Party. When

Zinoviev and Lenin came before the Peasant Congress to demand unconditional land seizure, they were accused of promoting civil war.[36] Lenin responded brilliantly by taking the offensive, admitting that Bolshevik policy was indeed a declaration of war against the propertied classes. He went on to contrast SR and Menshevik denunciations of peasant land seizure as "arbitrary" with the Bolshevik commitment to immediate satisfaction of the peasantry's just demands. Using the same arguments with which Chernov had attempted in vain to convince his fellow government ministers of the need to transfer land to government land committees, Lenin told the Peasant Congress of the peasantry's capacity for constructive and rational collective action. Peasant delegates were understandably more receptive than Prince L'vov to the suggestion that an organized seizure of land would not necessarily lead to a fall in agricultural productivity. According to Lenin, peasant organizations did not act blindly, lightly, or stupidly when they took to action. Enslaved for centuries by the landed gentry, the peasantry had cultivated the land poorly. Was it possible, Lenin asked, that they would cultivate the land in a worse manner once it was their own? Lenin claimed that peasant attempts to destroy their "intolerable bondage" to the gentry were not arbitrary. Action taken by a majority of peasants who were "careful enough in making decisions" was rather a "restitution of justice" and "a lawful decision of state significance."[37] Attempting to refute the charge that Bolsheviks were engaging in anarchist-style appeals for unorganized popular retribution and vengeance, Lenin emphasized that Bolsheviks favored a strong central government which repudiated all "bourgeois" conceptions of law and order. In his view, "The basic difference between ourselves and our opponents is in our respective understanding of what order is and what law is. Up to now law and order have been regarded as things that suited the landowners and bureaucrats, but we maintain that law and order are things that suit the majority of the peasantry." It was in this sense that Lenin argued that there was in fact greater order in the Russian countryside in the spring of 1917 than ever before, "because majority decisions were being made by the people."[38]

To Chernov's argument that land seizure would benefit peasants who were already rich and powerful, Lenin's response was quite honest and principled. He claimed that land seizure would bring freedom from the overwhelming evil of gentry domination, although it would not save the rural poor from exploitation. "You cannot eat land," as Lenin put it.[39] Without the money to buy livestock, tools, and seed, the poor would inevitably hire themselves out to the richer peasants. If private property were abolished and land transferred to the state for the use of all working people, agricultural laborers and poor peasants would still be forced to organize in defense of their own interests. At best, the poor would let themselves be guided by their own experience and by "their distrust of what the village sharks tell them, even though these sharks wear red rosettes in their buttonholes and call themselves 'revolutionary democrats.' "[40] In other words, the class struggle would continue, even after an organized seizure of gentry land by the peasantry.

According to Lenin, both the evils of capitalism and the suffering imposed by economic backwardness could be avoided if a worker–peasant revolution carried out an economic program based upon the common cultivation of land by agricultural laborers. And he concluded his speech to the Peasant Congress with a lengthy discussion of the merits of joint cultivation of large-scale agricultural enterprises. Lenin's emphasis upon the difficulties inherent in the Bolshevik solution indicated that just as in 1907 and 1908,[41] his appeals to the peasantry had both a short- and a long-term significance. Eager to rouse the peasant to fight for immediately popular objectives, Lenin nevertheless remained seriously concerned to develop a specifically Marxist political consciousness. As he put it:

> To be sure, joint cultivation is a difficult business and it would be madness of course for anybody to imagine that joint cultivation of the land can be decreed from above and imposed on people, because the centuries-old habit of farming on one's own cannot suddenly disappear, and because money will be needed for it. When we advise such a measure, and advise caution in the handling of it . . . we are not drawing that conclusion from our . . . socialist doctrine alone, but because we, as socialists, have come to this conclusion by studying the life of the West European nations.[42]

Universal labor service required concentration, determination and energy on the part "of each peasant and worker at his own place, at his own particular job which he knows and has been working at for years. It is not a thing that can be done by any sort of decree, but it is a thing that must be done. . . ."[43]

While Lenin had begun his speech with politically expedient emphasis upon the peasant's inherent good sense, his conclusions reflected an honesty and respect for his "backward" peasant audience which distinguished him from many other speakers at the congress. The joint cultivation of giant farms was hardly an issue to stir the enthusiasm of either communal or non-communal peasants. The absence of demagoguery in Lenin's conclusion may explain the meager support (some two dozen votes) given to the resolution the Bolsheviks introduced to the Peasant Congress.

At the same time, there were SR observers at the congress who noted with dismay the impact of Lenin's appeal for land seizure and the damaging political case which Bolsheviks were able to make against SR ministers in the coalition. Bolsheviks were particularly successful in embarrassing Chernov by pointing to the contradiction between SR party declarations and the fate of the Pereverzev order suspending land transactions. Why, they asked, was the order withdrawn at the same time that Chernov was telling the congress that such a measure was essential? Why were the SRs so ineffective? In the context of his party's failure to put its program into practice, there was something plaintive in the SR Derber's complaint that the Bolsheviks had stolen the SR program.[44] The congress passed Chernov's resolution advocating the transfer of land to the land committees by a comfortable margin.[45] But it would in practice prove extremely difficult to distinguish between the Bolshevik slogan of "organized seizure" and Chernov's "transfer." And the Bolsheviks were in fact more willing than the SR leadership to risk the consequences of immediate land "transfer" to the land committees.

Chernov was far better able to criticize the Bolsheviks than to explain his ineffectiveness within the coalition. He argued that Bolsheviks encouraged land seizure out of contempt for the revolutionary potential of the peasantry and respect for their numerical strength. In Lenin's slogans, Chernov saw a "wager on the strong" peasant who would seize the most land and brutally exploit the landless. Chernov argued that in fact Lenin feared that Bolsheviks would never come to power through democratic elections but only as a result of the economic chaos and civil war which would follow from arbitrary land seizure. In contrast, he claimed that the SRs were firmly opposed to the satisfaction of any peasant "instinct" for private ownership. As Chernov put it, "We are the servants of the people, but we are not subservient to them." SRs were unwilling, he said, to use the peasantry as cannon fodder for the Bolshevik idea of revolution.[46]

But the sincerity of Chernov's promise that the coalition would soon transfer land to legally constituted land committees was insufficient to restrain growing dissatisfaction within the SR Party itself, where "Bolshevik" demands for action were being echoed with increasing force. At the SR congress which met in late May 1917, a left-wing faction led by B. D. Kamkov, A. S. Spiridonova, and M. A. Natanson opposed coalition with the bourgeoisie and demanded an all-socialist government, immediate peace, and immediate action for the socialization of land.[47] Their efforts were defeated by the moderates who controlled the congress. Zenzinov and Gotz, convinced that the need for "defensive war" and a stable coalition were issues of more pressing concern than the land question, worked with other party moderates to engineer the passage of resolutions which repeated the demands of the Peasant Congress. In line with the views of Chernov, the "arbitrary" seizure of land was again condemned.[48] In response, the frustrated Left SRs took the step of establishing a secret information bureau to coordinate the activities of like-minded critics of the party leadership. In their view, the party's claim to be the legitimate representative of the peasantry was being put in jeopardy by government inaction on the land question.

The hard-won moderation reflected in the final resolutions of the SR Party and the Peasant Congress did not elicit any concessions on the agrarian question from non-SR members of the coalition. By June 15 Chernov was still promising that a decree suspending land transactions was imminent. While a "left" Kadet "Union of Evolutionary Socialism" was vainly attempting to salvage the remnants of the Kadet peasant policy,[49] most non-socialists in the coalition were becoming increasingly vocal in their opposition to any official encouragement of popular initiatives on the land question. In the judgment of Prince L'vov, the coalition president, the implementation of Chernov's policies would prejudice the Constituent Assembly's final decision on the land question. He argued that if land were transferred to land committees, a Constituent Assembly would not really decide but simply acknowledge a *fait accompli*.[50] Even if Chernov and his followers did not openly advocate land seizure, L'vov argued, they were using all the power of the Ministry of Agriculture to encourage peasants to believe that the ownership of land had already been transferred to the people. Why, he asked, would peasants feel any obligation to consider the rights of landowners if they were told that the land question was going to be decided in the interests of the peasantry? L'vov's analysis was of course quite well founded. Chernov did in fact hope that the countryside would remain peaceful if peasants were assured that the land question would be decided in their favor by the Constituent Assembly. At the same time, it should be noted that L'vov's desire to freeze property relations before the Constituent Assembly met did not lead him to support Chernov's plan for the suspension of land transactions. Similarly, his reliance on the Constituent Assembly for all solutions did not keep him from repeatedly agreeing to its postponement.[51]

In May and June, 1917, Lenin criticized the Soviet's inaction on the land question and appealed for organized land seizure by the peasantry. With little success, he urged an All-Russian Trade Union Conference meeting in Petrograd to establish unions of agricultural laborers, emphasizing that no government would help "the rural wage worker, the farmhand, the day laborer, the poor peasant, the semi-proletarian, if he does not help himself."[52] According to Lenin's political analysis, Mensheviks and SRs were acting as the guardians and tools of the bourgeoisie, with Chernov's prestige serving to reconcile the peasantry to the absence of any government-sponsored land reform.[53] He argued that this was a dangerous policy, because it was only a matter of time before the bourgeoisie would turn on its allies, and launch bloody and repressive attacks upon them. Just as the credulous and indecisive Louis Blanc had prepared the way for General Cavaignac in the "June Days" of 1848, so the concessions of Tsereteli and Chernov in the summer of 1917 were creating a situation in which the Cavaignacs (the Kadets) would support a military leader willing to use unlimited force against the poor.[54] Lenin claimed that if the Soviet's "revolutionary democracy" were truly democratic, in action and not only in rhetoric, it would place the interests of the masses above the interests of coalition with the capitalists. According to Lenin, popular support for the Soviet gave Soviet leaders both the right and the responsibility to govern Russia. Their timidity was shameful—no party had the right to refuse power. In fact the Bolsheviks were willing to take power at any time, Lenin stated, to the amusement of delegates at the June Congress of Soviets.[55] Without the Bolsheviks, Lenin warned, the Soviet, an institution "unparalleled and unprecedented anywhere in the world in strength," would be destroyed by the incessant and unnecessary compromises of its ministers in the coalition. Lenin bitterly reproached Soviet leaders for their refusal to govern, while holding them responsible for the errors and inadequacies of the existing government and especially for their inactivity on the agrarian question.[56]

According to Lenin, once the autocracy had fallen, the Soviet and the Provisional Government had been so concerned to establish laws to consolidate the gains of the revolution that they ignored the immediate and pressing poverty which really governed the lives of most people. Until the revolution the land belonged to the landlords; but this was not called anarchy, though it led to destruction, to "anarchy," and to the ruin of the land and the people. While the populists, the Mensheviks, and Kadet Minister Shingarev condemned the immediate seizure of land as anarchy, the Bolsheviks wanted an immediate seizure of land by the peasants in the best organized manner. There was no anarchy, Lenin claimed, in a decision for land seizure arrived at by the majority of the population in each locality. Was the decision of the majority to be called "anarchy"? Was it not more just to say that the decision of the minority was anarchy? Lenin argued that Minister Shingarev's recommendation that three hundred peasant families "voluntarily" make an agreement with one rich exploiter was an "anarchist" decision. "The decision of the majority of workers and peasants is not anarchy but the only guarantee of democracy. . . ."[57] Although such a defense had little to do with conventional definitions of "anarchy" and "democracy," it was quite consistent with peasant readiness to believe that demands for law and order had a definite upper-class bias, and it was well within the traditions of Marxist political analysis. For Lenin, the material conditions under which the peasant lived were deplorable, and this was the true social and economic content of bourgeois democratic law and order. He therefore appealed for peasant action and aligned the Bolsheviks with the peasants' most immediate demands.[58]

While granting this kind of "support" to the soviet, the Bolsheviks reserved to themselves the right of "complete freedom of agitation and demonstration"[59] in the days of June and July which were to bring down the First Coalition.

9

Lenin as Spokesman for Peasant Revolution: July–October 1917

> Opportunism? Of course. But the question is, where is the boundary beyond which a legitimate quest for the line of least resistance passes into an illegitimate submission to the force of circumstances?
>
> N. N. Sukhanov[1]

BETWEEN JULY AND OCTOBER 1917 Lenin's analysis of the Revolution, so controversial and unpopular when it was first formulated in the spring, was borne out by the actions of his political opponents.[2] During this period, the Soviet leaders in the Provisional Government conducted a sort of "holding operation" for a bourgeoisie with whom they found themselves increasingly at odds. SR moderates followed in the wake of their Menshevik counterparts, who sought in vain for individuals and groups willing to act in conformity with their conception of bourgeois-democratic revolution. At the same time, socialist government ministers, SRs and Mensheviks agreed to the suppression of violence in the cities and in the countryside without providing workers or peasants with any material stake in the maintenance of law and order. As a result, they were less and less able to convince the politically active Petrograd poor that Menshevik and SR good intentions would lead to any concrete improvement in the conditions under which they lived.

In this situation, Lenin's approach to the peasant question was clear and simple: he argued that the Soviet's failures were obvious, Soviet appeals for order spurious, and the revolutionary potential contained in peasant action against private property infinite. As his strategy developed in line with such arguments, he began to claim that the Bolsheviks were justified in seizing power in the name of the people, i.e., the peasants seizing land, the soldiers deserting from the front, the workers seizing factories.

The July Crisis

Ever since the "February Days," Kadet government ministers had been able to block any legal encroachment upon pre-revolutionary property relationships; in June they even managed to engineer the launching of a new military offensive against the Germans. But despite such achievements, Kadets were well aware that their successes might not be permanent. Each day brought them new reports of worker and peasant opposition or indifference to government authority, while the June military offensive, which had begun so well, ended in disaster. In this difficult situation, the continual "carping" of leftists like Chernov, who claimed to recognize the need for coalition with the bourgeoisie but felt free to engage in anti-bourgeois propaganda, became insupportable. On July 2, 1917, the Kadets withdrew from the coalition and confronted Soviet ministers with the prospect of sole responsibility for governing the country.

To the dismay of the Soviet leadership, the Kadet resignations brought thousands of workers, soldiers, and sailors into the streets of Petrograd to demand a transfer of all power to the Soviet. Many of the crowd's slogans were conspicuously pro-"Bolshevik," although the Bolsheviks of the Petrograd Central Committee were apparently unprepared for the size and scope of the unrest and uncertain of their ability to control the protesters. The frustration and growing anger of the populace with "their" socialist ministers was everywhere evident. In one well-documented incident, Chernov himself was assaulted by an enraged worker who shook his fist in Chernov's face and yelled, "Why don't you take power, you son of a bitch, when it's given to you?"[3]

The Rump Coalition was extremely careful and deliberate in its assessment of blame for the July crisis. Refusing to criticize the Kadets, Kerensky and Tsereteli concentrated exclusively upon the left-wing, "anarchist" threat to the revolution.[4] A number of Bolsheviks (including Kamenev and Trotsky) were arrested, *Pravda* was closed down, and

Lenin and a number of others went into hiding.[5] A resolution of the Joint Executive Committee of the Petrograd Soviet of Workers', Soldiers', and Peasants' Deputies called upon the government to "crush with an iron hand all anarchist outbursts."[6] With the arrival of loyal government troops from outside Petrograd, the coalition was able to survive the July days, although it has been correctly noted that the size of the demonstration indicated that increasingly revolutionary measures would be necessary to allay popular discontent.[7]

Lenin saw the Kadet withdrawal from the government as an attempt to frighten the Soviet ministers into accepting Kadet policies, and he predicted that this "Kadet strategy" would be successful. Given the Menshevik obsession with bourgeois-democratic revolution and the general political ineptitude of the SRs, he was certain that Tsereteli and Chernov would not call the Kadet bluff by transferring power to the Soviet or by enacting fundamental land reform. Instead, he argued, they would prefer to compromise the interests of their supporters by meeting Kadet terms for re-entry into the coalition.[8] According to Lenin, such conciliatory measures would be justified by the "illusory" belief that Russia was on the eve of a Constituent Assembly which would solve the agrarian question. In reality, Lenin argued, the bourgeoisie would delay elections to the Constituent Assembly and use increasingly coercive measures to deal with the spread of peasant violence. Eventually, the bourgeoisie's repressive actions would force the masses to entrust their fate to the proletariat. In what seemed a fantastically improbable conjecture in the aftermath of the "July Days," he claimed that the proletariat would then take power and bring about the socialist revolution.[9]

"Order" or Land Reform: Agrarian Priorities in July 1917

Debate on the agrarian question had long centered around three issues: the repeal of the Stolypin legislation; the suspension of rights to buy, sell, or lease land, and the legitimate power of the land committees created in April 1917. In the absence of the Kadets, the Rump Coalition moved cautiously to the Left and promised the peasantry some material improvement in their economic life. A declaration of July 8 stated that laws would be passed "in the near future" to empower land committees to regulate relations between peasants and landlords. As in the spring, it was emphasized that these changes were not to encroach upon existing private property relationships. All such questions were to be finally settled by the Constituent Assembly.[10]

By July 1917 opposition to such formulations had begun to come not only from the Bolsheviks, but from the increasingly dissident left wing of the SR Party. B. D. Kamkov demanded to know why SR leaders were attempting to placate the middle class instead of defending the interests of working people. A. S. Spiridonova argued that "illegality" and "arbitrary" action were a less serious danger than betrayal of the revolution; SR ministers had to be held responsible for the enactment of fundamental land reform and the withdrawal of Russia from the war.[11] Moving gradually toward a Bolshevik position, Left SRs emphasized class struggle in the countryside and called for immediate material aid to the poorest peasants. In a declaration issued on July 9, they welcomed the Kadet resignations of July 2, and warned the SR leadership against political reliance upon strata of the population which were opposed to revolutionary socialism.[12]

The impact of the Kadet withdrawal from the coalition was immediate and dramatic. Land transactions were suspended, the Stolypin legislation was declared null and void, and on July 16 Chernov issued an "Instruction" which empowered land committees to go "quite far" in satisfying any peasant demand which did not endanger the national economy. In addition, local committees were officially granted the right to manage all land left uncultivated by its owners.[13] *Izvestiia* enthusiastically claimed that it was "no accident" that at the same time that the Soviet and the Provisional Government were saving the revolution from the July disorders, the rights of laboring people were being defended. The new agrarian laws were, *Izvestiia* went on, a warning to all who tried to delay agrarian reforms, that the only basis for a coalition of "revolutionary democrats" with the "bourgeoisie" was the enactment of long-delayed labor and agrarian measures.[14] The Bolshevik perspective on the government's sudden action was quite different; as Trotsky brusquely commented in *Pravda*, the suspension of land transactions did not occur until the people had taken to the streets.[15]

In practice, however, it seemed that no coalition member except Chernov was willing to see the land committees go "quite far" in satisfying peasant demands. Chernov's "Instruction" was criticized, limited, and undermined almost immediately by the Menshevik Tsereteli, the minister of the interior, and by A. V. Peshekhonov, the SR minister of food, who viewed Chernov's "Instruction" as a dangerous threat to the maintenance of order and stability within the country. On July 17 Tsereteli issued a circular to *guberniia* commissars which condemned "arbitrary" land reforms and promised that appeals for land seizure would be punished "with all the force of the law."[16] On the following day, Peshekhonov issued a circular in which peasants were warned that "willful and illegal" acts against the landowners would be punished by the firmest and most energetic means.[17]

But in the days which followed, few SRs were able to hold to such a policy. Before July 17 SRs like Chernov, Bykhovskii, Gurevich, and Rakitnikov had consistently opposed land seizure as a process which could easily degenerate into a Stolypinist "wager on the strong," with the strongest able to seize the most land. But when peasants were arrested for "arbitrary action" in accordance with the circulars of Tsereteli and Peshekhonov, many of these same SRs joined with the Bolsheviks in angry protest. Bykhovskii claimed that peasants were driven to land seizure by the inaction of provincial land committees which excluded from membership any representatives of the organized peasantry.[18] And as for Chernov, the liberal *Russkia Vedomosti* noted quite correctly that he deplored in general terms the existence of illegal activity but refused to condemn actual cases of peasant attack upon private property rights.[19] In a speech to the Soviet Executive Committee, Chernov argued that arbitrary seizures were an attempt to counteract the chaos which existed in the absence of fundamental agrarian reforms; peasant violence would subside if land were transferred to the management of land committees.[20]

SRs had long criticized Lenin for his "anarchist" appeals to the peasantry. Yet after July 1917 the refusal of Chernov and of SRs to the left of him to choose between forcible maintenance of the status quo and the support of violent peasant action led him to explain the peasantry's illegal activity in what were essentially "Leninist" terms. Ever since the February days, Lenin had insisted that an unjust law was not binding, and that when "order" involved the oppression of the poverty-stricken majority of the population it was not really order.[21] His arguments formed part of a consistent and realistic bid for peasant support, and in the summer of 1917 he elaborated a theory, implicit in his earlier writings, to justify an appeal for spontaneous peasant action.[22] But when SRs, in contrast, made the argument that *actual* cases of land seizure reflected a desire for order, while seizures were *in principle* a source of chaos and a threat to the revolution, they exposed the muddleheadedness which was a major factor in their failures in 1917.

In contrast to such agonized attempts on behalf of the peasantry, Lenin simply held the SRs and Mensheviks responsible for the renewal of the war effort and for Russia's economic collapse. He pointed out that unlike the Bolsheviks, SRs and Mensheviks were free to organize. Enjoying widespread popular support and in control of the Soviet which held real power in Petrograd,[23] they nevertheless "shamefully" refused to make use of their power to shape Russia's foreign or domestic policy. Claiming to be moderate opponents of left- and right-wing extremism, Mensheviks and SRs foolishly ignored the fact that the class interests of the "moderate" bourgeoisie were hostile to the welfare of working people. Lenin insisted that whatever the Rump Coalition might pretend, land could not be transferred to the land committees without encroaching upon the bourgeois principle of private property. None of the reforms promised by the government would be enacted without revolutionary action against the bourgeoisie.[24]

On July 21, when a frustrated Chernov resigned from the government in the wake of Kadet denunciations of his "anarchism" and "pro-German sympathies," Lenin was able to argue that "even Chernov" was too radical for the bourgeoisie.[25] His resignation was followed by the brief withdrawal of Kerensky, and moderates on the Soviet's Executive Committee soon called for the re-entry of the Kadets into a "strong" coalition. In the words of Liber, speaking for the Organizational Committee of the Mensheviks, "We need the dictatorship of the Government to Save the Revolution, but [it must be] a creative dictatorship, and not a dictatorship of repressions."[26] Kerensky was given a free hand in the formation of a new coalition which included members of the Kadet Party, Chernov once again, and the Right SR Avksentiev as minister of the interior.[27]

In the necessarily ephemeral Bolshevik publications of July and August, Lenin denounced the new government as a "Bonapartist" dictatorship, predicting that Kerensky, like his French predecessor, would make unscrupulous promises to placate the peasantry while limiting his concrete actions to the restoration or maintenance of "order."[28] Although Lenin had argued since March that Bolsheviks had to win over the "Soviet majority," when the Soviet Executive Committee mobilized popular support for restrictions on Bolshevik freedom to speak, write, or organize, he began to emphasize the class nature of "majority rule." He cited Marx's analysis of the triumph of Louis Napoleon's majority dictatorship in France to prove that decisions made by "formal majorities" did not guarantee that the interests of politically unsophisticated workers and poor peasants would be served. Lenin went on to argue that since parliamentary institutions in a bourgeois society always reflected the interests of the bourgeoisie, even a Constituent Assembly would be meaningful only if it met after a new, anti-bourgeois revolution. Otherwise, a Russian Constituent Assembly would be as ineffective as the "democratic" Frankfurt Assembly in the German Revolution of 1848. Lenin set in contrast to the "Bonapartist manipulations" of Kerensky and the "futile parliamentarism" of Soviet moderates the superiority of a well-organized and well-armed Bolshevik minority. Such a minority, representing the true interests of the majority (the urban and peasant poor) might in his view be able to avoid the forms of bourgeois democracy which had served in the past only to perpetuate and maintain social and economic evils.[29]

The path which the Bolsheviks would follow to success in October was now roughly sketched out, but Lenin's intricate distinctions between farmhands, semi-proletarians, middle peasants, and the rural poor still remained difficult for even his most loyal supporters to fully comprehend. At the Bolshevik Sixth Party Congress, held in Lenin's absence,[30] shortly after the formation of the Second Coalition, the rudimentary level of Bolshevik understanding of Lenin's peasant policy was plain for all to see. Although Bolshevik propaganda had for months been emphasizing the necessity for alliance with the poorest peasantry, E. P. Preobrazhenskii still found it necessary to ask in August (1) for a concrete definition of the category of the "poorest peasant" to whom Bolsheviks were to appeal, and (2) for a description of the form that organizational cooperation between peasant and proletarian was to take.[31] Stalin's appalling response was to explain that the poorest peasants were obviously those seizing land in opposition to the admonitions of the "bourgeois" SRs. The particular form which proletarian–peasant alliance would take was not really important, Stalin went on: the revolution would create all the necessary organizational opportunities, and in any event, such problems would be solved by the transfer of power to the proletariat.[32]

The resolutions of the Sixth Congress were quite cautious. It was recognized that not only the upper strata of the petty bourgeoisie, but even part of the working class still believed in the "illusions" fostered by

SRs and Mensheviks. In this context, Bolsheviks were to prepare for the moment when the rural and urban poor would cross over to the side of the workers in the struggle to destroy the power of the bourgeoisie.[33] In the absence of Lenin (or even Trotsky), there was no Bolshevik attempt to take account of the growing bankruptcy of the socialist moderates in the late summer of 1917.

August–September: The Failure of Moderation

As Lenin had predicted, the Kerensky government did not order the much-discussed transfer of land to the management of the land committees. In *Izvestiia* and elsewhere, Chernov criticized the continued delay in the enactment of agrarian reform.[34] A conference of *guberniia* representatives from the Ministry of Agriculture sent a delegation to Kerensky in early August to "acquaint him" with the dangers of inaction on the agrarian question.[35] When Kerensky received the delegation, he told them of the extreme seriousness of the financial situation, emphasized the danger posed by the Ukrainian crisis, and promised to place the agrarian question on the agenda at the earliest possible time. Was it possible, as the SR Bykhovskii asked, that the "Revolutionary Provisional Government" would deal with the agrarian question in tsarist fashion, by demanding the restoration of order before it would consider urgently needed reform?[36]

In fact, the government did relapse into inactivity on the agrarian question after the brief flurry of lawmaking by the Rump Coalition in mid-July. A deadlock had clearly been reached: the coalition had condemned land seizure, but said that land might be taken from individuals who misused it. At the same time, local land committee members were arrested for acting "arbitrarily," i.e., for seizing private property which peasants believed to be unjustly held. Although the Main Land Committee had decided months before that land should be temporarily transferred to local land committees, all agricultural property remained in the hands of its former owners. As a Left SR sourly noted, Kerensky seemed able to exercise power to check Bolshevik and anarchist activity, but he was strangely incapable of exercising power for the purpose of encroaching on the rights of private property owners.[37] This view was not altogether fair; it vastly simplified the difficulties with which Kerensky had to deal and exaggerated the extent of his power to control events in the Russian countryside. At the same time, such overstatements by the Left SRs exposed and illuminated some undeniable government priorities.

Outside of government circles, hostility to a coalition with the Kadets increased in the late summer of 1917. While Left SRs demanded that their representatives in the coalition be held accountable for their failures to the party,[38] Lenin denounced what he called the government's suppression of peasant revolution.[39] From the country-side, peasants sent "mandates" to the All-Russian Congress of Peasant Deputies, calling for the immediate abolition of private ownership of land without compensation; but they no longer seemed as concerned to send their petitions or demands to the central government. Their initial enthusiasm dampened by government inaction on issues that concerned them most, peasants had by August begun in increasing numbers to ignore government directives, to seize land and to burn gentry estates by the thousands.[40] In reports submitted by the Petrograd Soviet's Agrarian Section in July and August, peasant disturbances were blamed upon the deliberate sabotage of landowners who refused either to cultivate or to rent their land to the peasants. According to these reports, peasants viewed the coalition government's committees, commissars, and ministers as defenders of the rich whose task it was to punish peasants who opposed the machinations of the landlords. At the same time, an increasingly significant segment of the troops sent to suppress agrarian uprisings refused to restore order in the countryside. Within the disintegrating Russian army, support for the transfer of land to the peasantry without compensation to former owners was increasingly commonplace. An enlisted man who had fought for three years in the war concluded his letter to the Bolshevik *Rabochii i Soldat* with a plea for the land "paid for with our blood."[41]

However such actions, sentiments, and evidence may be judged, it is clear that they did nothing to strengthen the government's authority or base of popular support. And in mid-August the Moscow State Conference was convened at least in part to bolster the faltering coalition. Unsurprisingly, the Bolsheviks refused to participate. Defying an appeal by the Moscow Soviet, they led a protest strike on August 12, the opening day of the conference. In contrast, moderate Soviet leaders made every effort to act "constructively", i.e., to satisfy both the Kadet demands for order and the calls for immediate action from the non-Bolshevik left. Repeatedly condemning the intransigence of the propertied class, they demanded the enactment of the land reforms promised on July 8. Chkheidze, speaking for the Soviet delegation, warned against land seizure and in a characteristically Menshevik formulation asked for immediate regulation of agricultural affairs *without any breach* in existing forms of landownership.[42] In a symbolic reconciliation between the "bourgeoisie" and the "revolution," Tsereteli and the industrialist Bublikov shook hands before an applauding audience, and *Izvestiia* fatuously commented that "everyone understood" that at that moment the acuteness of the class struggle had "significantly decreased."[43] But no concrete support was given by Bublikov, or the Kadets, even to the Provisional Government declaration of July 8. Not only did the Moscow Conference fail to resolve any policy conflict between Kadets on the one hand, and SR–Menshevik moderates on the other; it was equally unsuccessful as an effort to bridge the widening abyss between the Soviet's Executive Committee and its membership in Moscow and Petrograd. It was no longer obvious to Soviet delegates that the danger from the extreme left was equal to the danger from the right.[44]

Doing his best to exacerbate the difficulties which plagued his political rivals, Lenin claimed that Soviet leaders were too cowardly to admit that it was not anarchy but the Kadet Party which threatened the preservation and development of the revolution. He pointed out that the Second Coalition, dominated by *Soviet* ministers, was enacting all of the policies which the Kadet Party had attempted to put into practice in the spring of 1917. Rural disorders were suppressed by force, public meetings were closed by government order, and agrarian reforms were delayed. Claiming that fundamental changes could only be enacted by a Constituent Assembly, the Kerensky government nevertheless proposed, and the Soviet Executive Committee agreed to, the further postponement of elections.[45]

The Provisional Government's policy on elections to the Constituent Assembly had been a subject of controversy ever since the spring of 1917, when the Kadet foreign minister P. N. Miliukov openly expressed his fear of the outcome of elections in which war-weary Russian troops would participate and the Kadet N. A. Maklakov proposed postponement of elections until the end of the war. From that time onward, left-wing anti-Bolshevik writers from Sukhanov to the Right SR Vishniak attributed the repeated delays to pressures exerted on the government by members of the Kadet Party. According to Vishniak, it was only when the Bolsheviks scheduled demonstrations for June 18, 1917, that the First Coalition set September 17 as election day, in order "to distract the masses from their sympathy with the Bolsheviks and prevent the success of street demonstrations." Although socialists outnumbered Kadets in the government formed after the July crisis, Miliukov believed that the "real preponderance" in the cabinet "unconditionally belonged to the adherents of bourgeois democracy." On August 9, when the new coalition delayed elections until November 12, 1917, Miliukov called the postponement a "rectification of the political sin" committed by the First Coalition, namely the too-hasty call for elections in June.[46]

In late August, as Lenin warned that an anti-Soviet military coup was imminent, General L. G. Kornilov did in fact attempt to seize power. Certain that the "Bolshevik" soviets were pressuring the government toward a betrayal of Russia to the German enemy, Kornilov called for a government of national unity. Although Kornilov and his supporters possessed a level of education and training which in theory gave them some advantages in the sphere of military strategy, the outcome of his effort at counterrevolution was decided above all by the spontaneous initiative of untutored workers, who tore up the railway tracks leading to Petrograd; by soldiers, who fraternized with Kornilov's troops and undermined their loyalty to their officers; and also by the more organized efforts of the Soviet Executive Committee. The Kornilov affair seemed to vindicate the Bolshevik claim that it was the Right rather than the Left which was responsible for violence against the revolution.

From his place of hiding, Lenin immediately demonstrated an uncommon ability to take his sudden political good fortune in stride. In a flood of enthusiastic directives to the Bolshevik Central Committee, he demanded that workers, soldiers, and peasants "*carried away*" in their desire to suppress the Kornilov revolt be encouraged to "beat up the Kornilovist officers" who wanted to return political power and ownership of the land to Russia's former masters. At the same time, Lenin offered as a "compromise" to reintroduce the slogan of "All Power to the Soviets." While admitting that "*Our party, like every other political party*," wanted political domination for itself,[47] he argued that the Bolsheviks were now willing to support the Soviet because they wanted a peaceful development of the revolution. The Menshevik Sukhanov drily noted in this connection that Lenin's compromise was offered for the sake of the increasing Bolshevik strength in the Petrograd and Moscow soviets.[48] For in the wake of Kornilov's attempted coup, Bolsheviks had won majorities in both of these political bodies, and Trotsky was elected president of the Soviet in Petrograd.

Toward a Theory of Marxist Peasant Revolution

Before 1917 Mensheviks had frequently attacked Lenin as a cynic or a utopian on the peasant question, while relying on their own Marxist belief in the unreliability of the petty bourgeoisie to justify attitudes of condescension and contempt for the peasantry. Certainly, evidence of opportunism had never been difficult to find in Lenin's writings, although it was no more true for him than for any other political leader that opportunism necessarily invalidated his real political insights or defined the overall character of his theory and practice. In August 1917, for example, Lenin suggested that Bolsheviks make use of SR slogans in favor of "socialization" and the "prohibition of wage labor." Since peasants would be likely to support these slogans and the SR Party had not officially used them in 1917, Lenin had no compunction about using them in Bolshevik propaganda. He tough-mindedly recognized that whatever confusion might result would be likely to benefit the Bolsheviks. In the current political situation, with Bolsheviks attempting to lead the peasants toward socialism and liberal politicians, Mensheviks, and SRs engaged in the effort to reconcile them to some form of capitalism,[49] Lenin argued that the use of formerly "empty" SR slogans was eminently justified.[50]

Rejecting what he called the abstractness of the Menshevik claim that Russian economic backwardness posed an insuperable obstacle to socialist development, Lenin argued instead that the real, concrete problem in 1917 was whether Russia's economic difficulties could be overcome without significant encroachments upon private property rights, i.e., without decisive steps toward socialism.[51] Using many of the ideas he had opposed in earlier disputes with Trotsky over the theory of permanent revolution, Lenin claimed that the war had so greatly accelerated the self-destructive growth of world monopoly capitalism that neither the proletariat nor the revolutionary petty bourgeoisie (the peasants) could any longer confine themselves to the framework of capitalism. In 1917, he claimed that the imperialist war was the eve of the socialist revolution—not only because of the increasing militance of the proletariat ("no uprising will create socialism if it has not ripened economically . . ."),[52] but because the state monopoly capitalism which existed in Russia in 1917 provided the fullest *material* preparation for socialism. With a ponderous enthusiasm which failed to disguise the glaring inadequacies of his economic evidence, he concluded that "monopoly capitalism was that rung on the historical ladder between which rung and the one called socialism there are no intermediate rungs."[53] Such assertions failed to convince any but the already converted that Russia had suddenly become a highly developed capitalist society. But however superficial his arguments, Lenin's economic analysis was intended to justify his constructive response to the political realities of his time. In contrast to the fears which had driven Mensheviks and SRs to join in a coalition with the Kadets, Lenin insisted that the dangers involved in peasant land seizure were always outweighed by the benefits to be gained through the experience of collective attacks upon bourgeois property. Resting his hopes upon the rise of revolutionary consciousness among the peasantry, he consistently refused to consider seriously and in depth the problems which might arise if the Bolsheviks rose to power on a wave of peasant unrest: "Life will show what modifications will be necessary. This is the last thing to worry about. We are not doctrinaires. Our philosophy is not a dogma, but a guide to action."[54] Bolsheviks could not claim to predict the exact methods of achieving socialism. As Marxists they could know the direction of change and the significance of the various class forces involved, "but concretely and practically" the means by which socialism will be established "will be learned from the *experiences of the millions* when they take up the task."[55]

It is important to emphasize at this point that such optimistic expressions of faith in the ability of the masses to make practical decisions about the life that would emerge in the process of the destruction of bourgeois property were not an aberration in Leninist theory or practice. His concern with organization and discipline had always been balanced by a positive interpretation of the consequences of spontaneous peasant action when it actually occurred in 1903, 1906, and 1917. Lenin's enthusiasms were complex. He praised the peasantry while insisting that, in general, it was petty capitalist in outlook. He ignored the peasant commune and found no socialist implications in the fact that so many peasant petitions and resolutions reflected a belief in the need for social control over the land, the basic means of production. At the same time, although peasants remained for him at best only second-rate socialist material,[56] Lenin argued that their attacks on private property reflected a willingness to break with traditional habits of obedience which held immense political significance. Each time peasants placed themselves outside the law they came a step closer to understanding that existing laws and institutions formed part of a system of economic, social, and political exploitation. Their spontaneity was, as Lenin had claimed in *What Is To Be Done?*, a form of "embryonic consciousness," and what better circumstances could there be for the growth and development of consciousness than a time of revolution? In *State and Revolution*, written in the summer of 1917, at the height of his enthusiasm for the peasant movement, Lenin went on to claim that the revolutionary transfer of land to the people could even provide a basis for the emergence of humane values in a cooperative socialist society. The political awareness and the experience gained in the process of nationalization would count heavily among the factors which Lenin hoped could develop in peasants and proletarians the ability to administer the rationalized economy they inherited from the bourgeoisie.[57]

Perhaps a key to understanding Lenin's simultaneous commitment to discipline and spontaneity may be found in the necessary link he conceived between spontaneous mass action and Bolshevik leadership. The possible unreliability of the peasant as socialist was always to be mitigated by the organizational and educational abilities of politically conscious proletarians, i.e., by the Bolshevik Party.

> If the peasants wanted to be small landholders, let them. The confiscation of landed property would undermine the capitalist economy and *with the rule of the proletariat in the center* the rest would get along by itself. The transfer of political power to the proletariat is the fundamental problem. After that, everything essential in peasant demands is possible.

Although peasants might at first want individual ownership, Lenin cited Engels to prove that they would soon come to recognize the advantages of socialist agriculture. The confiscation of land would undermine the banks, the confiscation of livestock would undermine capital, and under the rule of the proletariat "the rest will get along *by itself*."[58]

Such statements do not merely demonstrate the shallowness of Lenin's economic analysis or his awareness of the propaganda value of optimistic and uncomplicated solutions. They epitomize the simplicity which lies at the core of the tough-minded strategy of Leninism. Lenin believed that the experience and understanding of workers and peasants would be immeasurably deepened by revolutionary action and by the policies of a Bolshevik-led government. He was certain that working people were capable of recognizing their "real" enemies and would be won over to the socialist cause by the demonstrable benefits of a more productive and humane, scientifically organized socialist economy. This was the sort of faith which had sustained Lenin during the darkest days of the Stolypin era, and it came to his aid during his months of hiding in the summer of 1917.[59]

As far as the peasant and his "defenders" were concerned, Lenin's optimism gave his appeals to soldier–peasant deserters and "arbitrary" land committees a devastating effectiveness. With the aid of vaguely worded and enthusiastic formulations on the subject of building socialism, he was able to avoid dwelling on the socioeconomic issues for which his Marxism had no real solution. Unequaled in his political insights, he left the complexities of economics and sociology to his political rivals, who were engulfed by them in September and October 1917.

Toward the Seizure of Power

At the Democratic Conference which opened on September 14, 1917, Chernov opposed all proposals of coalition with the Kadets and suggested that if agreement with non-socialist elements proved impossible, a "popular" ministry should be formed. In response, the Menshevik Skobelev put forward the familiar argument that Russia's future depended upon the willingness of the bourgeoisie to develop the Russian economy and establish the material basis for socialism. "Leninist" appeals for the arrest and hanging of industrialists or landlords were in Skobelev's view no substitute for a real program for economic transformation. Referring with well-merited humility to the activities of SRs and Mensheviks between May and September, Skobelev concluded that "the experience of the last four months justifies me in saying that in the field of economics this new socialist government will have no more brilliant successes than the old type of Provisional Government."[60] By the time the Democratic Conference met, the Bolsheviks controlled a majority in the Petrograd Soviet.[61] Their support came not only from the many new members of the Bolshevik party, but also from Left SRs who found intolerable the unlimited capacity for compromise exhibited by SR ministers in the coalition. Because they demanded that the Soviet seize power and transfer land to the peasantry, Left SRs were denounced by party loyalists as "Bolsheviks" who cynically appealed for action without knowing how they could realize the goals in which they claimed to believe.[62] But such charges did not touch the key issue which concerned the dissidents they were attacking; moderates were not able to make a compelling case for peacefully awaiting the future actions of the Kerensky government.

The Bolsheviks presented a single resolution at the Moscow Democratic Conference and then withdrew, preferring to focus instead upon the Petrograd Soviet as the more receptive and powerful of the two assemblies. Trotsky, speaking in defense of the Bolshevik agrarian policy before the Soviet, encountered little opposition. As he put it,

> They tell us that our program is unrealizable, that we interfere with work, but is it really true that we have prevented Chernov from carrying out land projects in the Provisional Government? And are we really responsible for the arrest of many members of land committees, and when they appear before the court, do we tell them that it would be better not to take the landlord's land? [Laughter, applause][63]

The Soviet subsequently passed a resolution demanding the immediate transfer of land to the land committees until the Constituent Assembly.

In late September moderate Mensheviks and SRs agreed to form a Third Coalition, led once again by Kerensky and including ten "socialist" and six "non-socialist" ministers. The Kadet P. N. Miliukov was not alone in believing that the basis for agreement on the new coalition was the "readiness of the representatives of the Democratic Conference to abandon all their positions of principle."[64] Using Chkheidze's August formula for "the regulation of agricultural relations without any break in existing forms of landownership," the coalition promised that "the most energetic measures," including use of the army, would be taken to quell manifestations of "anarchy in the countryside."[65]

Unlike many other promises made by the coalition, this one was kept. As the incidence of estate burnings and food riots rapidly escalated in September and October, the government resorted to the use of armed force more frequently than during the spring and summer combined.[66] At the same time, the Kerensky government postponed the implementation of land reform and again delayed elections to the Constituent Assembly. The hopes of Soviet moderates now turned to a Pre-Parliament established by the Democratic Conference and including a large percentage of Kadets and organizations willing to support them.[67] *Izvestiia* appealed for revolutionary unity, arguing that if the Pre-Parliament were enthusiastically supported any government in "revolutionary Russia" would have to be responsible to it.[68] With its reliance first upon the Moscow Conference and then upon the Pre-Parliament to somehow save the revolution, the self-confidence of the non-Bolshevik left had reached a new low.

Lenin, having decided in September that the time was ripe for the seizure of power, paid little attention to Menshevik and SR attempts to save Russia from the dangers of "extremism." His writings during this period were overwhelmingly concerned with the development of justifications for Bolshevik rule. The spread of "peasant revolution," the growth of popular hostility to any coalition with the "bourgeoisie," and the establishment of Bolshevik majorities in the Moscow and Petrograd Soviets in September 1917 seemed to him a fulfillment of the necessary conditions for a Bolshevik seizure of power. Lenin warned of capitalist sabotage, supporting his charges with data taken from reports issued by the Petrograd Soviet's economic section.[69] He found evidence of right-wing "conspiracy" in the failure of the minister of the interior to mention the soviets in his speeches about the institutions necessary for the "regeneration of the revolution."[70] And, Lenin asked, what if the SRs cooperated with the Kadets in the elections for the Constituent Assembly—could the Bolsheviks then accept the decision of a majority created out of the machinations of irresponsible and cowardly SRs and Kadets?[71] By threatening to resign from the party and agreeing to Trotsky's condition that the seizure of power be in the name of the Soviet, Lenin was able to convince his reluctant followers, over strong opposition, to accept his plan for a seizure of power led and organized by the Bolshevik Party.[72]

As plans for the insurrection went forward, Lenin's political rivals attempted to find explanations for the shift in popular sentiment toward the Bolsheviks. Mensheviks commonly expressed the view that support for Bolshevism was nothing more than an expression of the "formless dissatisfaction of the people," who were backward, illiterate, and all too responsive to political demagoguery. SR moderates tended to attribute popular dissatisfaction to the absence of agrarian legislation.

Many were like V. S. Pankratov, who argued that it was the delay of land reform rather than peasant violence which posed the threat of anarchy.[73] The SR Rakitnikov was as insistent as Lenin that the arrests and "persecution" of peasant members of the land committees had to end before there could be any talk of the struggle against anarchy.[74] One SR repeated the pathetic accusation of May: the Bolsheviks had no right to leadership on the agrarian question.[75]

The confused nature of SR "leadership" on the agrarian question was demonstrated by the party's choice of S. M. Maslov as minister of agriculture in the Third Coalition. In September Maslov had shocked many members of his party by his support for land reform projects which required peasants to render payment to their landlords for the allotments they cultivated. Yet in late September Maslov was chosen by the SR Party to carry out a plan to transfer land to the land committees without compensation—to implement the program he opposed.[76] As Lenin pointed out, when Maslov's plan was officially formulated it included a requirement that peasants pay rent which was to be transferred in part to the "rightful owner," that is, to the former landlord.[77] The SR *Delo Naroda* subsequently called for the enactment of the "Maslov plan," but deplored any unauthorized or violent peasant attempts to put it into practice.[78] Maslov's proposal was presented to the Provisional Government on October 15. On October 18 it was announced that despite the opposition of several ministers, the law would soon be passed,[79] since all were aware of the urgency of reform. But the Maslov plan was neither passed nor implemented.

In contrast to government delay and confusion, Lenin argued, a Bolshevik government would act immediately to abolish private property and transfer all land to the land committees. Banks and key industrial enterprises would be nationalized, he said, since such measures would more evenly distribute the burdens of war without harming the middle peasants, the Cossacks, or the small handicraftsmen.[80] As he wrote in October, "Any government which hesitates to introduce these measures is worthy of being overthrown; only a government that had realized these measures will be a government of all the people."[81]

The by now familiar pattern of government promises of economic reform and decrees prohibiting "arbitrary peasant action" continued to repeat itself as the last details of the plan for the Bolshevik seizure of power were being completed. According to Lenin,

> What is needed for the uprising is . . . a mood of despair among the broad masses who *feel* that nothing can now be saved by half measures; that you cannot "influence" anybody; that the hungry will "smash everything, destroy everything, even anarchically" if the Bolsheviks are not able to lead them in a decisive battle.[82]

By late October 1917 such conditions had been amply met.

The Political Triumph

Bolshevik strength, and the success of Bolshevik organizing activities within the army, did not go unnoticed by the Kerensky government, which began in October to issue orders for the transfer of pro-Bolshevik army regiments from the capital. The recalcitrant mood of the army in Petrograd was indicated in a declaration by regiments of the garrison on October 16 which stated that they intended to disobey Kerensky's marching orders and remain in Petrograd. According to Trotsky, "This was the silent rising which in advance decided the outcome of the contest."[83] On October 23 Kerensky banned the Bolshevik newspaper *Rabochii Put'*. On October 24 he announced to a meeting of the Pre-Parliament that a new police search for Lenin was under way, and promised that Trotksy would soon be arrested. That evening at a meeting of delegates to the Second All-Russian Congress of Soviets scheduled to open on the following day, F. I. Dan, speaking for the Menshevik Central Committee, promised immediate peace negotiations and land reform. But from the floor came the cries, "Too late!"[84]

On October 25, 1917, the Bolsheviks seized power with the support or at least the neutrality of most of the workers and soldier – peasants of Petrograd. At the Congress of Soviets which opened on that day, they were able to muster a two-thirds majority (with the support of the Left SRs, three-fourths of the votes of the Congress). The new government's Land Decree of October 26, taken largely from the so-called 242 peasant mandates and from the SR agrarian program, abolished private property in land. Henceforward all land was to be part of a national land reserve, and every citizen willing to work was to be granted an allotment. Local land committees and soviets were to decide the size of each allotment according to the number of adult workers or the consumption needs of the prospective farmer's family. The land was to be subject to periodic repartition in order to safeguard the principle of equal rights to the land. According to Lenin, "The root of the matter is that the peasantry should be given the assurance that there are no more large landed proprietors in the village. . . . Let the peasants themselves decide all questions, let them build their own life."[85] The Bolshevik Land Decree was a striking demonstration of respect for the massive and triumphant peasant struggle for the Russian land. As a Bolshevik document, it was unique in its sanction of the communal and labor-oriented traditions which Marxists had been at great pains to ignore or deny ever since the last decades of the nineteenth century.

IV

Conclusion

10

The Meaning and Implications of Lenin's Triumph

I

THE BOLSHEVIK LAND DECREE of October 1917 was "un-Marxist" in its respect for communal peasant traditions. Its terms were populist, and the non-Bolshevik left were quite right to recognize its politically expedient, even opportunist character. The more usual Marxist insistence on the obsoleteness of peasants and peasant institutions had a history which began with Plekhanov and Lenin's nineteenth-century assertions that the commune played no significant role in Russian rural life, continued with Shestakov's 1905 speech denouncing peasant seizure of gentry land as an economically reactionary measure, and culminated with Sukhanov's warning against peasant "intervention" in the revolutionary process in March 1917. Bolshevik willingness to grant so much autonomy to peasants in October was clearly related to the narrowness of their political base. But like the earlier proposals which had marked Lenin's approach to a revolutionary peasant strategy, the promises made in the Bolshevik Land Decree were not simply a cynical concession to the petty bourgeoisie. Optimistic hopes that ordinary people were capable of making rational and progressive economic and political decisions had always surfaced in Lenin's writings in times of popular upheaval.

As we have seen, Russia's Marxist tradition was rooted in a denial of the sociological insights which Marx himself had praised in the work of populists like Daniel'son. In the late nineteenth and early twentieth centuries, Russian Marxists ignored the social relations of peasant

communal agriculture except when they fit narrow economic categories which were derived from West European history. They thus
insisted that the peasantry lacked historically significant forms of social
organization, although the commune, which was pronounced mori-
bund in 1885, survived and even increased its power and influence
until it was forcibly destroyed by the Soviet regime in the 1920s. If
peasants were "backward," Marxists focused upon their economic
obligations to a semi-feudal landlord and state. If they were "modern,"
Marxists examined peasant participation in class conflict over the issues
of wages, property, and profit. Defined always by their resemblance to
some other social group, they were "really" either serfs or entrepreneurs
or proletarians, but for Marxists they never seemed to be "really"
peasants.

The use of Western categories of "feudalism" or "capitalism" to sum
up, explain, and evaluate peasant behavior yielded some important
insights and a host of misunderstandings. The events and patterns of activity which most closely resembled the experience of Western Europeans
were most clearly understood. The myriad disadvantages of pre-
capitalist village life were exposed in great detail; Marxists permitted no
sentimental idealization of the peasant solidarity which led to pogroms
against the unfortunate outsider, or the bestial ignorance which led
peasants to distrust and betray the radical intellectual. Sensitive as well
to the abundant manifestations of Russian rural capitalism, they were
able to see that the commune could function to disguise kulak
domination of the poor. Marxists sought and, unsurprisingly, they
found kulak and proletarian tendencies in the majority of the peasant
population, the middle peasants who neither hired labor nor hired
themselves out to work for others.

On the other hand, from the Western-centered perspective of
Russian Marxism the majority became mysteriously unimportant, a
sort of empirical impurity in a larger "world-historical" analysis. Kulak
and proletarian minorities were crucial; the rest of the peasant
population, significant only as it resembled these two groups, was held
to possess no traditions or social relations. Marxists were unable to
explain and therefore tended to ignore the persistently collective
patterns of rural unrest and economic decision-making among peasants they labeled "capitalist," "semi-feudal," or "proletarian." They
ignored as well the evidence and recommendations of most turn-of-the-
century economists who found in the commune an economically and
socially viable institution. Instead, Marxists referred to commune

peasants as proprietors and responded to their appeals for the abolition of private property in land with assertions that such concerns were essentially "bourgeois" (Lenin) or with arguments that peasants had to be freed from their foolish notions of "leveling" in question of land use (Martov). Unaware that peasants reentered the communes in increasing numbers during that pre-war period, Bolsheviks and Mensheviks found no constructive socialist significance in the peasantry's successful efforts to return the *otrubshchiki* to the communes in the course of 1917.

In Lenin's thinking, such mistaken assumptions existed from the outset in tension with his total commitment to revolution-making. Whatever the ostensible topic of his early writings, his intention was always to assess the fighting capacity of his political rivals and to establish the broadest possible social basis for a Russian revolutionary movement. Even his superficial arguments for the existence of advanced rural capitalism in 1917 were a product of such concerns. Like the young Marx, who had exaggerated the ripeness of the capitalist West for socialist revolution in the 1840s, Lenin exaggerated the degree of Russia's development and claimed in the 1890s that the countryside was already dominated by a rural bourgeoisie. Neither Marx nor Lenin was insincere in putting forward his "scientific" exaggerations; such unrealistic judgments were quite common among both the proponents and the critics of capitalism in the late nineteenth and early twentieth centuries. At the same time, these were politically expedient judgments for both Marx and Lenin: a capitalist system seething with class conflict obviously provided brighter prospects for a German or a Russian revolutionary than the alternative of a supposedly stagnant "medieval" society.

Lenin soon relinquished the claims put forward so authoritatively in *The Development of Capitalism in Russia* (1899). During the "miniature revolution" of 1902 he did not repeat the ludicrous assertion that Russian rural life centered on the class struggle between rapacious kulaks and desperate proletarians. Instead, he emphasized the anti-feudal character of peasant unrest, admitting that in their battles against the old order, farmhands and "semi-proletarians" had fought side by side with middle peasants and kulaks. In the future (so Lenin's argument went), this rural solidarity would disappear. The rural poor would break with the kulaks and a section of the middle peasants in order to fight for a socialist revolution. In 1903 Lenin set himself to distinguish a substantial revolutionary segment of the peasantry from the unreliable petty bourgeoisie. He therefore presented evidence which suggested that the experience of the allotment-owning rural poor made them somehow at the same time both fighters against feudalism and proletarian supporters of socialism. Although in *Capital* and elsewhere in Marx's writings it was precisely the "pygmy property" of the peasantry which functioned to prevent them from acting as unconditional opponents of the existing order, Lenin argued in 1903 that peasants were made so desperate by the difficulties of survival on their meager allotments of land that they became receptive to the appeal of revolutionary socialism. By departing from a rigid analysis of class according to wage labor or ownership of the means of production, Lenin left himself vulnerable to attack by the many Menshevik and Bolshevik proponents of ideological purity. This was a serious matter within the Marxist community, where consistency was one of the highest terms of approbation and inconsistency, contradiction, or even flexibility carried a distinct aura of opportunism. It is possible that a more straightforward attempt to fill in some of the gaps which Marx himself had recognized in his theory might have impressed Lenin's critics, although the fate of the "populist-Marxist" Daniel'son does not offer very much hope on this score. As for Lenin, he continued to refer to the "rural poor" in his writings of the early 1900s, but always concerned himself more with proving that his ideas were truly Marxist than with developing this category into a useful tool of analysis. Lenin remained extremely cautious as a social theorist; his response to charges of opportunism was to demonstrate to his critics that all of his ideas on the peasant question were extracted without revision from the pages of *Capital*.

During the debates and struggles of 1905, Lenin responded to renewed political opportunity with enthusiasm, common sense, and little theoretical precision. The outbreak of popular violence and the formation of mass political organizations convinced him that revolutionary socialists had to risk a struggle for victory. Certain that further capitalist development was necessary to prepare the material foundations for socialism, Lenin argued that "proletarian" Social Democrats, aided by the rural poor, were more suited to this task than the bourgeoisie. Such insights set him apart from the Mensheviks and from many fellow "Leninists" who feared that popular organizations like the All-Russian Peasant Union or the St. Petersburg Soviet all too often revealed dangerous tendencies toward blind spontaneity, "economism," and lack of principle. With what Professor Ulam has called "his engaging faith in the common man,"[1] Lenin responded to such criticisms with the repeated assertion that the proletariat and the peasantry would be responsible for whatever gains the revolution might achieve. Revolutionary socialists in the midst of revolution could not, in his view, ask the poor to sacrifice their lives so that political power might pass into the hands of an exploitative bourgeoisie. Instead, they had to take responsibility for guiding the nation through the most radical and rapid of capitalist developments.

During this period, as Lenin praised revolutionary peasants for fighting longer and harder than Russian liberals, Mensheviks sought in vain for a revolutionary, or at least a moderately progressive, bourgeoisie which would extend urban patterns of social organization to the Russian village. Finding support in *Capital* for their belief in large-scale capitalist enterprise, Mensheviks considered peasant demands for land dangerous, because they might result in an economically reactionary fragmentation of the gentry estates. Their reading of Russian history was equally anti-peasant; Mensheviks pointed out that in the past, revolutionary peasant movements all too often degenerated into pogroms against the Jews. But the most powerful argument put forward by Mensheviks in 1906, one which would return to haunt them in 1917 (and the Bolsheviks after October), was that Marxists who seized power prematurely would be hopelessly compromised by the effort to implement the historically necessary task of capitalist economic development. In such conflicts it became painfully obvious that Russian Marxists had defined for themselves a choice between the political sterility of the Mensheviks and a Leninist voluntarism which was often indistinguishable from opportunism. In consequence, they could look forward to the dismal possibility of either immediate or future betrayal of their proletarian supporters.

It was characteristic of Lenin's political style and the specific character of his political genius that most of his political judgments about liberals, SRs, and Mensheviks appeared unfair when they were first advanced, but were borne out in the future. As Lenin had predicted, Kadet leaders would compromise with the autocracy in the aftermath of 1905, in order to defend "Russia" against a frighteningly primitive "rabble." Moderate and right-wing SRs, as if in confirmation of Lenin's contemptuous dismissal of his opponents as petty bourgeois intellectuals, were paralyzed by the concrete implications of their efforts to fight on behalf of a peasantry imbued with prejudices and selfish interests as well as revolutionary potential. Between 1906 and 1917 Gotz, Zenzinov, Avksentiev, and S. M. Maslov had come to believe that a long civilizing process was needed before an anarchic, greedy, and bigoted peasantry might be capable of creating a socialist society. The Mensheviks had been the first Russian socialists to lay claim to this perspective, and in the years before the outbreak of the February Revolution they held fast to the belief that the bourgeoisie was the historically designated agent of political and economic progress. Pessimism and ideological principle turned the non-Bolshevik left reluctantly toward the Kadets, who in their turn discovered an ever-increasing number of redeeming qualities in the more traditional forms of order.

In contrast, Lenin argued that the merit of the revolutionary peasantry lay precisely in its resistance to "civilized," parliamentary change. Centuries of "lawful" oppression by the gentry had made peasants less responsive to the liberal argument that there existed a kind of law and justice which benefited rich and poor alike. Their skepticism and their willingness to do battle with the gentry created abundant opportunities for the development of revolutionary consciousness. In 1903, 1906, and afterward, Lenin was content to rely on the strategy of consciousness-raising whenever it was linked with freedom of agitation for Bolshevik organizers and a process of unconditional struggle against the existing order. During the Stolypin period, Lenin argued that if land were nationalized in a revolution led by Social Democrats, practical experience and Social Democratic propaganda could convince even the small producer that his prosperity depended upon socialization of the means of production. And by 1917 he had come to believe that, with all its shortcomings, the peasant majority of the population would inevitably decide the immediate outcome of any Russian social revolution.

II

The social revolution which began in February 1917 made it imperative that Russian revolutionary leaders decide whether they wanted an uneducated peasantry to sweep away preexisting property relations and weaken a potentially democratic "bourgeois" government. In this context, Lenin's capacity for enthusiasm and optimism about the educational benefits of peasant violence, and his certainty that "educated" peasants would listen to Bolshevik propagandists, made it easier for him to face the disintegration of traditional order than the

Mensheviks who had opposed the centralist tendencies of his *What Is To Be Done?*. Lenin argued in 1917 that peasant attacks upon private property were a form of rough justice, a rational way to destroy the old order and develop in peasants the confidence that they could build a new one. While he did not deny that peasants and soldiers might engage in cruel and excessive violence, Lenin seemed to understand far better than any of his political rivals (1) that social revolution was an attack upon the foundations of social order, and (2) that a single-minded focus on popular "excesses" was inappropriate in a professional revolutionary. He argued that Marxist revolutionaries worthy of the name could not agree with the Menshevik Sukhanov that "those hungry, frightened and not politically conscious soldiers posed as great a threat to the revolution as did the organized forces of tsarism." Revolutionaries could not equate misdirected acts of popular violence with the violence inflicted by an exploitative upper class.

At the same time, it should be noted that Lenin was quite reluctant to face the objective problems of political administration in time of revolution. Certainly any Russian government would have found it difficult to rule a nation whose citizens were in the habit of debating whether or not to obey its every law, prohibition, and sanction. Worse yet, the specter of universal political disobedience coincided with the murder of landlords and representatives of the Provisional Government, as well as the destruction of gentry livestock, farm buildings, and agricultural machinery. After a spring and summer filled with rural unrest, one estimate indicates that in September alone peasants in the province of Tambov destroyed 105 estates. Their compatriots in Penza put the torch to 164 in September and October, and food riots erupted everywhere, from Saratov to Archangel.[2] In this crisis-ridden context it was understandable that the government might hesitate to institute sweeping changes, and appoint most officials instead of taking the time to organize democratic elections. By any standard, these were confusing times. But for this very reason it is all the more significant that between February and October the policies of the Provisional Government were not at all confused or contradictory. Quite consistently, landowners were appointed as provincial and *uezd* commissars to replace the old provincial governors and vice-governors. On the *volost* level, these new officials were instructed to "draw into the work of these committees local landowners and all the intelligent forces of the countryside."[3] On the land question, the government did not

haphazardly and inconsistently implement policies which were sometimes leftist and sometimes conservative. In the course of 1917, as
peasants laid claim to the land on the basis of labor, occupation, and
birthright, the government quite *rigidly* refused to implement land
reform.

From the outset, Mensheviks were more concerned to ensure
bourgeois stability and order than they were to encourage popular
initiatives by a citizenry unused to the exercise of significant economic
or political power. At the same time, their willingness to delay land
reform and to subordinate the Soviet to the Provisional Government
revealed not only a lack of political imagination, but a stunning
insensitivity to the needs and wishes of the economically disadvantaged
elements of Russian society. Refusing to provide the masses with any
material grounds for faith in the government's future policies,
Menshevik and SR ministers established a pattern of fearful response to
the threat of chaos and anarchy which contrasted dramatically with
Bolshevik insistence on the constructive aspects of popular activity. The
significance of the difference between Lenin and the non-Bolshevik left
would not be lost upon the peasants and soldiers who in 1917 had just
begun to "intervene," as Sukhanov had put it, in the revolutionary
process. As the revolution continued, they would turn in increasing
numbers toward Lenin and toward the Bolshevik political organizations which supported their actions as appropriate and necessary.

Lenin's emphasis on the material consequences of the actions of his
opponents was thus not only in the best Marxist tradition; it was a
politically brilliant tactic in a society where land came before political
freedom in the popular demands of the majority of the population.
Ignoring the difficulties of economic and political administration which
were independent of questions of class, he wrote of the devastating
impact of Provisional Government policies upon the already wretched
living standard of the poorer soldiers and peasants. This was for him the
real meaning of the commitment to productivity, military defense, and
the rule of law which characterized the Provisional Government even
after the SRs and Mensheviks became its leading ministers.

The charge that Lenin was obsessed with the political aspects of the
revolution needs to be balanced against the fidelity to political
compromise in defense of law and order which characterized the Soviet
leadership before October 1917. The revolutionary abnegation prac-
ticed by Mensheviks and SRs did not mean that they acted in defense of

their ideals. Lenin helped to expose the concrete and specific failures of men unable (in the case of Chernov) or unwilling (in the case of Tsereteli) to act as responsible and revolutionary political leaders. The Mensheviks in 1917 were paralyzed by their intellectual consistency, the SRs by their general inconsistency.

Once the autocracy had fallen, Lenin argued that it was nonsense for Bolsheviks to fight for the right to establish or approve a politically enlightened bourgeois regime. The dual power shared between the "bourgeois" Provisional Government and the Petrograd Soviet, which Lenin characterized as a "revolutionary-democratic dictatorship of the proletariat and the peasantry," meant to him that Russia had already progressed beyond the stage of the bourgeois-democratic revolution. When, after the Kornilov affair, Bolsheviks began to win majorities in the Petrograd and Moscow soviets and peasant rioting swept the countryside, he called for a Bolshevik seizure of power.

In justifying a Bolshevik-led revolution, Lenin did not emphasize the peasant love of property, a theme that usually emerged in his writings in time of revolutionary decline. Instead, he sought out the aspects of peasant behavior upon which revolutionary Marxists might place their hopes. He argued that the soviet movement in the countryside was a product of the exploited peasantry's desire to shape their economic and social life by collective action. He claimed that the experience of common action against the landlords during the course of the revolution had broken down their former isolation from one another and from the more advanced social classes. Peasant committees were managing land and sending delegates to congresses and soviets. Once the masses had begun to question and disregard authority which contradicted what they considered their interests and collectively went on to take control of their lives, Lenin refused to impose any limits upon the potential for political or social transformation.

His most optimistic hopes were evident in *State and Revolution* (August 1917), a work which also revealed that Lenin was something of a novice at the task of conceiving how to build socialism in a peasant society. Like any anarchist, Lenin argued that when inexperienced working people took over the accounting and control of the state's economic and political institutions, they would come to understand that they could decide the issues which "experts" had dealt with so incompetently under the tsarist regime. Like any statist, Lenin assumed that the central guidance of the party in power would guarantee that progressive tendencies would always be fostered. Politically conscious Bolshevik leaders would be able to correctly assess the true interests of the urban proletariat and the rural poor, the common sense of a revolutionary people would permit the resolution of any surviving social conflict, and the evolution of political consciousness would eventually abolish the distinction between the masses and their "proletarian" leaders.[4] *State and Revolution* embodied the contradictory insights and goals of Leninism on the peasant question. It was a declaration of faith in popular creativity developed through revolutionary action, Marxist political education, and a reliance on the incorruptible wisdom of the revolutionaries Lenin had conceived in *What Is To Be Done?*. As a plan for social reconstruction, *State and Revolution* was less sophisticated and carefully thought out than contemporary populist literature on relations between state and citizen, or between city and countryside.[5] But *State and Revolution* reflected quite well Lenin's fundamental but inchoate belief that the seizure of power by politically conscious Bolsheviks in the midst of widespread rejection of established authority could not help but make "everything" somehow different. Lenin was absolutely certain that the conditions of life for the poor would inevitably improve after the Bolsheviks took power. As he wrote on October 1,

> when tens of millions of people who have been crushed by want . . . see from experience and *feel* that state power has passed into the hands of the oppressed classes, that the state is helping the poor to fight their landowners and capitalists, is *breaking* their resistance . . . only then, for every *ten thousand* overt and concealed enemies of working class rule . . . there will arise a *million* new fighters who had been politically dormant, writhing in the torments of poverty and despair, having ceased to believe that they were human, that they had the right to live, that they too could be served by the entire might of the modern centralized state, that contingents of the proletarian militia could, with the fullest confidence, also call upon *them* to take a direct immediate, daily part in state administration.[6]

The effectiveness of such appeals cannot be reduced to Lenin's manipulative ability to make peasants believe that Bolsheviks who despised them were nevertheless somehow on their side.

In fact, we may not learn as much from debates over Lenin's cynicism or sincerity as we can by considering the debilitating burden which the Marxist tradition had imposed upon the Russian revolutionary activist. Ever since the late nineteenth century, obsessions with capitalism in the countryside, contempt for the semi-feudal "dark forces," and awareness of the individualistic property fanatics and the bigots among the peasants had blinded Russian Marxists to much evidence about the agricultural economy, about the widespread resistance to the Stolypin reforms, and about the collectivist notions of peasants who demanded abolition of private property in land. This meant that, paradoxically enough, when Lenin insisted in conventional Marxist terms that the bourgeoisie was the master of the Russian countryside or that the rural proletariat was the most radical force in the peasant movement, he was most out of touch with the realities of rural life.

Given his failure to resolve the conflict between his Marxism and his political insight, Lenin's faith in the future and his refusal to deal in depth with the economic issues for which his Marxism had no real solution were equally crucial to his success as a spokesman for peasant revolution in 1917. In contrast, Mensheviks held fast to their economic principles and joined with the SRs in sacrificing political integrity and popular support in their futile effort to confront head-on the issue of economic backwardness. In this context, Lenin's willingness to gloss over the immense difficulties which might follow from a Bolshevik seizure of power was not simply a proof of hyprocrisy. Like other effective political leaders, he was frequently evasive, inconsistent, mistaken and stubbornly optimistic. Despite the contradictions and inadequacies of his economic and sociological analysis, his political response to the peasant question was both healthy and rational from the point of view of a revolutionary activist. Political greatness is neither a simple nor perhaps even a wholly admirable trait. But surely we must recognize it in Lenin, who triumphantly responded to the exigencies of circumstance while remaining committed to a set of principles which set some limits both to compromise and to opportunism. He was quite willing to simplify on a number of key issues because he was always confident that a government led by revolutionary Marxists could not help but surpass the bourgeoisie in the pursuit of social justice.

The weaknesses of Lenin's analysis, which were essentially the weakness of the Marxist tradition to which he was so loyal, would not pose difficulties until after the Bolsheviks seized power. After October, amidst the ravages of world war, civil war, and Allied intervention, as Bolsheviks attempted in vain to make good on their immensely generous promises of material security, they would attribute their difficulties to the petty bourgeoisie in every possible guise. The intellectual, the small businessman, and above all the peasantry were held responsible for problems of administration and economic reconstruction. Fears of the kulak flourished in official circles, as peasant communes carried out an unprecedented equalization of land on behalf of the poor without any help from the Soviet authorities.[7] In this situation, it was indeed unfortunate for Russia's peasants that Lenin's political gifts were more difficult to transmit to his heirs and supporters than the doctrinaire economics and sociology which he had put forward before 1917. But this is indeed another, though not unrelated, story.

Finally, it needs to be said that the contradictions that have been outlined here in such detail were by no means either uniquely Russian or uniquely Marxist. In China, Cuba, and elsewhere, Marxists also began with the assumption that peasants were economically obsolete and hopelessly unreliable in a political sense. And in agrarian societies the world over, proponents of economic development would share Lenin's hope that the peasantry would find in itself the wisdom and good sense to accept the unconditional triumph of the city over the countryside. Historically, this process was always (at least initially) the triumph of a minority over the majority and a challenge to democratic sensibilities. The evolution of Lenin's peasant policy was therefore at once a specifically Russian problem, a challenge to Marxist theory, and an aspect of one of the most intractable dilemmas of rural development.

Notes

INTRODUCTION

1. See the insightful and original discussion in John Berger, "Peasants and Progress," *New Society*, January 5, 1978.

2. A profoundly important examination of the reasons why the writings of Marx have so often aroused interest and heartfelt support in developing societies is contained in Adam Ulam, *The Unfinished Revolution* (New York, 1960).

3. Marcel Liebman, *Leninism under Lenin* (London, 1975) p. 172.

4. Neil Harding, *Lenin's Political Thought: Theory and Practice in the Democratic Revolution* (New York, 1977), pp. 85–108.

5. After 1905, Lenin himself would admit that he had been guilty of "exaggeration" in the 1890s.

6. S. P. Trapeznikov, *Leninizm i agrarno-krest'ianskii vopros*, 2 vols. (Moscow, 1967).

1. THE LESSONS OF THE MARXIST CLASSICS

1. See Esther Kingston-Mann, "Marxism and Russian Rural Development: Problems of Evidence, Experience and Culture," *American Historical Review* 86 (October 1981): 731–52.

2. A particularly interesting discussion of Marx's quite unrigorous use of the term "peasant" may be found in V. M. Chernov, *K teorii klassovoi bor'by* (Moscow, 1906), pp. 19–20.

3. Karl Marx, "Rent of Land" (1844), in *Karl Marx: Early Writings*, ed. T. B. Bottomore (London, 1963), pp. 117–18.

4. "Communist Manifesto," *Basic Writings on Politics and Philosophy by Karl Marx and Friedrich Engels*, ed. Lewis Feuer (New York, 1959), p. 18.

5. Ibid., pp. 31–32.

6. Ibid., pp. 37–39.

7. "Address to the Communist League" (1850), in *A Hand-Book of Marxism*, ed. Emile Burns (New York, 1935), p. 67.

8. Ibid., p. 69.

9. *The Eighteenth Brumaire of Louis Bonaparte* (Chicago, 1918), p. 73.

10. Ibid., p. 58.

11. Ibid., pp. 125–26.

12. *The Class Struggle in France* (Moscow, 1965), p. 119.

13. Ibid., p. 63.

14. *Eighteenth Brumaire*, p. 150.

15. *Class Struggle in France*, p. 165.

16. Engels's *Germany in 1848* was a series of articles which Marx had asked him to write in 1851. That the articles were written and published under Marx's name, often without any criticism or corrections added, is an indication of the trust and agreement which existed between the two men. Friedrich Engels, *The German Revolutions: Peasant Wars in Germany* and *Germany in 1848: Revolution and Counter-Revolution*, ed. Leonard Krieger (Chicago, 1967), pp. 222–23, 230.

17. *Peasant Wars in Germany*, p. 32.

18. Karl Marx, *Capital* (London, 1909) 1: 13.

19. Ibid., p. 23.

20. Ibid., p. 13.

21. *Capital* 3: 945–46.

22. Ibid.

23. See note 3.

24. *Capital* 3: 730, 884–85, 938–45.

25. See Lenin's discussion of nationalization in Chapters 2 and 6, and V. M. Chernov's *K voprosu o kapitalizme i krest'ianstve* (Nizhni-Novgorod, 1905), pp. 7–8.

26. *Capital* 1: 835.

27. Within the First International, Marx had voted in 1869 for a resolution favoring land nationalization against the French, who argued that such a program would be unpopular with the peasantry. In 1870, Marx's draft for the International stated that only public ownership of land would restore to the majority of the population the property which had been stolen from them in the past by means of conquest. In the same year, Engels's preface to the second edition of *Germany in 1848* suggested that the small peasant could easily be convinced of the necessity for accepting proletarian leadership: if they were serfs or tenants, the small peasants would "logically" look to the working class for leadership. And for Engels, the small peasant landowners, crushed by the weight of financial burdens unjustly imposed upon them, were somehow objectively comparable to tenant farmers in their needs and demands. When the Commune uprising took place, neither Marx nor Engels had made any attempt to reconcile such politically optimistic suggestions with the pessimistic implications of Marxist economic theory.

28. Marx, "Letter to Kugelmann" (1871), in *Civil War in France* (New York, 1968), pp. 85–86.

29. Ibid., p. 60.

30. See Chapter 6, note 28, for example.

2. POPULISTS AND MARXISTS: THE "RUSSIAN" AND "WESTERN" PATHS TO SOCIALISM

1. England's preeminence as a model for Russian rural development is discussed in detail in Esther Kingston-Mann, "Transforming the Russian Countryside: A 'Western'

and a 'Russian' Path" (Paper presented at the National Seminar on the Social History of Twentieth-Century Russia, University of Pennsylvania, January 1982).

2. I. V. Kireevskii, *Polnoe sobranie sochinenii* (Moscow, 1911) 1: 214–15.

3. A. S. Khomiakov, *Polnoe sobranie sochinenii* (Moscow, 1900–1904) 3: 105, 115–16, 465.

4. The best recent study is D. G. Atkinson, "The Russian Land Commune and the Revolution" (Ph.D. diss., Stanford University, 1970); a classic turn-of-the-century investigation is K. R. Kachorovskii, *Russkaia obshchina: Vozmozhno li, zhelatel'no li, eia sokhranenie i razvitie* (St. Petersburg, 1900).

5. Kireevskii, *Polnoe sobranie sochinenii* 1: 209.

6. V. G. Belinskii, *Selected Philosophical Works* (Moscow, 1956), pp. 534–35.

7. A. M. Herzen, *Sobranie sochinenii* (Moscow, 1954–65) 12: 306–12.

8. The Prussian Baron Augustus von Haxthausen was the first scholar to attempt a systematic empirical investigation of the repartitional land commune. Although he believed that the commune functioned to stabilize a society dominated by a landed nobility, his work was used by Herzen and other populists as a basis for their belief in the socialist potential of the Russian peasantry. Augustus von Haxthausen, *The Russian Empire, Its People, Institutions and Resources*, 2 vols. (London, 1856).

9. Herzen, *Sobranie sochinenii* 7: 319–22.

10. A. E. Lositskii, *Vykupnaia operatsiia* (St. Petersburg, 1908), pp. 16–19; and D. I. Shakhovskoi, "Vykupnye platezhi," in *Velikaia reforma*, ed. A. K. Dzhivelagov (Moscow, 1911) 6: 114–16.

11. N. G. Chernyshevskii, *Polnoe sobranie sochinenii* (Moscow, 1948) 5: 378–79.

12. Quoted in Rose Glickman, "An Alternative View of the Peasantry: Raznochintsy Writers of the 1860's," *Slavic Review* 31, no. 4 (1973): 697.

13. Chernyshevskii, *Polnoe sobranie sochinenii* 1: 419. It was ironic that despite his tough-mindedness, Chernyshevskii's impact upon the radicals of his generation was pre-eminently moral. In his stoic response to political persecution and exile, and in the lessons of his novel *What Is To Be Done?*, courage, dignity, and comradeship emerged as the test of commitment to socialist ideals. Free of self-doubt, immune to feelings of condescension or cynicism toward the masses, Chernyshevskii's Rakhmetov and Vera Pavlovna embodied the personal, intellectual, and moral satisfactions of life spent in service to the people.

14. See discussion in Deborah Hardy, "Consciousness and Spontaneity in 1875: The Peasant Revolution Seen by Tkachev, Lavrov and Bakunin," *Canadian Slavic Studies* 4, no. 4 (1970): 705.

15. P. L. Lavrov, *Izbrannye sochineniia na sotsial'no-politicheskie temy* (Leningrad, 1934) 2: 135.

16. The information on relations between peasants and "their" radicals is taken from Daniel Field, "The 'Movement to the People' of 1874 Reconsidered" (Paper presented at the Historians' Seminar of the Russian Research Center, Harvard University, May 1, 1981). A valuable discussion of the Chigirin incident may be found in Field, *Rebels in the Name of the Tsar* (Boston, 1976).

17. Stepniak [S. M. Kravchinskii], *Underground Russia: Revolutionary Profiles and Sketches from Life* (New York, 1885), p. 262.

18. Maureen Perrie, *The Agrarian Policy of the Russian Socialist-Revolutionary Party from Its Origins through the Revolution of 1905–1907* (Cambridge, England, 1976) pp. 16–17.

19. Alan Kimball, "The First International and the Russian Obshchina," *Slavic Review* 32, no. 3 (1973): 491–514.

20. The image of peasant hostility to schooling has been challenged by the research of Ben Eklof, "Peasant Sloth Reconsidered: Strategies of Education and Learning in Rural Russia before the Revolution," *Journal of Social History* 14, no. 3 (1981): 362–66.

21. According to official accounts, there were 224 factory strikes between 1870 and 1879; see A. M. Pankratova, Introduction, "Osobennosti formirovaniia i bor'by proletariata Rossii v 60–80–x godakh xix veka," in Pankratova, ed., *Rabochee dvizhenie v Rossii v xix veke: Sbornik dokumentov i materialov* (Moscow, 1950) 2, pt. 1, p. 45.

22. See discussion in Kingston-Mann, "Marxism and Russian Rural Development," p. 735.

23. N. K. Mikhailovskii, *Sochineniia* (St. Petersburg, 1896–97) 1: 169–74.

24. P. N. Tkachev, *Izbrannye sochineniia na sotsial'no-politicheskie temy* (Moscow, 1923) 3: 274, 90–93, 263–66. Lenin's *What Is To Be Done?* and "To the Rural Poor" were a response to the same concerns which drove Tkachev to advocate a "Jacobin" seizure of power.

25. Marx, "Letter to Mikhailovskii" (1877), in *Selected Correspondence of Karl Marx and Friedrich Engels, 1846–1895* (New York, 1944), pp. 354–55.

26. Marx, "Letter to Zasulich" (1881), in *Selected Correspondence*, p. 412. Marx worked very carefully on this formulation. For earlier drafts of this passage, see ibid., pp. 400–421. A brilliant discussion of the relationship between Marx and his first Russian disciples is contained in Andrzej Walicki, *The Controversy over Capitalism* (Oxford, 1969), pp. 179–94.

27. In Marx's own words, Daniel'son's work was "in the best sense of the word 'original' ": *Selected Correspondence*, p. 383.

28. K. Marks and F. Engels's, *Sochineniia* (Moscow, 1961) 27: 684.

29. Quoted in V. Ia. Iakovlev [V. Bogucharskii], *Iz istorii politicheskoi bor'by v 70-kh i 80-kh gg.* (Moscow, 1912), p. 470.

30. Quoted in V. Vagan'ian, *G. V. Plekhanov: Opyt kharakteristiki sotsial'no politicheskikh vozzrenii* (Moscow, 1924), p. 54.

31. G. V. Plekhanov, *Sochineniia* (Moscow, 1923) 2: 225.

32. Nevertheless, as late as 1880 Plekhanov remained an ambivalent populist. He believed that industrial workers would provide the "chief forces" for a revolutionary socialist movement. The Russian worker's rural ties sustained an interest in the land question at the same time that his urban surroundings provided him an escape from the stultifying influences of peasant life. Plekhanov justified his continuing concern with the peasantry on the basis of the still insignificant number of urban workers and the relatively low level of Russian industrial development. Although these reasons remained valid for at least the next two decades, they did not prevent Plekhanov from making his way toward Marxism. See Lev Deutsch, "Kak G. V. Plekhanov stal marksistom," *Proletarskaia Revoliutsiia* 7 (1922): 118.

33. Plekhanov, *Sochineniia* 10: 129.

34. Ibid. 2: 361–62.

35. Quoted in Leopold Haimson, *Russian Marxists and the Origins of Bolshevism* (Cambridge, Mass., 1955), p. 23. Lev Tikhomirov, an editor of *Zemlia i Volia*, joined *Narodnaia Volia* in 1879. By 1900 he was not a populist or a revolutionary but a partisan of the extreme Right.

36. A detailed discussion of the findings and conclusions of Orlov and other leading economists may be found in Steven Grant, "The Peasant Commune in Russian Thought, 1861–1905" (Ph.D. diss., Harvard University, 1973), pp. 269–72.

37. In fact, the writings of leading populists from Vorontsov and Daniel'son to A. A. Karelin and N. A. Karyshev were devoted to the problem of dealing with the problems raised by the undeniable existence of capitalist practices within the Russian rural economy.

38. Plekhanov, *Sochineniia* 2: 271.

39. *Perepiska K. Marksa i F. Engel'sa s russkimi politicheskimi deiatel'iami* (Moscow, 1951), p. 334.

40. Quoted in *Reminiscences of Marx and Engels* (New York, n.d.), p. 320.

41. Engels, "Letter to Zasulich" (1885), in Deutsch, *Gruppa 'osvobozhdenie truda'* 3: 26–27.

42. Plekhanov, *Sochineniia* 2: 221–22.

43. N. K. Mikhailovskii, *Literaturnye vospominaniia i sovremennaia smuta* (St. Petersburg, 1900) 2: 270–73. Both the extent and causes of the famine are still under debate. The evidence and the implications of the famine remain as problematic and difficult to interpret today as they were in the nineteenth century. See Richard Robbins, *Famine in Russia, 1891–92: The Imperial Government Responds to a Crisis* (New York, 1975); James Simms, Jr., "The Crisis of Russian Agriculture at the End of the Nineteenth Century: A Different View," *Slavic Review* 36, no. 3 (1977): 377–98; and G. M. Hamburg, "The Crisis in Russian Agriculture: A Comment," *Slavic Review* 37, no. 3 (1978): 381–86.

44. V. P. Vorontsov, *Krest'ianskaia obshchina* (St. Petersburg, 1892), pp. 459–600.

45. N. F. Daniel'son, *Ocherki nashego poreformennago khoziaistva* (St. Petersburg, 1893), p. 113.

46. Plekhanov, *Sochineniia* 7: 269.

47. Ibid. 3: 411.

48. Plekhanov, *Dela i dni: Istoricheskii zhurnal* (1921) 2: 91, quoted in Baron, *Plekhanov*, p. 77.

3. Lenin as an Orthodox Marxist

1. The most striking example of the shift away from support for the commune may be found in the writings of Witte himself. The transformation of his views is discussed in I. V. Chernyshev, *Agrarno-krest'ianskaia politika Rossii* (Petrograd, 1918), pp. 250–64.

2. See discussion in Grant, "Peasant Commune," pp. 269–72.

3. Engels, "La Question Paysanne en France et Allemagne" (1894), *Cahiers du Communisme*, 1955; idem, *The Mark* (New York, 1928). Engels's discussion of primitive communism in *The Origins of the Family, Private Property and the State* (1895) also provided some basis for efforts to construct a politically constructive socialist peasant policy, but no practical or theoretically consistent political strategy was suggested or developed in either *Origins* or *The Mark*.

4. According to a recent study, German small producers were quite successful in domestic and foreign competition, and able to adapt their three-field system and other traditional practices to the demands of modern economic life. See Robert G. Moeller, "Peasants and Tariffs in the Kaiserreich: How Backward Were the *Bauern?*" *Agricultural History* 55, no. 4 (1981): 371–84.

5. Quoted in Harvey Goldberg, *The Life of Jean Jaurès* (Madison, Wisc., 1962), p. 183. The meaning of the Jaurès challenge is discussed in Gustav Landauer, "The Guesdists and the Small Farmer: Early Erosion of French Marxism," *International Review of Social History* 6 (1961): 214.

6. Engels, "La Question Paysanne," p. 1481.

7. Eduard David, *Sozialismus und Landwirtschaft* (Berlin, 1903) 1: 49, 698–99. See also Peter Gay, *The Dilemma of Democratic Socialism* (New York, 1962), pp. 162–63, 194–95.

8. Georg von Vollmar, in *Modern Socialism*, ed. R. C. K. Ensor (New York, 1907), pp. 220–26.

9. Ibid., p. 227.

10. Kautsky, *Die Agrarfrage* (Stuttgart, 1899), pp. 106–15.

11. Karl Kautsky, *The Class Struggle (The Erfurt Program)* (Chicago, 1910), p. 217. See also discussion in *Agrarfrage*, pp. 64–193, 296–300.

12. Quoted in Lenin, "Chto takoe 'druz'ia naroda' i kak oni voiuiut protiv sotsial-demokratov" (1894), in *Polnoe sobranie sochinenii*, 5th ed. (Moscow, 1971–75) (cited hereafter as *Soch.*) 1: 191–92.

13. Ibid., p. 193.

14. Ibid., p. 241.

15. Ibid., p. 251.

16. Lenin, "Ekonomicheskoe soderzhanie narodnichestva . . ." (1895), *Soch.* 1: 451.

17. Lenin, "Chto takoe 'druz'ia naroda' . . .," *Soch.* 1: 259–60.

18. See discussion in Kingston-Mann, "Transforming the Russian Countryside," pp. 15–22.

19. Lenin, "Ot kakogo nasledstva my otkazyvaemsia" (1897), *Soch.* 1: 528. It is interesting to compare Lenin's evaluation of the populists with the equally negative but anti-Bolshevik position of Oliver Radkey: "The effort to derive an advanced collectivist society from the primitive collectivism of the past, restricting intervening forms of development to as narrow a scope as possible or eliminating them entirely, is a distinctive feature of Populism." "Chernov and Agrarian Socialism Before 1918," in *Continuity and Change in Russian and Soviet Thought*, ed. E. Simmons (Cambridge, Mass., 1955), p. 65.

20. Lenin, "Ot kakogo nasledstva . . . ," *Soch.* 1: 214. This was not an isolated statement in Lenin's early writings. See, for example, his assertions in 1894 that the Russian bourgeoisie was "already everywhere in control of the people's labor," "the 'depeasantization' of the countryside is established beyond question," or in 1895, that "the entire mass of the village folk work for capital," "capital is dominant in the countryside," etc. "Chto takoe 'druz'ia naroda' . . . ," *Soch.* 1: 278, 237–38, and "Ekonomicheskoe soderzhanie narodnichestva . . . ," *Soch.* 1: 395.

21. Lenin, "Chto takoe 'druz'ia naroda' . . . ," *Soch.* 1: 213–14.

22. Lenin, "Ekonomicheskoe soderzhanie narodnichestva . . . ," *Soch.* 1: 240–41. Among the "reactionary" tendencies of the populists, Lenin noted their support for the inalienability of the peasants' allotments and their opposition to the further development of a money economy.

23. See, for example, A. A. Mamalui, *Lenin ob agrarnykh otnosheniiakh v Rossii* (Kharkov, 1960), pp. 87–88; S. P. Trapeznikov, *Agrarnyi vopros i leninskaia agrarnaia programma v trekh russkikh revoliutsiiakh* (Moscow, 1963), pp. 39–41.

24. Lenin, "Ekonomicheskoe soderzhanie narodnichestva . . . ," *Soch.* 1: 416–17.

25. Lenin, "Chto takoe 'druz'ia naroda' . . . ," *Soch.* 1: 301.

26. Lenin, "Proekt i ob"iasnenie programmy sotsial-demokraticheskoi partii" (1895), *Soch.* 2: 86.

27. Nationalization, or the transfer of landed property to the state, was considered a bourgeois measure because it freed capital for investment in the improvement of

agricultural techniques. Lenin, "Chto takoe 'druz'ia naroda' . . . ," *Soch.* 1: 299. For Marx's discussion of nationalization, see Chapter 1, note 27.

28. Lenin, "Zadachi russkikh sotsial-demokratov" (1897), *Soch.* 2: 448–9.

29. "Manifest rossiiskoi sotsial-demokraticheskoi rabochei partii," *Pervyi s"ezd RSDRP* (Moscow, 1959), p. 79.

30. Chernov, *K voprosu o kapitalizme i krest'ianstve,* pp. 26–28.

31. Lenin, "Proekt programmy nashei partii" (1899), *Pervyi s"ezd RSDRP,* p. 68.

32. Ibid., p. 70.

33. Exaggerated claims for the profundity of what was after all a rather modest if lengthy book review are made in E. G. Vasilievskii, *Agrarnyi vopros v rabotakh V. I. Lenina 1883–1915* (Moscow, 1964), p. 10. Lenin himself noted that the review was intended for submission to a liberal journal, and contained no exposition of his revolutionary political views. The review was not published until after the October Revolution.

34. Lenin, *Razvitie kapitalizma v Rossii, Soch.* 3: 64.

35. A detailed and useful discussion of Lenin's "natural history of capitalism" approach to understanding conditions in the Russian countryside may be found in Neil Harding, *Lenin's Political Thought: Theory and Practice in the Democratic Revolution* (London, 1977). Harding emphasizes Lenin's concern with wage labor as proof that capitalism was dominant (although relatively undeveloped) in the 1890s. As Harding sets out Lenin's arguments, they bear a certain resemblance to those made by the populist Mikhailovskii for the peasant commune in the 1870s. While Lenin claimed that capitalism represented a progressive and higher "type" of system at a low level of development, Mikhailovskii made the same argument on behalf of the commune. In both cases, however, the reader is led to ask what exists and is highly developed at the time that the preferred system (either capitalism or the commune) is at such a primitive level. See Lenin, "Ekonomicheskoe soderzhanie . . . ," *Soch.* 1: 466–67, and Harding, *Lenin's Political Thought,* pp. 86–107. After 1905, Lenin admitted that he had been mistaken in his arguments on capitalist dominance in the 1890s. See Chapter 6, note 7.

36. Lenin, *Razvitie kapitalizma, Soch.* 3: 118–19.

37. Ibid., pp. 167, 135.

38. Ibid., p. 170.

39. V. P. Vorontsov, *Sud'ba kapitalizma v Rossii* (St. Petersburg, 1882), pp. 108, 117. According to Vorontsov, the separation of industry from agriculture which Marx described as part of the capitalist process meant that the peasant's sole source of income was derived from farm work. His income as a tiller of the soil was insufficient for the payment of taxes or for the development of improved agricultural techniques. In Vorontsov's judgment, the agricultural crisis which would inevitably result from such a situation would be so serious that even capitalist industry would be unable to flourish.

40. Lenin, *Razvitie kapitalizma, Soch.* 3: pp. 587–602.

41. It is useful to consider Lenin's argument in the light of George Lukacz's later investigations of the disjunction between "objective" economic conditions and "proletarian" consciousness. See Lukacz, *History and Class Consciousness* (London, 1971), pp. 51, 71–75, 81.

42. Boguslaw Galeski, *Basic Concepts of Rural Sociology* (Manchester, England, 1972), p. 107. Galeski rather illogically concludes that Lenin's approach nevertheless provides "a basis for determining the relative weight of class groups in the peasant stratum and for analyzing the genesis of the Russian rural structure."

43. Lenin, *Razvitie kapitalizma, Soch.* 3: 185–87, 191–98.

44. Ibid., p. 246. While Witte rested his hopes on sturdy entrepreneurs rather than rebellious proletarians, both Lenin and Witte considered capitalism an unsurpassed form of schooling. As Witte wrote in 1899, "no matter how significant the promotion of enlightenment, that road is too slow. . . . The natural school of industry is first of all a lively industry. . . . The first investment of savings awakens in man the restlessness of enterprise, and with the first investment the powerful stimulus of personal interest calls forth such curiosity and love of learning as to make an illiterate peasant into a railway builder, a bold and progressive organizer of industry. . . ." Witte, "An Economic Policy for the Empire," in *Readings in Russian Civilization,* ed. Thomas Riha (Chicago, 1968) 2: 434.

45. Lenin, "Chto takoe 'druz'ia naroda' . . . ," *Soch.* 1: 191–93.

46. See Struve's *Kriticheskie zametki k voprosu ob ekonomicheskom razvitii v Rossii* (St. Petersburg, 1894), pp. 280–82. Lenin denounced Struve's objectivism in his "Ekonomicheskoe soderzhanie narodnichestva . . . ," *Soch.* 1: 396–98.

47. Although Plekhanov had discussed the issue of rural differentiation in some detail in *Our Differences* (1885) and in other works, S. P. Trapeznikov has argued that Plekhanov treated the peasantry as a "homogeneous mass": Trapeznikov, *Agrarnyi vopros,* pp. 58–59.

48. Lenin was quite consistent on this point. In an exchange with P. P. Maslov over a government decision to raise grain prices, Lenin argued that higher prices would stimulate capitalist development. In Lenin's view, the merits of rapid development outweighed any regrets for the peasant suffering which might result from the rise in prices. Lenin, "K voprosu o khlebnykh tsenakh" (1897), *Sochineniia,* 3rd ed. 2: 3–4; and "Pis'ma P. Maslovu i Iu. Martovu o tsenakh na khleb" (1897), 2: 583–84.

49. It should be noted that hard truths are not necessarily more valid than the truths of the "tender-minded." Vorontsov's argument that Russia lacked a domestic market for her industry and would be unable to compete with her more advanced Western capitalist rivals is not less plausible than the ideas of Lenin and Witte as an explanation of why the economic gap between Russia and Germany, Japan, and the U.S.A. (estimated in terms of per capita growth) was larger in 1913 than it had been in 1861. See R. W. Goldsmith, "Economic Growth of Tsarist Russia, 1860–1913," *Economic Development and Cultural Change* 9 (1961): 442–43, 474–75.

4. Proletarian Theory and Peasant Practice: Lenin, 1901–4

1. See Adam Ulam, *The Bolsheviks* (New York, 1965), p. 214, and H. Willets, "Lenin and the Peasants," in Leonard Schapiro and P. B. Reddaway, ed., *Lenin the Man, the Theorist, the Leader* (New York, 1967), pp. 218–20, for examples of the prevailing Western scholarly view.

2. Quoted in Lenin, "Bor'ba s golodaiushchimi" (1901), *Soch.* 5: 283. See also B. B. Veselovskii, ed., *Krest'ianskoe dvizhenie 1902 goda* (Moscow, 1923), p. 109; and Robinson, *Rural Russia,* pp. 138–45.

3. Witte's proposed agrarian program is discussed in detail in T. H. von Laue, *Sergei Witte and the Industrialization of Russia* (New York, 1962).

4. V. I. Gurko, *Features and Figures of the Past* (Stanford, Calif., 1939), pp. 691–701; and I. P. Belokonskii, *Zemskoe dvizhenie* (Moscow, 1914), pp. 153–54.

5. *Revoliutsionnaia Rossiia*, January, 1902, no. 3; and reference in Oliver Radkey, *The Agrarian Foes of Bolshevism* (New York, 1958), p. 56.

6. *Revoliutsionnaia Rossiia*, June 25, 1902, no. 8. The whole of this issue was devoted to the peasant question.

7. Quoted in P. B. Struve, "Predislovie," *Samoderzhavie i zemstvo* (Stuttgart, 1903), p. lviii. For a general discussion of the liberal position during this period, see George Fischer, *Russian Liberalism from Gentry to Intelligentsia* (Cambridge, Mass.), 1958, pp. 126–31; and Victor Leontowitsch, *Geschichte des Liberalismus in Russland* (Frankfurt am Main), 1957, pp. 255–77.

8. Struve, "Predislovie," p. lxii.

9. See Miliukov's article "Ot russkikh konstitutsionnalistov," in *Osvobozhdenie*, June 18, 1902, no. 1, and his *Vospominaniia, 1859–1917*, vol. 1 (New York, 1955), p. 236.

10. *Osvobozhdenie*, June 18, 1902, no. 1; September 18, 1902, no. 7; March 19, 1903, no. 19.

11. Ibid., June 18, 1902, no. 1.

12. Ibid., October 18, 1903, no. 9.

13. P. N. Miliukov, *Russia and Its Crisis* (Chicago, 1905), p. 218. See also pp. 290, 335, 340.

14. Quoted in Fischer, *Russian Liberalism*, p. 147.

15. Ibid., 147–51.

16. Lenin, "Vnutrenee obozrenie" (1901), *Soch.* 5: 307.

17. See Chapter 3, pp. 41–42.

18. Lenin, "Agrarnyi vopros i 'kritiki Marksa' " (1901), *Soch.* 5: 100–113, 141–56.

19. In this connection, the Social Democratic agrarian program was to be a guide for "the activities of those forces that cannot find an outlet anywhere except in the rural localities . . .": "Rabochaia partiia i krest'ianstvo" (1901), *Soch.* 4: 435–36.

20. For example, Lenin, "Bor'ba s golodaiushchimi" (1901), *Soch.* 6: 284.

21. For example, Lenin, "Rabochaia partiia i krest'ianstvo" (1901), *Soch.* 4: 433–36.

22. It is especially interesting to read "To the Rural Poor" in conjunction with Lenin's discussion of the development of political consciousness in *What Is To Be Done?* (1902). See *Soch.* 6: 28–58.

23. Lenin, "K derevenskoi bednote" (1903), *Soch.* 7: 131–33.

24. See Robinson, *Rural Russia*, pp. 64–94.

25. Lenin, "K derevenskoi bednote," *Soch.* 7: 134.

26. Ibid., pp. 135, 139–41. For an account of forged imperial manifestos distributed during the famine and rebellions of 1902, see Veselovskii, *Krest'ianskoe dvizhenie 1902 goda*, pp. 100 and 104, and *Osvobozhdenie*, August 2, 1902, no. 4.

27. Lenin, "K derevenskoi bednote," *Soch.* 7: 166.

28. Ibid., pp. 142–44, 146, 156.

29. Ibid., pp. 143–44.

30. For Lenin, rural proletarians were not necessarily landless peasants. Any peasant who survived by working for others and/or renting out his allotment was included by Lenin within the proletariat. This departure from a strict interpretation of class according to relation to the means of production was justified by Lenin as being consistent with the conditions of life for a peasant who had no "real" control over anything but the sale of his labor. Ibid., p. 151.

31. Ibid., p. 165.

32. Ibid., pp. 182, 48–49.

33. Ibid., pp. 161–64.

34. Ibid., pp. 192, 159–60.

35. Ibid., pp. 170–76.

36. Ibid., pp. 138, 166.

37. Ibid., p. 178.

38. See Chapter 3, notes 3 and 11.

39. Lenin, "K derevenskoi bednote," *Soch.* 7: 189.

40. Ibid., p. 192.

41. Ibid., p. 178.

42. Ibid., p. 196.

43. Ibid., pp. 201–3.

44. I have verified the accuracy of approximately one-half of Lenin's citations from statistical collections. Although Robinson's emphasis is different, his statistics support Lenin's contentions: Robinson, *Rural Russia*, pp. 133–35, 268–69; and *Leninskii sbornik* 19: 348–49.

45. The liberal Union of Liberation took shape in the summer of 1903 as a clandestine organization which established "front groups," i.e., legal organizations not officially connected with it. The founders of the Union of Liberation "had little use for a large membership, mass following, or even for the provisional branches it had set up." As noted by Fischer, these tactics "best suited the times and Union of Liberation make-up and organization." Fischer, *Russian Liberalism*, pp. 151–52. The SR penchant for secrecy and conspiracy was well known. See Radkey, *Agrarian Foes of Bolshevism*, pp. 47–88.

46. A discussion of this issue would go beyond the scope of this chapter, but it is worth suggesting that the practical political importance of the controversy may have been exaggerated at the time by all Russian Marxists, and later by Soviet and Western scholars. The RSDLP continued in practice to be both conspiratorial and indisciplined in both its Bolshevik and Menshevik wings up to, and including, 1917. The question of an open, "free," decentralized political organization versus a "closed," disciplined, and centralized one would of course have enormous significance after 1917.

47. See Chapter 2, note 33.

48. Lenin, "Zamechaniia na vtoroi proekt programmy Plekhanova" (1902), *Soch.* 6: 228.

49. Lenin, "Dopol'nitelnye zamechaniia po kommissionyi proekt programmy" (1902), *Soch.* 6: 256.

50. Lenin, "Agrarnaia programma russkoi sotsial-demokratii" (1902), *Leninskii sbornik* 3: 346.

51. Emphasis as given in quotation in "Agrarnaia programma russkoi sotsial-demokratii" (1902), *Soch.* 6: 311–12; quotation without emphasis in "Agrarnaia programma russkoi sotsial-demokratii" (1902), *Leninskii sbornik* 3: 329–30.

52. Ibid., *Soch.* 6: 347, 353–54.

53. Liber, Egorov, and Makhov, *Vtoroi s"ezd RSDRP: Protokoly i'iul'–avgust 1903* (Geneva, 1903), pp. 208, 210–12, 219–21.

54. Martynov, *Vtoroi s"ezd*, p. 215.

55. Zhordaniia, Urutadze, and Gusev, *Vtoroi s"ezd*, pp. 216, 207, 222.

56. Lenin, *Vtoroi s"ezd*, p. 213.

57. Trotsky, *Vtoroi s"ezd*, p. 228; see also p. 212.

58. The reference to violence as a defining characteristic of revolutionary action was interesting here; Lenin never allowed anyone else to employ this usage. Lenin *in Vtoroi s"ezd*, p. 213, and "Rech' pri obsuzhdenii agrarnoi programmy 31 i'iulia," *Soch.* 7: 280–81.

59. Lenin, *Vtoroi s"ezd*, p. 229.

60. Ibid., pp. 420–24.

61. Liber, *Vtoroi s"ezd*, pp. 211, 218–21, 241–44. Trapeznikov's assertion that the scantiness of the agrarian program adopted at the congress (with no specific provision for separate organization of the rural proletariat, or for nationalization of land) was due in large part to the hesitations of the Mensheviks is inaccurate. Lenin fought for and won acceptance of a program which demonstrated his own failure to meet the criticism of men like Liber. His program was supported by Plekhanov and Martov, among others. See Trapeznikov, *Agrarnyi vopros*, pp. 89–90.

62. Plekhanov, *Vtoroi s"ezd*, p. 199.

63. Trotsky answered Liber with the argument (a peculiar one for a historical materialist) that in areas where there were few survivals of feudalism, Social Democrats would proletarianize the peasantry "politically, before they are proletarianized economically": *Vtoroi s"ezd*, p. 212.

64. Martov, *Vtoroi s"ezd*, p. 242.

65. See Lenin's discussion in "Shag vpered, dva shaga nazad" (1904), *Soch.* 8: 217–18; and see note 31.

66. Populists had long questioned the moral right of a group which welcomed the ruin of the peasant majority of the population to speak for the exploited people of Russia. The SRs were no more ready than nineteenth-century populists had been to accept the idea that History required that they observe and encourage competition and eventual ruin for the peasant population.

67. *Revoliutsionnaia Rossiia*, June 25, 1902, no. 8, and January 15, 1903.

68. Lenin, "Pochemu sotsial-demokratiia dolzhna ob"iavit' reshitel'nuiu i bezposhchadnuiu voinu sotsialistam-revoliutsioneram?" (1902), *Soch.* 6: 375.

69. Lenin, "Vul'garnyi sotsializm i narodnichestvo" (1902), *Soch.* 7: 44.

70. This view was expressed by Miliukov in *Osvobozhdenie*'s first issue, on June 18, 1902.

71. Lenin, "Zemskaia kampaniia i plan 'Iskry'" (1904), *Soch.* 8: 75–98.

72. Lenin, "Chto delat'" (1902), *Soch.* 6; see especially pp. 28–58.

73. "Rabochaia partiia i krest'ianstvo" (1901), *Soch.* 4: 433–36.

74. "Rech' pri obsuzhdenii agrarnoi programmy 31 i'iulia," *Soch.* 7: 280–81.

75. "Shag vpered, dva shaga nazad" (1904), *Soch.* 8: 218–20. In this connection, Lenin praised Trotsky's designation of the critics of his agrarian program as "philistines": "Given the overwhelming necessity of an alliance between the proletariat and the peasantry, the skepticism and political farsightedness of Makhov and Egorov are more harmful than any shortsightedness."

76. "Otvet na kritiku nashego proekta programmy" (1903), *Soch.* 7: 226.

5. The Outbreak of Revolution: The Challenge of Peasant Militance in
1905 and 1906

1. Lenin, "Doklad ob uchastii sotsial-demokratii vo vremennom revoliutsionnom pravitel' stve" (April 18, 1905), *Soch.* 10: 134.

2. See, for example, P. N. Miliukov, *Vospominaniia, 1859–1917* (New York, 1955) 1: 224.

3. See G. Gapon, *Istoriia moei zhizni* (Berlin, 1925), pp. 96–97; see also Walter Sablinskii, *The Road to Bloody Sunday: Father Gapon and the St. Petersburg Massacre of 1905* (Princeton, N. J., 1976).

4. In fact, rural and urban unrest did not seem to coincide in the early months of the revolution. The number of strikes increased in January, lessened in February and March, increased again in April; peasant disorders were relatively insignificant in January and markedly increased in February and March. S. M. Dubrovskii, *Krest'ianskoe dvizhenie v revoliutsii 1905–07gg.* (Moscow, 1956), p. 42.

5. "Zapiski A. S. Ermolova," *Krasnyi Arkhiv* 8 (1924): 51–52.

6. *Zakonodatel'nyi akty perekhodnogo vremeni*, ed. N. I. Lazarevskii (St. Petersburg, 1907), p. 18.

7. The list of Chirikovo's demands was published in *Revoliutsionnaia Rossiia*, June 15, 1905, no. 169, cited in Ettore Cinnella, "La social democrazia e il muovimento contadino nella revoluzione russa del 1905," *Studi storici* 15 (1974): 502–3.

8. *Istoriia SSSR s drevneishikh vremen do nashikh dnei* vol. 6, *Rossiia v periode imperializma 1900–1917 gg.*, ed. A. L. Sidorov et al. (Moscow, 1968), p. 124.

9. In contrast to the Marxists, liberal economists and publicists like A. I. Chuprov, A. A. Manuilov, and P. N. Miliukov did not base their predictions and proposals upon the assumption that economic progress required the destruction of all links between the small peasant and the land.

10. Belokonskii, *Zemskoe dvizhenie*, pp. 272–73.

11. Nathan Smith, "The Constitutional-Democratic Movement in Russia, 1902–1906" (Ph.D. diss., University of Illinois, Urbana, 1958), p. 346.

12. See, for example, L. E. Shishko, "Staryi marksizm i sovremennaia sotsial-demokratiia," *Russkoe Bogatstvo* (May 1906); and V. M. Chernov, "K voprosu o 'polozhitel'nykh' i 'otritsatel'nykh' storonakh kapitalizma," *Russkoe Bogatstvo*, (April 1901), pp. 222–34.

13. See Chernov as quoted in Maureen Perrie, "The Russian Peasant Movement of 1905–1907: Its Social Composition and Revolutionary Significance," *Past and Present*, (November 1972), p. 15.

14. S. M. Dubrovskii, "Krest'ianskoe dvizhenie 1905 goda," *Krasnyi Arkhiv* 9 (1925): p. 74.

15. Lenin, "Sotsial-demokratiia i vremennoe revoliutsionnoe pravitel'stvo," *Vpered*, March 30, 1905, no. 14. In 1905 Lenin claimed that he responded to the peasant revolution as Marx had reacted to the Paris Commune. And it was certainly true that like Marx, Lenin seemed devoid of any fear that the revolutionary efforts of workers and peasants might ever be exerted in vain. In 1905 Lenin argued that peasant unrest provided real opportunities for effective revolutionary activity, while Mensheviks focused above all upon Russian backwardness and in particular upon the prevalence of rural ignorance and prejudice. It is instructive in this connection to contrast the lessons which Lenin and the Menshevik Martov attempted to derive from the Paris Commune. Lenin argued that the Commune provided examples of the technique of partisan warfare, the possibility for proletarian–peasant cooperation, and the dangers of liberal treachery, while Martov feared the danger of a "tragic" repetition of the Paris Commune—the

defeat and harsh repression of a revolution in which the proletariat had prematurely seized power. See Lenin, 'Ob ulichnoi bor'be," *Vpered*, March 10, 1905, no. 11. Martov's statement appeared in *Iskra*, May 15, 1905, no. 26. See also the general discussion in Israel Getzler, *Martov* (Cambridge, 1967), pp. 96–113, and Lenin's statement of July 1905: "When we study the lessons of the Paris Commune we should imitate, not the mistakes it made, . . . but its successful practical measures which indicate the correct path . . .": *Soch.* 11: 132.

16. For a discussion of the "revolutionary-democratic dictatorship of the proletariat and the peasantry" in which voluntaristic and deterministic elements in Lenin's writings are analytically separated, see K. I. McKenzie, "Lenin's Revolutionary-Democratic Dictatorship of the Proletariat and the Peasantry," in *Essays in Russian and Soviet History*, ed. J. S. Curtiss (Leiden, 1963), pp. 149–63.

17. Lenin, "K derevenskoi bednote" (1903), *Soch.* 13: 74; and see Chapter 4, notes 39 and 40.

18. Lenin, "Sotsial-demokratiia i vremennoe revoliutsionnoe pravitel'stvo," (March 30, 1905). According to Lenin's formulation of 1903, the rural poor were the farm hands and peasants who owned a tiny plot of land and one horse. See Chapter 4, note 30.

19. Lenin, *Soch.* 10: 44–52; 11: 215–24; 11: 282–91.

20. Vladimirov and Vorovskii, *Tretii s"ezd RSDRP, aprel'–mai 1905 goda: Protokoly* (Moscow, 1959), pp. 240–41.

21. Lenin, *Soch.* 9: 357.

22. Lenin, *Vpered*, March 10, 1905, no. 11. SR leaders were in fact as sensitive as Lenin was to the dangers of "adventurism." Chernov saw a real danger in what he called the "arbitrary seizure of individual parcels of land by individual peasants." Cited and discussed in Perrie, "Russian Peasant Movement," p. 151.

23. Lenin, *Tretii s"ezd*, p. 454.

24. Lenin, *Tretii s"ezd*, p. 227.

25. Many on the left wing of the Kadet Party were committed to a radical limitation of property rights in the interests of the peasantry, and even among the more conservative, there were few defenders of the unconditional rights of property. On the Left, see, for example, N. N. Chernenkov, *K kharakteristike krest'ianskogo khoziaistva* (Moscow, 1905), vol. 1, p. 1; and on the Right, N. Ia. Gertzenshtein, *Agrarnyi vopros* (Moscow, 1906).

26. Lenin, *Vpered*, April 7, 1905, no. 15.

27. Lenin, *Vpered*, March 10, 1905, no. 11.

28. Iu. O. Martov, *Iskra*, March 17, 1905, no. 93.

29. As Martynov put it, the middle class was posed with the dilemma of stagnation under an absolutist system or progress in a popular revolution. *Dve diktatury* (Geneva, 1905), pp. 58–60.

30. *Iskra*, May 15, 1905, no. 100.

31. Trotsky assumed that Western Europe was on the verge of a socialist revolution which might be sparked by the current upheaval in Russia. He considered the success of international revolution crucial to the establishment of Russian socialism because of the "petty bourgeois" character of the Russian peasantry. Only with the aid of the Western European proletariat did it seem possible to Trotsky that Russia's proletarian minority would be able to overcome the peasantry's inevitably "reactionary" pressure. See Trotsky, *Itogi i perspektivy* (Moscow, 1919; first published 1906), pp. 39–41, p. 73.

32. *Pervaia obshcherusskaia konferentsiia partiinykh rabotnikov*, published as an appendix to *Iskra*, May 15, 1905, no. 100.

33. According to a letter from the Saratov Committee of the RSDRP published in *Proletarii*, the expropriation of modern gentry estates by petty bourgeois proprietors could only be supported if it accelerated the rate of rural economic development. *Proletarii*, July 20, 1905, no. 10.

34. V. M. Chernov, *Revoliutsionnaia Rossiia*, July, 1905, no. 70.

35. A. R. Gotz, *Revoliutsionnaia Rossiia*, July, 1905, no. 70.

36. Lenin, "Dve taktiki sotsial-demokratii v demokraticheskoi revoliutsii" (July 1905), *Soch.* 11: 38.

37. See Chernov's earlier discussion in *Revoliutsionnaia Rossiia*, February–March, 1904, no. 42.

38. Lenin, "Dve taktiki . . . ," *Soch.* 11: 34.

39. Ibid., p. 39.

40. E. I. Kiriukhina, "Vserossiiskii krest'ianskii soiuz v 1905g.," *Istoricheskie zapiski* 50 (1955) 1: 103–4. Congress delegates were not, however, agreed on the question of compensation for the land they wanted to take from the gentry.

41. *Protokoly uchreditel'nogo s"ezda Vserossiiskogo soiuza krest'ianskikh deputatov* (St. Petersburg, 1905), pp. 12–17.

42. Ibid., p. 48.

43. S. M. Dubrovskii and B. B. Grave, eds., *Agrarnoe dvizhenie v 1905–1907gg.* (Moscow–Leningrad, 1925), 1: 114–15; Perrie, "Russian Peasant Movement," p. 135.

44. Lenin, "Otnoshenie sotsial-demokratii k krest'ianskomu dvizheniiu" (September 1905), *Soch.* 11: 222.

45. After the publication of the October Manifesto, some forty thousand peasants assembled in Sumi uezd in Kharkov province to demand land and liberty, and went on to establish committees to organize for an agricultural strike until their demands were met. See discussion in Cinnella, "La social democrazia," p. 541.

46. Lenin, "Pervaia pobeda revoliutsii" (October 25, 1905), *Soch.* 12: 32.

47. Ibid., p. 33.

48. Lenin, "Nashi zadachi i sovet rabochikh deputatov" (November 2, 1905). *Soch.* 12: 63. In the autumn of 1905, even Plekhanov briefly referred to the peasantry as a potential substitute for the unreliable bourgeoisie: Plekhanov, *Sochineniia* 13: 350. Such comments were rare in Plekhanov's writings, and he did not develop this one any further. See also discussion in S. H. Baron, "Plekhanov and the 1905 Revolution," in Curtiss, *Essays in Russian and Soviet History*, pp. 133–48.

49. See discussion in Marcel Liebman, *Leninism under Lenin* (London, 1975), pp. 88–89.

50. V. M. Chernov, *Pered burei* (New York, 1953), pp. 251–59.

51. Lenin, "Melkoburzhuaznyi i proletarskii sotsializm," *Soch.* 12: 40.

52. Lenin, "Proletariat i krest'ianstvo" (November 12, 1905), *Soch.* 12: 94.

53. See discussion in Smith, "Constitutional-Democratic Movement," pp. 498–99.

54. Cited in J. F. Zimmerman, "Between Revolution and Reaction: The Russian Constitutional-Democratic Party, October 1905–June 1907" (Ph.D. diss., Columbia University, New York, 1968), p. 144.

55. Lenin, "Rezoliutsiia po agrarnomu voprosu konferentsii "bol'shinstva" v Tammerforse" (December 17, 1905), *Soch.* 12: 148; and "Boikotirovat' li gosudarstvennuiu dumu?" (January 1906), *Soch.* 12: 158.

56. Dubrovskii and Grave, *Agrarnoe dvizhenie*, 1: 114-15.

57. See discussion in R. T. Manning, "Zemstvo and Revolution: The Onset of the Gentry Reaction, 1905-1907," in Leopold Haimson, ed., *The Politics of Rural Russia in 1905-1914* (Bloomington, Ind., 1979), pp. 43-49.

58. Lenin, "Peresmotr agrarnoi programmy rabochei partii" (March 1906), *Soch.* 12: 265.

59. Lenin, *Protokoly: Chetvertyi (ob"edinitel'nyi) s"ezd RSDRP, aprel'–mai 1906 goda* (Moscow, 1959), p. 127 (cited hereafter as *Protokoly: Chetvertyi s"ezd*).

60. Dan, ibid., pp. 80-81.

61. Ibid., pp. 56-57.

62. Maslov, ibid., pp. 522-23.

63. Dan, ibid., p. 81.

64. Maslov, ibid., p. 56.

65. Ibid., pp. 522-23.

66. Plekhanov, ibid., pp. 59-61.

67. Stalin, ibid., p. 79; see also pp. 77 and 117-18.

68. In vol. 3, pt. 6 of *Capital*, Marx described the process of nationalization, the transfer of land rent to the state, as a bourgeois measure which accelerated the growth of rational capitalist investment. Marx referred to the American Homestead Act as a capitalist measure which enabled farmers to invest in their own land the rent money they would otherwise have been required to pay out as rent. Lenin claimed that nationalization was a bourgeois measure which was appropriate to Russia's current stage of historical development, and likely to appeal to peasants demanding the abolition of private landed property. He did not develop this argument very fully in 1906, but he would return to it again and at length in the period before 1917. See especially Lenin, *Soch.* 16: 268-70, 294-95, 316-20; and *Soch.* 19: 339-44. See also Chapter 1, note 24.

69. Lenin, *Protokoly: Chetvertyi s"ezd*, pp. 131-33.

70. Ibid.; and *Soch.* 13: 29.

71. Lenin, *Protokoly: Chetvertvi s"ezd*, pp. 131-33.

72. Despite Lenin's repeated disclaimers, his perspectives were clearly in line with Trotsky's. In fact, ideas of permanent revolution were not uncommon among the more "activist" revolutionaries in 1905. See Maureen Perrie, "The Socialist Revolutionaries on 'Permanent Revolution,'" *Soviet Studies* 24, no. 2 (1973): 411-13.

73. Lenin's emphasis upon peasant consciousness and popular creativity may be traced back to his analysis of spontaneous action (or "embryonic consciousness," as he referred to it in *What Is To Be Done?*). *Soch.* 7: 96.

74. Lenin, *Protokoly: Chetvertyi s"ezd*, p. 133.

75. In support of Lenin's contention, it may be noted that when Georgian Mensheviks were confronted with unexpected successes in building a rural revolutionary movement in the Caucasus, they ignored the Menshevik program for "municipalization." See Leopold Haimson, 'Preface' to G. Urutadze, *Vospominaniia* (Stanford, 1968), p. viii.

76. Lenin *Protokoly: Chetvertyi s"ezd* pp. 127-28; and see earlier statements in *Soch.* 11: 290, and 12: 263-66.

77. *Protokoly: Chetvertyi s"ezd*, pp. 526-27.

78. Lenin, "Doklad ob ob"edinitel'nom s"ezde RSDRP" (April 1906), *Soch.* 13: 19-20.

79. Lenin, "Vopros o zemle i bor'ba za svobodu" (May 19, 1906), *Soch.* 13: 122-23;

and "O sovremennom politicheskom polozhenii" (May 28, 1906), *Soch.* 13: 175–76.

80. The Trudoviks were non-aligned peasant delegates to the first duma who banded together to fight for the transfer of land to the peasantry and the transformation of the duma into something like a Constituent Assembly. An interesting Soviet discussion of the Trudoviks may be found in D. A. Kolesnichenko, "Agrarnye proekty Trudovoi 'gruppy' v I Gosud. dume," *Istoricheskie zapiski*, 82 (1968), pp. 44–47.

81. See, for example, the discussion of the Kadet I. I. Gessen's position in Zimmerman, "Between Revolution and Reaction," p. 191.

82. As Lenin had written in May 1906, "Taken by themselves, the SRs are nothing. But as exponents of the spontaneous aspirations of the peasantry, the SRs are part of the broad, mighty revolutionary-democratic masses without whose support the proletariat cannot even think of achieving the complete victory of our revolution": "Krest'ianskaia ili "trudovaia" gruppa" (May 11, 1906), *Soch.* 13: 97. See also "Kadety, trudoviki i rabochaia partiia" (May 24, 1906), *Soch.* 13: 146–47.

83. "Kadety, trudoviki i rabochaia partiia," *Soch.* 13: 146–47.

84. See Chernov's early formulation in *Revoliutsionnaia Rossiia*, March 1904, no. 42.

85. The Trudovik proposal that locally elected committees prepare materials for land reform was criticized in the Kadet newspaper *Rech'* as a measure likely to establish new centers for the organization of rural unrest: Zimmerman, "Between Revolution and Reaction," p. 211.

86. "Kadety, trudoviki i rabochaia partiia," *Soch.* 13: 147.

87. Ibid., pp. 146–47.

88. Hans Heilbronner, "Aerenthal in Defense of Russian Autocracy," *Jahrbücher für Geschichte Osteuropas* 17 (1969): 393–94.

89. "Rospusk dumy i zadachi proletariata" (mid-July 1906), *Soch.* 13: 307.

90. Quoted in Robinson, *Rural Russia*, p. 189.

91. "Eserovskie Mensheviki" (September 19, 1906), *Soch.* 13: 405.

92. "Bor'ba za vlast' i 'bor'ba' za podachki" (June 14, 1906), *Soch.* 13: 221.

93. "Rospusk dumy i zadachi proletariata," *Soch.* 13: 319.

6. A Strategy for Marxist Bourgeois Revolution, 1907–16

1. For a detailed and illuminating discussion of the gentry's emergence as a conservative force, see R. T. Manning, *The Crisis of the Old Order in Russia* (Princeton, N. J., 1982).

2. In the 1820s and 1830s, Prussian reformers claimed that a property-owning peasantry served as the best defense against the dangers of proletarian revolution. According to the influential economist Robert von Mohl, "The landowner, in the enjoyment of a home, participates in the preservation of lawfulness, peace and order in the state, while a propertyless mass of agricultural day laborers is easily inclined to any kind of change." A general discussion of the transformation of German public sentiment on the peasant question may be found in John Gagliardo, *From Pariah to Patriot: The Changing Image of the German Peasant, 1770–1840* (Lexington, Ky. 1975), pp. 238–42.

3. Stolypin's decree of November 9, 1906, allowed a householder with allotment land held in communal tenure to separate from the commune and claim a share of common land as private property. Would-be separators were hampered at first in their efforts to

establish separate, private farms, since most allotments were made up of scattered strips of land which could not be enclosed without permission of the communal assembly. To accelerate the separation process, in 1911 the government required communes either to consolidate peasant plots on request or to pay the peasant a financial indemnity for the land involved. In the same year, repartitional tenure was abolished in favor of hereditary holdings in every commune where no general redistribution had taken place since 1861.

4. *Obrazovanie*, March 1907, no. 3.

5. *Otgoloski: sbornik* (St. Petersburg, 1907), pt. 5.

6. For Lenin, the "cowardice" of the Kadets in 1905 and 1906 had demonstrated the bankruptcy of the bourgeoisie, who wanted to "change the old regime but not to fight it, to 'renovate' tsarism but fear[ed] its overthrow": "Za chto borot'sia?" (March 23, 1910), *Soch.* 19: 212.

7. "Agrarnaia programma sotsial-demokratii v pervoi russkoi revoliutsii" (November–December 1907), *Soch.* 16: 268–69.

8. "Agrarnyi vopros v Rossii k kontsu XIX veka" (1908), *Soch.* 17: 72.

9. Ibid., pp. 215–21; and "Proekt rezoliutsii o sovremennom momente i zadachakh partii" (December 1908), *Soch.* 17: 325–26.

10. According to Lenin, the American Civil War had broken up the slave plantations of the South and created the conditions for the most rapid and free development of capitalism. See "Agrarnaia programma sotsial-demokratii . . . ," *Soch.* 16: 270.

11. Ibid., p. 302.

12. Ibid., pp. 294–95, 316–20. The sources in Marx are in *Capital* 3:2 and *Theories of Surplus Value*, vol. 2, ch. 1. Both chapters suggest that in a purely economic sense, the landowner was superfluous in capitalist society.

Lenin dismissed P. P. Maslov's suggestion that small farms could more easily raise productivity through intensive cultivation, while large farms were superior in their capacity to use modern technology in a rational fashion. For Lenin, big farms were superior to small in every respect. It is interesting that Maslov's argument is accepted (without reference to its source and with the implication that it is in fact Lenin's argument) in the final work of the Soviet scholar S. M. Dubrovskii. See Dubrovskii, *Sel'skoe khoziaistvo i krest'ianstvo Rossii v periode imperializma* (Moscow, 1975), pp. 183–84. Lenin's arguments may be found in "Agrarnaia programma sotsial-demokratii . . . ," *Soch.* 16: 285–92, and "Kapitalisticheskii stroi sovremennogo zemledeliia" (September 11, 1910), *Soch.* 19: 339–44; Maslov's position is presented in his *Agrarnyi vopros v Rossii* (St. Petersburg, 1908) 1: 661, 2: 341–45, 451–56; and idem, *Teoriia razvitiia narodnago khoziaistva* (St. Petersburg, 1910), pp. 325–26.

13. See the discussion of his view of the rural poor in Chapter 4.

14. "Pis'mo I. I. Skvortsov-Stepanovu" (December 16, 1909), *Proletarskaia Revoliutsiia* 28, no. 5 (1924): 104.

15. "Agrarnaia programma sotsial-demokratii . . . ," *Soch.* 16: 267–68.

16. Ibid., p. 248.

17. Between 1907 and 1917 such phrases were extremely common in Lenin's articles and speeches. See, for example, "Proekt rechi po agrarnomu voprosu vo vtoroi gosudarstvennoi dume" (late March 1907), *Soch.* 15: 139; "Piatidesiatiletie padeniia krepostnogo prava," *Soch.* 21: 180.

18. "Agrarnyi vopros v Rossii k kontsu XIX veka," *Soch.* 17: 103–5.

19. "Agrarnaia programma sotsial-demokratii . . . ," *Soch.* 16: 265-66.

20. In *What Is To Be Done?* (1902) and "To the Rural Poor" (1903), it was through revolutionary struggle and a grasp of the fundamental truths of Marxism that bourgeois intellectuals "became" proletarian Social Democrats, and the rural poor became socialists. The audacity and initiative which brought Lenin so close to opportunism were rooted in a consistent optimism about the transforming power of revolutionary consciousness. At the Stockholm Congress of 1906, Plekhanov had equated Lenin's notion of "popular creativity" (*narodnoe tvorchestvo*) with the tactics of the Narodnaia Volia (*narodovolchestvo*) of the last decades of the nineteenth century. In 1907 Lenin frankly admitted that the victory of peasant revolution "required an exceptionally favorable combination of circumstances." Focusing on Plekhanov's criticism, he argued that it "requires what from the standpoint of the philistine or the philistine historian are very 'optimistic' assumptions; it requires tremendous peasant initiative, revolutionary energy, class consciousness, organization, and rich popular creativity. All that is beyond dispute, and Plekhanov's philistine jokes at the expense of the latter phrase are only a cheap way of dodging a serious issue." Lenin's comments are in "Agrarnaia programma sotsial-demokratii . . . ," *Soch.* 16: 325; the clearest statement of Plekhanov's position may be found in *Protokoly: Chetvertyi s"ezd*, pp. 59-60. See also discussion in Chapter 4.

21. "Po tornoi dorozhe!" (April 16, 1908), *Soch.* 17: 31.

22. "Agrarnaia programma sotsial-demokratii v russkoi revoliutsii" (August 1908) *Soch.* 17: 172-73.

23. "Na dorogu!" (January 28, 1909), *Soch.* 19: 360.

24. "Agrarnyi vopros v Rossii k kontsu XIX veka" (1908), *Soch.* 17: 64.

25. As F. I. Dan wrote: "All the forces of bourgeois society are sure to rebel against the 'dictatorship' of the feudal gentry. . . . The gentry's 'dictatorship' is bound to propel even the big bourgeoisie into the opposition": *Otzvuki* (St. Petersburg, 1907), pp. 4-5.

26. Plekhanov, *Obrazovanie*, January 1907, no. 1.

27. See discussion in Getzler, *Martov*, p. 124, and Martov's later statement in *Zhizn'*, January 1910, no. 1.

28. "Predislovie k russkomu perevodu pisem K. Marksa k L. Kugelmanu" (February 5, 1907), *Soch.* 14: 378-79; "Agrarnaia programma sotsial-demokratii v russkoi revoliutsii" (August 1908), *Soch.* 17: 170-71; "Ob otsenke tekushchego momenta" (November 1, 1908), *Soch.* 17: 272-73; "Na dorogu!" (January 28, 1909), *Soch.* 17: 360.

29. In the second duma, Sviatopolk-Mirsky argued that the peasants were like sheep, unable to manage without the guidance of landlords who were as shepherds to them. Lenin used the cattle image to which I have referred in "Piatidesiateletie padeniia krepostnogo prava" (February 8, 1911), *Soch.* 20: 141-42. See also "Pamiati kommuny" (April 14, 1911), *Soch.* 20: 222; and Lenin's citation of Engels in support of this kind of analysis in "Po tornoi dorozhe!" (April 16, 1908), *Soch.* 17: 34.

30. "Agrarnaia programma sotsial-demokratii . . . ," *Soch.* 16: 360-61.

31. "Sila i slabost' revoliutsii" (April 1907), *Soch.* 15: 223.

32. See, for example, "Krizis menshevizma" (December 7, 1906), *Soch.* 14: 156-58; "Plekhanov i Vasiliev" (January 7, 1907), *Soch.* 14: 238-39; and "Vtoraia duma i vtoraia vol'na revoliutsii" (February 11, 1907), *Soch.* 14: 380-85.

33. "Proekt rechi po agrarnomu voprosu vo vtoroi gosudarstvennoi dume" (March 1907), *Soch.* 15: 131-34.

34. *Londonskii s"ezd RSDLP: Polnyi tekst protokolov* (Paris, 1909), pp. 301–2.

35. Martov, *Londonskii s"ezd*, p. 303.

36. Plekhanov, *Londonskii s"ezd*, p. 113.

37. Tsereteli, *Londonskii s"ezd*, p. 152.

38. Tsereteli, *Londonskii s"ezd*, p. 158; Cherevanin, p. 187.

39. Abramovich, *Londonskii s"ezd*, p. 293.

40. Trotsky, *Londonskii s"ezd*, pp. 295–96.

41. Like Lenin, Trotsky responded to political opportunity as an activist, but he disagreed with Lenin's assessment of the peasantry and criticized the bitterness of Lenin's polemics against the Mensheviks. Trotsky continued to hope that with the aid of a revolutionary European proletariat, Russian Social Democrats could lead the proletariat in a revolution which would end in the establishment of socialism. Before 1917 Lenin agreed with the Mensheviks on the bourgeois limits of any Russian revolution. As we shall see, Trotsky's agreement with Lenin on the issue of revolutionary leadership did not bring the two into any sort of political alliance in the years before the February revolution.

42. Luxemburg, *Londonskii s"ezd*, p. 105.

43. *Londonskii s"ezd*, pp. 454–55.

44. According to government statistics published in 1907, 10 million peasant households held 73 million *desiatiny* of land, while 28,000 landlords owned 62 million *desiatiny*: Robinson, *Rural Russia*, pp. 268, 270.

45. Lenin, "Agrarnaia programma sotsial-demokratii . . . ," *Soch*. 16: 354–61.

46. Quoted in "Agrarnaia programma sotsial-demokratii . . . ," *Soch*. 16: 364–65.

47. The figures are Lenin's. "Agrarnye preniia v III dume" (December 1, 1908), *Soch*. 17: 315.

48. Ibid.

49. "Kak ne sleduet pisat' rezoliutsii" (March 19, 1907), *Soch*. 15: 94; "Miagko steliut, da zhestko spat' " (March 25, 1907), *Soch*. 15: 115.

50. P. P. Maslov, *Obshchestvennoe dvizhenie v Rossii v nachale XX veka*, ed. Iu. O. Martov, P. P. Maslov, and A. N. Potresov (St. Petersburg, 1908) 1: 661.

51. Quoted in Lenin, "Agrarnye preniia v III dume," (December 1, 1908), *Soch*. 17: 313.

52. "Kak sotsialist-revoliutsionery podvodiat itogi revoliutsii i kak revoliutsiia podvela itogi sotsialistam-revoliutsioneram" (January 7, 1909), *Soch*. 17: 345.

53. "L. N. Tolstoi i sovremennoe rabochee dvizhenie" (November 28, 1910), *Soch*. 20: 40–41, and "L. N. Tolstoi (November 16, 1910), *Soch*. 20: 19–24.

54. "Lev Tolstoi, kak zerkalo russkoi revoliutsii" (September 11, 1908), *Soch*. 17: 209–11. See also "L. N. Tolstoi" (November 16, 1910), *Soch*. 20: 20–24; "L. N. Tolstoi i sovremennoe rabochee dvizhenie" (November 28, 1910), *Soch*. 19: 39–40; "Tolstoi i proletarskaia bor'ba" (December 18, 1910), *Soch*. 19: 70–71; "L. N. Tolstoi i ego epokha," *Soch*. 20: 103.

55. Lenin, "Nekotorykh chertakh sovremennogo raspada" (July 2, 1908), *Soch*. 17: 142. See also "Neskol'ko zamechanii po povodu 'otveta' P. Maslova" (October–November 1908), *Soch*. 17: 268. Chernov's theory of land socialization is spelled out in his *K voprosu o kapitalizme i krest'ianstve*, pp. 4–14; see also Perrie, *Agrarian Policy*, pp. 143–85. Lenin's comment is from the postscript in *Soch*. 16: 413.

56. In this passage, rationality was defined by Lenin as a commitment to enact

historically necessary economic and political tasks. Lenin, "Agrarnaia programma sotsial-demokratii . . . ," (November–December 1907), *Soch.* 16: 215. See also "Novaia agrarnaia politika" (February 19, 1908), *Soch.* 16: 422–23.

57. "Proekt rechi po agrarnomu voprosu vo vtoroi gosudarstvennoi dume" (March 1907), *Soch.* 15: 159.

58. "Dve utopii" (October 1912), *Soch.* 22: 120–21.

59. Atkinson, "Russian Land Commune," p. 86.

60. See discussion of the *otrub* and the *khutor* in Atkinson, "Russian Land Commune," pp. 66–67, and Robinson, *Rural Russia*, pp. 208–44.

61. M. Egorov, "Krest'ianskoe dvizhenie v tsentral'noi chernozemnoi oblasti v 1907–1914 godakh," *Voprosy Istorii*, 1948, no. 5, pp. 14–15.

62. Veselovskii, *Krest'ianskoe dvizhenie 1902 goda*, p. 109.

63. A. M. Anfimov, *Rossiiskaia derevnia v gody pervoi mirovoi voiny* (Moscow, 1962), p. 174. For a different interpretation of the government's policy, see D. W. Treadgold, *The Great Siberian Migration* (Princeton, 1957), pp. 159–80.

64. According to Anfimov, by 1913, arrears in payments to the Peasant Land Bank were equal to half the entire sum loaned out annually. By 1915, arrears mounted to 68%: *Rossiiskaia derevnia*, p. 327.

65. Ibid., pp. 82–83, and E. G. Vasilievskii, *Ideinaia bor'ba vokrug Stolypinskoi agrarnoi reformy* (Moscow, 1960), p. 88.

66. "Reformizm v russkoi sotsial-demokratii" (September 1, 1911), *Soch.* 20: 305–18; see also "Razoblachennye likvidatory" (May 9, 1910), *Soch.* 19: 59–66.

67. "O zadachakh S. D. v bor'be s golodom" (January, 1912), *Soch.* 21: 145.

68. "Pomeshch'e zemleustroistvo" (May 21, 1913), *Soch.* 23: 174. In that same year, when the government introduced a bill to prevent the fragmentation of individual holdings, Lenin argued that such an attempt to protect small landed proprietors was a reactionary policy: "Novye mery zemel'noi reformy" (August 29, 1913), *Soch.* 23: 406–7.

69. "O chernosotenstve" (September 26, 1913), *Soch.* 24: 18.

70. Ibid., p. 19.

71. "Melkoe proizvodstvo v zemledelii" (July 18, 1913), *Soch.* 23: 283.

72. Lenin, "Detskii trud v krest'ianskom khoziaistve," *Soch.* 23: 212; and "Prikrashivanie burzhuazii levonarodnikami" (April 6, 1914), *Soch.* 25: 63.

73. Atkinson, "Russian Land Commune," p. 64.

74. Ibid., p. 101.

75. Ibid., pp. 95–99.

76. Ibid., p. 101. Scholarly opinion on the results of the Stolypin reform is divided. Many Kadet and Populist writers agreed with Lenin's evaluation. See, for example, I. V. Mozzukhin, *Agrarnyi vopros v tsifrakh i faktakh deistvitel'nosti* (Moscow, 1917), p. 48; and N. P. Oganovskii, *Individualizatsiia zemlevladeniia v Rossii i ee posledstviia* (Moscow, 1917), p. 49. The agreement of Soviet scholars may be taken as a matter of course, but see especially S. P. Trapeznikov, *Agrarnyi vopros*, pp. 190–235.

Other scholars, including Pavlovsky, Treadgold, and Antsiferov, have emphasized the positive aspects of the reform. Atkinson has suggested that "Soviet historians who view the Stolypin reforms negatively as part of the inevitable growth of capitalism with its attentuating ills, have tended to inflate the extent of the movement out of the commune. But in this respect they are bed-fellows of many Western historians": "Russian Land

Commune," pp. 62–63. Western and Soviet agreement may be explained in terms of the Westernization of educated observers of Russian agriculture during this period, but the issue clearly needs further study.

77. N. N. Sukhanov, *Marksizm i narodnichestvo* (Berlin, 1915), p. 28.

78. See discussion in Manfred Hildermeier, "Neopopulism and Modernization: The Debate on Theory and Tactics in the Socialist Revolutionary Party, 1905–1914," *Russian Review* 34, no. 4 (1975): 453–75.

79. See notes 26–28.

80. "Priemy burzhuaznoi intelligentsii protiv rabochikh" (June 1914), *Soch.* 25: 324–25.

81. "Demokratiia i narodnichestvo v Kitae" (July 5, 1912), *Soch.* 21: 403–4.

82. "Obnovlennyi Kitai" (November 8, 1912), *Soch.* 22: 191. See also "Demokratiia i narodnichestvo v Kitae" (July 5, 1912), *Soch.* 21: 403–5.

83. "Angliiskie liberaly i Irlandiia" (March 12, 1914), *Soch.* 24: 365.

84. "Itogi diskussii o samoopredelenii" (July 1916), *Soch.* 30: 54.

85. "Porazhenie Rossii i revoliutsionnyi krizis" (September 1915), *Soch.* 27: 27.

86. "Sotsializm i voina" (July–August 1915), *Soch.* 26: 330.

87. "O dvukh liniiakh revoliutsii" (November 20, 1915), *Soch.* 27: 79.

88. "Neskol'ko tezisov—ot redaktsii" (October 13, 1915), *Soch.* 27: 50; see also "Doklad o revoliutsii 1905 goda" (January 1917), *Soch.* 30: 316–23.

7. Problems of Order and Revolution: February–April 1917

1. Bernard Pares, *My Russian Memoirs* (London, 1931), p. 423.

2. See discussion in W. G. Rosenberg, *Liberals in the Russian Revolution* (Princeton, 1974), pp. 79–80.

3. See discussion in Graeme Gill, *Peasants and Government in the Russian Revolution* (New York, 1979), pp. 23–73.

4. A. F. Kerensky and R. P. Browder, *The Russian Provisional Government, 1917* (Stanford, Calif., 1961) 2: 584–85.

5. *Russkiia Vedomosti*, April 18, 1917.

6. Quoted in Gill, *Peasants and Government*, p. 29.

7. P. N. Miliukov, *Istoriia vtoroi russkoi revoliutsii* (Sofia, 1921–23), pt. 1, p. 48.

8. The SR-Bolshevik appeal is reproduced in A. S. Shliapnikov, *Semnadtsatyi god* (Moscow, 1926) 1: 261–62.

9. *Delo Naroda*, March 15, 1917.

10. Alexandrovich, a member of the SR Party, was one of the authors of the SR-Bolshevik manifesto of March 2. N. N. Sukhanov, *Zapiski o revoliutsii* (Berlin and Moscow, 1922) 2: 279.

11. On March 7, 1917, the Menshevik newspaper *Rabochaia Gazeta* reassured the Provisional Government in the following terms: "Members of the Provisional Government, the proletariat and the army await your orders to consolidate the revolution and make Russia a democracy." The Menshevik position is considered in detail in John D. Basil, "Political Decisions Made by the Menshevik Leaders in Petrograd during the Revolution of 1917" (Ph.D. diss., University of Washington, 1966).

12. I. G. Tsereteli, *Izvestiia*, March 21, 1917; E. Z. Morokhovets, *Agrarnye programmy*

rossiiskikh politicheskikh partii v 1917 godu (Leningrad, 1929), pp. 56 and 70. See also Oskar Anweiler, "The Political Ideology of the Leaders of the Petrograd Soviet in the Spring of 1917," *Revolutionary Russia*, ed. Richard Pipes (Cambridge, Mass., 1968), p. 127.

13. See discussion in *Protokoly: Chetvertyi s"ezd*, pp. 522–23.

14. For example, *Rabochaia Gazeta*, March 5, 1917, and March 17, 1917.

15. V. B. Stankevich, *Vospominaniia 1914–1919 g.* (Berlin, 1920), pp. 71–77.

16. Sukhanov, *Zapiski o revoliutsii*, 1: 201–2. Although Sukhanov was an ex-SR who had written in 1915 about the essential agreement between SRs and Marxists on the peasant question (see his *Marksizm i narodnichestvo*), his assessments of peasant action in *Zapiski* are consistently fearful and contemptuous.

17. Hildermeier, "Neopopulism and Modernization," pp. 462–64.

18. Unlike the Mensheviks (or the Bolsheviks before 1917), the SR Party program did not recognize the inevitability of capitalist development as a prerequisite for the establishment of socialism.

19. *Delo Naroda*, March 15, 1917, and April 6, 1917.

20. "Revoliutsiia i krest'ianstvo," *Pravda*, March 30, 1917, no. 21. On the other hand, an editorial of March 7 announced that "of course there is no question among us of the downfall of the rule of capital, but only of the downfall of the rule of autocracy and feudalism."

21. M. I. Kalinin, "O zemle," *Pravda*, March 12, 1917, and "Revoliutsiia v derevne," *Pravda*, March 28, 1917. Professor Ferro is incorrect in his statement that *Pravda* paid no attention to the agrarian question in the first weeks of the revolution. See Marc Ferro, "The Aspirations of Russian Society," in *Revolutionary Russia*, p. 151.

22. L. B. Kamenev, "Bez tainoi diplomatii," *Pravda*, March 15, 1917.

23. J. V. Stalin, "O voine," *Pravda*, March 16, 1917. In an introduction to a collection of articles published in 1925, Stalin noted that in March and April 1917 there was a "certain wavering" among the majority of the Bolshevik Party on these and other issues. See Stalin, "Predislovie," *Na putiiakh k oktiabriu* (Moscow, 1925).

24. Lenin went on to "request and insist that the theses from No. 47 of the *Social-Democrat* (10-13-15) be reprinted." In his "theses" of 1915, Lenin had predicted that if the peasant petty bourgeoisie shifted to the left at a decisive moment, the proletariat could lead and conquer Russia for the revolution.

An interesting discussion of Lenin's difficulties with Bolshevik opposition may be found in E. N. Burdzhalov, "O taktike bolshevikov v marte–aprel'e 1917 goda," *Voprosy Istorii*, 1956, no. 4, pp. 38–56.

25. Lenin, "Zadachi proletariata v nashei revoliutsii" (April 10, 1917), *Soch.* 31: 164.

26. "Nabrosok tezisov 4 (17) marta 1917 goda," *Leninskii sbornik* 2: 321–22.

27. "Pis'ma o taktike" (April 8–13, 1917), *Soch.* 31: 133–34, and "Pis'ma iz daleka" (1), *Pravda*, March 21, 1917. The question of Bolshevik leadership of the Russian revolution was as controversial in 1917 as it had been in 1905, when Lenin had argued that "revolutionary proletarian consciousness" of the type he had described in *What Is To Be Done?* would allow Bolsheviks to lead a bourgeois-democratic revolution without irrevocably compromising their right and ability to lead in a future socialist revolution. This idea was scorned and rejected by the Mensheviks in 1906, in 1917, and in the intervening period. See D. W. Treadgold, *Lenin and His Rivals* (New York, 1955), pp. 183–85, and Getzler, *Martov*, pp. 104–6.

28. This peculiar formulation seems understandable only in terms of the distorting influence of Marxist tradition, since no Russian at the time could have believed that peasants were supporting workers who were seizing land. It was perhaps to Lenin's credit that he often failed to use this phraseology. "Pis'ma iz daleka" (5) (March 26, 1917), *Soch.* 31: 56.

29. Ibid.

30. "Pis'ma iz daleka" (3) (March 11, 1917), *Soch.* 31: 41.

31. Lenin, "Pis'ma iz daleka" (5), *Soch.* 31: 56.

32. Lenin, "S"ezd krest'ianskikh deputatov," *Pravda*, April 16, 1917.

33. Lenin, "O zadachakh proletariata v dannoi revoliutsii," *Pravda*, April 7, 1917. Attorneys and professors of law were in fact very heavily represented within the Central Committee of the Kadet party. According to Rosenberg, on the eve of 1917 half were lawyers, professors of law or legal history. Among Miliukov's closest advisers were the trained legal minds of Nabokov, Vinaver, and Rodichev. See Rosenberg, *Liberals in the Russian Revolution*, pp. 201–2.

34. "O zadachakh proletariata . . . ," *Pravda*, April 7, 1917.

35. A. L. Sidorov et al., ed., *Velikaia oktiabr'skaia sotsialisticheskaia revoliutsiia: dokumenty i materialy*, vol. 3, *Revoliutsionnoe dvizhenie v Rossii v aprel'e 1917g: Aprel'skii krizis* (Moscow, 1958), p. 596.

36. "Rezoliutsiia Vserossiiskogo Soveshchaniia Soveta Rab. i Sold. Dep. po krest'ianskomu i zemel'nomu voprosam," *Izvestiia*, April 6, 1917.

37. *Izvestiia*, April 16, 1917.

38. Quoted in N. N. Avdeev, *Khronika sobytii: Revoliutsiia 1917 goda* (Moscow, 1923–30) 1: 51.

39. Lenin, "O dvoevlastii," *Pravda*, April 9, 1917.

40. Lenin, "Doklad na sobranie bol'shevikov-uchastnikov Vserossiiskogo soveshchanii sovetov rabochikh i soldatskikh deputatov" (*Pravda*, April 4, 1917), *Soch.* 31: 110.

41. Lenin, "Pis'mo o taktike" (April 8–13, 1917), *Soch.* 31: 133.

42. See Chapter 4, notes 28–34.

43. Sukhanov, *Zapiski* 3: 36.

44. Such views are similar to those put forth by various groups of Russian anarchists. But Lenin insisted that the soviets were not a substitute for but a higher form of state power. See, for example, "O dvoevlastii," *Pravda*, April 9, 1917, or "O zadachakh proletariata v dannoi revoliutsii," *Pravda*, April 7, 1917.

45. Sukhanov, *Zapiski* 1: 284–85.

46. Kamenev, "Nashi raznoglasiia," *Pravda*, April 8, 1917.

47. Zinoviev, "Ob"edinitel'nyi udar," *Pravda*, April 8, 1917.

48. Lenin, "Dobrovol'noe soglashenie mezhdu pomeshchikami i krest'ianami?" *Pravda*, April 15, 1917, no. 33.

49. Lenin, "Rezoliutsiia ob otnoshenii k vremennomu pravitel'stvu," *Pravda*, April 18, 1917.

8. The Burden of Political Opportunity: April–July 1917

1. Engels, *The Peasant Wars in Germany*, p. 135.

2. Tsereteli, *Vospominaniia* 1: 117; and *Izvestiia*, April 6, 1917, no. 33.

3. Despite the overwhelming sentiment within the Soviet against an expansionist war, the Miliukov note made it provocatively clear that the liberal imperial dream of Constantinople and the Straits was more compelling than the prosaic reality of the Kadet need for socialist support in order to remain in power.

4. Tsereteli, *Vospominaniia* 1: 88–89.

5. Ibid., p. 89.

6. See Chapter 6, note 77.

7. The Bolshevik A. S. Shliapnikov called for immediate popular demonstrations and Fyodorov urged the "Soviet democracy" to assume power, while Kamenev more moderately stated that if the Soviet permitted demonstrations, the Bolsheviks would support them as a method of raising the level of political consciousness among the masses. Tsereteli, *Vospominaniia* 1: 88, 97, and 101.

8. Lenin, "Krakh," *Pravda*, April 20, 1917, no. 36; and "S ikonami protiv pushek, s frazami protiv kapitala," *Pravda*, April 21, 1917, no. 37.

9. "I. G. Tsereteli i klassovaia bor'ba," *Pravda*, April 29, 1917, no. 44.

10. The idea of democratically elected committees to prepare land reform had been suggested as early as 1906. At that time, Kadets had proposed equal representation for peasants and landlords. The committees were never established. Kerensky and Browder, *Russian Provisional Government* 2: 528–32. See also P. Pershin, "Krest'ianskie podgotovki oktiabr'skoi sotsialisticheskoi revoliutsii," *Voprosy Istorii* 7 (1938): 70.

11. See discussion of this issue by J. L. H. Keep, who argues that the composition of the land committees established in April gave "excessive" weight to popularly elected officials, particularly at the local level: *The Russian Revolution: A Study in Mass Mobilization* (New York, 1977), pp. 164–65.

12. Lenin, "Dobrovol'noe soglashenie mezhdu pomeshchikami i krest'ianami?" *Pravda*, April 15, 1917.

13. Lenin, *Sed'maia (aprel'skaia) konferentsiia RSDRP Petrogradskaia obshchegorodskaia RSDRP (bol'shevikov): Protokoly* (Moscow, 1958), p. 68.

14. Ibid., pp. 72–73.

15. Ibid.

16. Ibid., p. 68. Precisely defined, semi-proletarians were peasants who could not survive without part-time work for a wage. However, ever since his "To the Rural Poor" (1903), there were times when Lenin merged this group with the mass of ruined peasants who did not hire themselves out to the gentry or the kulaks. One suspects that Lenin's merging of proletarian and semi-proletarian interests was related to his recognition of the obvious numerical insignificance of the proletariat.

17. Rykov, *Sed'maia (aprel'skaia) konferentsiia*, pp. 106–7.

18. Ibid., pp. 111–12.

19. Gill, *Peasants and Government*, p. 125. See also P. N. Pershin, *Agrarnaia revoliutsiia v Rossii* (Moscow, 1966) 2: 344.

20. *Sed'maia (aprel'skaia) konferentsiia*, pp. 72–73.

21. Ibid., pp. 72–74, 86–88, 189.

22. *Angarskii*, ibid., pp. 90–91.

23. *Lenin*, ibid., pp. 101–3.

24. Ibid., p. 245.

25. Radkey, *Agrarian Foes of Bolshevism*, p. 174.

26. Rosenberg, *Liberals in the Russian Revolution*, pp. 128–29.

27. V. M. Chernov, *Izvestiia*, May 9, 1917, no. 61.

28. Chernov, *Izvestiia*, May 14, 1917, no. 66.

29. The Pereverzev order is reproduced in Avdeev, *Revoliutsiia 1917 goda* 2: 164; cancellation of the order is cited on p. 202.

30. A. S. Posnikov, *Izvestiia Glavnogo Zemel'nogo Komiteta* (cited hereafter as *IGZK*), July 1–15, 1917, no. 1, p. 10.

31. Ibid., p. 11.

32. N. Ia. Bykhovskii, ibid., p. 12.

33. Chernov, ibid., p. 12.

34. Chernov, *Delo Naroda*, May 25, 1917, no. 17.

35. V. Gurevich, "Vserossiiskii krest'ianskii s"ezd i pervaia koalitsiia," *Letopis revoliutsii* 1: 192–93.

36. Ibid., p. 187. *Izvestiia Vserossiiskogo soveta krest'ianskikh deputatov*, May 13, 1917, no. 5; Radkey, *Agrarian Foes of Bolshevism*, pp. 244–47; and Lenin, "S"ezd krest'ianskikh deputatov" (*Pravda*, April 6, 1917, no. 34), *Soch.* 31: 273.

37. Lenin, "Rech' po agrarnomu voprosu" (*Izvestiia Vserossiiskogo soveta krest'ianskikh deputatov*, May 25, 1917, no. 14), *Soch.* 32: 172.

38. Ibid., p. 174.

39. Ibid., p. 176; "Zametka," *Pravda*, June 7, 1917, no. 75.

40. Lenin, "Rech' po agrarnomu voprosu," *Soch.* 32: 182.

41. Lenin's earlier agrarian proposals had only promised the peasantry a "more or less" human life. See Chapter 6, note 17.

42. Lenin, "Rech' po agrarnomu voprosu," *Soch.* 32: 185.

43. Ibid., p. 186.

44. Quoted in Avdeev, *Revoliutsiia 1917 goda* 2: 185.

45. Ibid., pp. 294–95.

46. Chernov, *Delo Naroda*, May 24, 1917, no. 56, and *Delo Naroda*, June 5, 1917, no. 67.

47. Radkey, *Agrarian Foes of Bolshevism*, p. 194.

48. Ibid., pp. 183–84.

49. Rosenberg, *Liberals in the Russian Revolution*, pp. 150–51.

50. Tsereteli, *Vospominaniia* 1: 447–50, 464–65.

51. L. Kochan, "Kadet Policy in 1917 and the Constituent Assembly," *Slavonic and East European Review*, January 1967, p. 190; and see discussion in Gill, *Peasants and Government*, p. 93.

52. All Bolshevik proposals to the conference were defeated. Lenin, "O neobkhodimosti osnovat' soiuz sel'skikh rabochikh Rossii" (1), *Pravda*, June 24, 1917, no. 90; and (2), *Pravda*, June 25, 1917, no. 91.

53. Lenin, "Velikii otkhod," *Pravda*, June 8, 1917, no. 76.

54. Lenin, "Iz kakogo klassovago istochnika prikhodiat i 'pridut' Kaven'iaki?" *Pravda*, June 16, 1917. According to a letter Lenin wrote to Karl Radek at the time, "Things here mostly resemble the eve of the June days of 1848. The Mensheviks and SRs are surrendering all and everything to the Kadets (= the Cavaignacs). *Qui vivra verra.*" *Soch.* 49: 443–44.

55. Lenin, "Rech' t. Lenina na Vserossiiskom s"ezda sovetov r.i.s.d.," *Pravda*, June 16, 1917, no. 83.

56. Lenin, "Chudesa revoliutsionnoi energii," *Pravda*, June 27, 1917, no. 92, and "Praviashchiia i otvetsvennaia partiia," *Pravda*, June 18, 1917, no. 85.

57. Lenin, "Zapugivanie naroda burzhuaznymi strakhami," *Pravda*, May 4, 1917, no. 48.

58. For the application of this type of argument to "democracy," see "I. G. Tsereteli i klassovaia bor'ba," *Pravda*, April 29, 1917, no. 44; it is applied to the concept of the "majority" in "O konstitutsionnikh illuziiakh," *Rabochii i Soldat*, August 4–5, 1917, nos. 11 and 12, and to "anarchy" in "Nad kem smeetes'? Nad soboi smeetes'!" *Pravda*, June 3, 1917, no. 72.

59. Lenin, "Rech' ob otnoshenii k Vremennomu Pravitel'stvu," *Pravda*, June 16, 1917, no. 83.

9. LENIN AS SPOKESMAN FOR PEASANT REVOLUTION: JULY–OCTOBER 1917

1. Sukhanov, *Zapiski o revoliutsii* 2: 200.

2. See, for example, Lenin, "Nabrosok tezisov 4 (17) marta 1917 goda," *Leninskii sbornik* 2: 321–2; and "O zadachakh proletariata v dannoi revoliutsii," *Pravda*, April 7, 1917, no. 26.

3. Miliukov, *Istoriia vtoroi russkoi revoliutsii*, vol. 1, pt. 1, p. 244.

4. See, for example, I. G. Tsereteli, *Izvestiia*, March 21, 1917, no. 20.

5. In the process, the government released information suggesting that Bolsheviks were in the pay of the Germans. Browder and Kerensky, *Russian Provisional Government* 3: 1364, 1378–79, 1370–77.

6. *Izvestiia*, July 11, 1917, no. 114.

7. Radkey, *Agrarian Foes of Bolshevism*, pp. 360–61. A. Rabinowitch, *Prelude to Revolution* (Bloomington, Ind., 1968), pp. 206–36.

8. Lenin, "Na chto mogli rasschityvat' kadety, ukhodia iz ministerstva?" July 3, 1917, *Leninskii sbornik* 4: 315–16.

9. *Pravda*, July 4, 1917, no. 99; Lenin, "O konstitutsionnikh illiuziiakh" (July 26, 1917; *Rabochii i Soldat*, nos. 11–12, August 14–15, 1917), *Soch.* 34: 34–38; and "K lozungam" (mid-July 1917), *Soch.* 34: 15.

10. *Izvestiia*, July 9, 1917, no. 113.

11. *Delo Naroda*, July 19, 1917, no. 104.

12. I. Z. Steinberg, *Ot fevralia po oktiabr'* (Berlin, 192—), p. 89.

13. *IGZK*, August 1–5, 1917, nos. 3–4, p. 3.

14. *Izvestiia*, July 15, 1917, no. 113.

15. Trotsky, *Rabochii i Soldat*, July 24, 1917, no. 2.

16. Browder and Kerensky, *Russian Provisional Government* 2: 563–64.

17. A. V. Peshekhonov was a founder of the right-wing Popular Socialist Party. At the June Congress of Soviets, he explained the reasons for the food crisis in the following fashion: "The whole difficulty lies, not in overcoming the resistance of the bourgeoisie, which gives way in everything, but in winning over the toiling masses, who must be summoned to the most exacting labor and the indispensable sacrifices. If we succeed in overcoming these psychological difficulties of the masses, and in drawing them after us, then we shall solve our problems." Quoted in Sukhanov, *Zapiski o revoliutsii* 4: 237.

18. Radkey, *Agrarian Foes of Bolshevism*, p. 107.

19. *Russkia Vedomosti*, August 4, 1917, no. 177.

20. "Rech' Chernova," *Izvestiia*, July 21, 1917, no. 123.

21. Lenin, "Zapugivanie naroda burzhuaznymi strakhami," *Pravda*, May 4, 1917, no. 48, and "Rech'," *Izvestiia Vserossiiskogo soveta krest'ianskikh deputatov*, May 25, 1917, no. 14.

22. Lenin's theory of Marxist peasant revolution is discussed in detail later in this chapter.

23. "Uroki revoliutsii" (written late July, published in *Rabochii*, August 31, 1917, no. 9), *Soch.* 34: 66–69.

24. "Tri krizisa" (July 7, 1917, published in *Rabotnitsa*, July 19, 1917, no. 7), *Soch.* 32: 430–32.

25. "Uroki revoliutsii" (written late July, published in *Rabochii*, August 31, 1917, no. 9), *Soch.* 34: 66–69.

26. *Izvestiia*, July 22, 1917, no. 124.

27. *Izvestiia*, July 23, 1917, no. 125.

28. Lenin, "Nachalo Bonapartizma," *Rabochii i Soldat*, July 29, 1917, no. 6.

29. Lenin, "O konstitutsionnikh illiuziiakh," *Rabochii i Soldat*; July 26, 1917, no. 3.

30. Lenin had been in hiding since the July Days and did not risk open political activity until the Bolshevik seizure of power.

31. Preobrazhenskii, *Shestoi s"ezd RSDRP bol'shevikov avgust 1917 goda: Protokoly* (Moscow, 1958), p. 116.

32. Stalin, *Shestoi s"ezd*, pp. 123–24.

33. Ibid., pp. 253–56. It should be noted that in August many Bolsheviks were still in hiding; others, like Trotsky, were in prison.

34. "Vremennoe Pravitel'stvo i agrarnyi vopros-rech' Chernova," *Izvestiia*, August 11, 1917, no. 141.

35. *Delo Naroda*, August 4, 1917, no. 118.

36. Bykhovskii, *Delo Naroda*, August 6, 1917, no. 121.

37. Steinberg, *Ot fevralia po oktiabr'*, p. 93.

38. Ibid., p. 113.

39. Lenin, "Otvet," *Rabochii i Soldat*, July 27, 1917, no. 3.

40. K. G. Kotel'nikov and V. A. Meller, eds., *Krest'ianskoe dvizhenie v 1917 godu* (Moscow, 1927), p. 323.

41. A. L. Sidorov et al., eds., *Velikaia Oktiabr'skaia sotsialisticheskaia revoliutsiia, Dokumenty i materialy: Revoliutsionnoe dvizhenie v Rossii v avguste 1917 g., Razgrom Kornilovskogo miatezha* (Moscow, 1929), pp. 307–8.

42. *Izvestiia*, August 15, 1917, no. 144.

43. *Izvestiia*, August 16, 1917, no. 145.

44. Radkey, *Agrarian Foes of Bolshevism*, p. 279.

45. Lenin, "Bumazhnye rezoliutsii," *Rabochii*, August 26, 1917, no. 2. It is interesting to note that Radkey, critical of the Soviet from another point of view, agrees with Lenin's analysis: see *Agrarian Foes of Bolshevism*, p. 149.

46. See M. Vishniak, *Vserossiiskoe uchreditel'noe sobranie* (Paris, 1932), p. 76, and P. N. Miliukov, *Istoriia vtoroi russkoi revoliutsii* (Sofia, 1921) 1, pt. 2, pp. 44–48, 91; and general discussion in L. Kochan, "Kadet Policy in 1917 and the Constituent Assembly," *Slavonic and East European Review*, 1967, pp. 183–92.

47. Lenin, "Pis'mo v Tsk MK, PK i chlenam sovetov," *Sochineniia*, 3rd ed., 21: 63.
48. Lenin, "O kompromisakh," *Rabochii Put'*, September 3, 1917, no. 3; and Sukhanov, *Zapiski o revoliutsii* 5: 91.
49. Lenin, "Iz dnevnika publitsista," *Rabochii*, August 30, 1917, no. 6.
50. Lenin, "Pis'mo k I. T. Smil'gu," September 27, 1917, published in *Pravda*, November 7, 1917, no. 255.
51. Lenin, "Russkaia revoliutsiia i grazhdanskaia voina," *Rabochii Put'*, September 16, 1917, no. 12.
52. Lenin, "Groziashchaia katastrofa i kak s nei borot'sia" (written September 10–14, 1917, published late October, 1917), *Soch.* 34: 190–93.
53. Ibid., p. 193.
54. Lenin, "Iz dnevnika publitsista," August 29, 1917, *Rabochii*, no. 5.
55. Ibid.
56. See, for example, Lenin, "Doklad o revoliutsii 1905 goda" (January 9, 1917), *Soch.* 30: 306–10; and see Chapter 6, pp. 118–20.
57. Lenin, "Gosudarstvo i revoliutsiia" (written August–September 1917), *Soch.* 33: 44–45, 101–2.
58. Lenin, "Iz dnevnika publitsista," *Rabochii*, August 19, 1917, no. 5.
59. The extent of Lenin's revolutionary faith was revealed in his frank admissions of error after 1917. See, for example, Lenin, "Rech' o dopolneniiakh k zakonoproektu SNK 'O merakh ukrepleniia i razvitiia krest'ianskogo sel'skogo khoziaistva' po fraktsii RKP (b) VIII s"ezda soveta" (December 14, 1920), *Soch.* 42: 187–89. Lenin's later recognition of Bolshevik misconceptions must of course be seen within the context of his revolutionary commitment: "For every 100 of our mistakes, there are 10,000 great and heroic acts—but if the situation were reversed, if there were 10,000 mistakes to every 100 of our correct acts, all the same our revolution would be and will be unconquerable in the eyes of world history, because for the first time not a minority, not only the rich, not only the educated, but the real masses, the enormous majority of the workers themselves build up a new life, with their own experience deciding the most difficult problems of a socialist organization." "Pis'mo k amerikanskim rabochim" (*Pravda*, August 20, 1918), no. 178 *Soch.* 37: 61.
60. "Rech' Skobeleva," *Izvestiia*, September 17, 1917, no. 173.
61. On September 1, 1917, the Petrograd Soviet adopted a Bolshevik resolution by a vote of 279 to 115; by September 9, when the Mensheviks and SRs in the presidium of the Soviet Executive Committee offered to resign, another Bolshevik resolution passed by a vote of 519 to 414.
62. See the statements of the Left SR A. A. Karelin, "Demokraticheskaia konferentsiia," *Delo Naroda*, September 14, 1917, no. 154; and his critics, A. Lezhnev, "Bol'sheviki v derevne," *Delo Naroda*, September 22, 1917, no. 161, and I. A. Prilezhaev, "Levaia fraktsiia sotsialistov-revoliutsionerov," *Delo Naroda*, September 26, 1917, no. 164.
63. *Izvestiia*, September 13, 1917, no. 169.
64. Miliukov, *Istoriia vtoroi russkoi revoliutsii* 1, part 3, p. 65.
65. *Delo Naroda*, September 27, 1917, no. 165. Although nothing came of its decision, on September 28 the Provisional Government decided to establish local committees (including representatives of the central authority) to restore a measure of rural stability. See *Krasnyi Arkhiv*, 1936, pp. 96–97.

66. Gill, *Peasants and Government*, p. 135.

67. Sukhanov, *Zapiski o revoliutsii* 6: 239–40.

68. *Izvestiia*, September 26, 1917, no. 182.

69. The seizure of land, livestock, and implements by the rural poor and evidence of hostility to the "capitalists" provided Lenin with his reasons for claiming that the majority of the population was in sympathy with the Bolshevik position. See "Uderzhat' li bol'sheviki gosudarstvennuiu vlast'?" (October 1917), *Soch.* 34: 296–99.

In "Groziashchaia katastrofa i kak s nei borot'sia," written in mid-September, Lenin referred to a resolution recently passed by the Economic Section of the Soviet which condemned the "harm" caused by the government's raising of grain prices. *Soch.* 34: 188–90.

70. *Izvestiia*, September 12, 1917, no. 168; Steinberg, *Ot fevralia po oktiabr'*, p. 118.

71. Lenin, "Bol'sheviki dolzhny vziat' vlast'" (written September 12–14, 1917) in *Proletarskaia Revoliutsiia* 2, (1921): 63.

72. Lenin, "Krizis nazrel," *Rabochii Put'*, October 7, 1917, no. 3; and see Isaac Deutscher, *The Prophet Armed: Trotsky 1879–1921* (New York, 1954), pp. 290–314.

73. See editorial in *Izvestiia*, October 5, 1917, no. 189, and V. S. Pankratov, "Tragediia derevnii," *Delo Naroda*, October 6, 1917, no. 173.

74. N. I. Rakitnikov, "Voina i zemlia," *Delo Naroda*, October 7, 1917, no. 174.

75. Avdeev, *Revoliutsiia 1917 goda* 2: 185.

76. The SR move is reminiscent of the action taken by the French revolutionary government in 1848 which placed the "social" or national workshops, under the authority of Alexandre Marie, a man who opposed their creation: Priscilla Robertson, *Revolutions of 1848: A Social History* (Princeton, 1952), p. 70.

See discussion of the SR action in E. Z. Morokhovets, *Agrarnye programmy rossiiskikh politicheskikh partii v 1917 godu* (Leningrad, 1928), p. 56.

77. Gill, *Peasants and Government*, p. 136.

78. *Delo Naroda*, October 18, 1917, no. 183.

79. Ibid.

80. Lenin, "Zadachi revoliutsii," *Rabochii Put'*, September 27, 1917, no. 21.

81. Lenin, "Pis'mo k tovarishcham" (October 17, 1917, published October 19–21, 1917, *Rabochii Put'*, nos. 40–42), *Soch.* 34: 413.

82. Lenin, "Zadachi revoliutsii," *Rabochii Put'*, October 26, 1917, no. 47.

83. Quoted in Deutscher, *Prophet Armed*, pp. 307–8.

84. Atkinson has noted that in a session of the Provisional Government which met on the same day it was said that "with winter approaching the crisis of land relations is perceptibly abating": "Russian Land Commune," p. 115.

85. Lenin, "Doklad o zemle" (October 25, 1917), *Soch.* 35: 27.

10. The Meaning and Implications of Lenin's Triumph

1. Professor Ulam uses this phrase in a wholly different context, to describe Lenin's too credulous faith in a Bolshevik associate of plebeian origin, despite evidence that he was a spy. See Ulam, *Bolsheviks*, p. 215.

2. Gill, *Peasants and Government*, pp. 142–44.

3. Ibid., p. 196 and p. 25.

4. Lenin, "Gosudarstvo i revoliutsiia" (August–September 1917), *Soch.* 33: 44–45, 101–2.

5. See, for example, V. M. Chernov, *Konstruktiv'nyi sotsializm* (Moscow, 1907), or B. D. Kamkov, *Gosudarstvo i trud* (Moscow, 1911).

6. Lenin, "Uderzhat li bolsheviki gosudarstvennuiu vlast'?" (October 1, 1917), *Soch.* 34: 328–29.

7. The equalization process in the countryside is discussed in Teodor Shanin, *The Awkward Class* (Oxford, England, 1972), pp. 145–61.

Glossary

appanage lands   lands which provided financial support to members of the Imperial family other than the tsar's immediate family.

barshchina   forced labor service rendered by a serf to his or her master.

black hundreds   a term used to refer to a number of extremist propaganda and paramilitary organizations dedicated to the defense of autocracy and Great Russian tradition against the threat allegedly posed by Jews, masons, radicals, and cosmopolitans of every variety.

cabinet lands   lands which provided financial support to the tsar and his immediate family.

Cherny Peredel (lit. Black Repartition)   an organization devoted to propaganda and agitation in the countryside and opposed to the political and terrorist focus of the *Narodnaia Volia* (People's Will). Both groups were formed in 1879 when the older Land and Liberty group (*Zemlia i Volia*) split apart over the issue of political terror.

dvorianin (pl. *dvoriane*)   a noble, a member of the landholding gentry.

desiatina (pl. *desiatiny*)   Russian unit of land area equal to 2.7 acres.

duma   representative assembly proposed by the tsarist regime under pressure of revolutionary agitation in 1905. The first duma met in 1906 and was soon dismissed. Between 1906 and 1917, the government repeatedly rewrote the electoral laws in order to obtain more conservative majorities and attempted to evade the promise of legislative power granted to the duma in the heat of revolution. In 1917 the fourth and most conservative of the dumas was in session.

guberniia   province, main administrative unit of the Russian Empire.

intelligenty (sing. *intelligent*)   members of the intelligentsia.

khutor   enclosed, self-contained farm, including the house and farm buildings of the peasant household.

Kadet abbreviation of Constitutional Democratic Party. Russia's liberal party, whose first congress met in 1905.

kulak (lit. fist) rich peasant; pejorative term commonly used to refer to peasants who lent money at high interest or otherwise exploited their neighbors.

mir repartitional land commune. See *obshchina*, and discussion in Chapter 2.

muzhik peasant, often a pejorative term.

Narodnaia Volia (lit. People's Will) revolutionary terrorist organization which in 1879 split from the older Land and Liberty party (*Zemlia i Volia*); it was dedicated to the "disorganization of the state" and responsible for the assassination of Alexander II in 1881.

obshchina term first used by the Slavophiles in the 1840s to refer to the repartitional land commune. See *mir*, and discussion in Chapter 2.

Octobrists those previously associated with the liberal movement who believed that with the October Manifesto of 1905 the government had conceded all that was necessary for the rational reform of Russian society. See discussion in Chapter 5.

otrabotka peasant labor rendered as payment for land rented from a landlord, or as repayment for loans of grain or money, or as compensation for damage which a peasant's cow might cause to the fields, etc. This practice was reminiscent of the *barshchina*, or forced labor system, of the pre-emancipation era.

otrezki (lit. "cut-off lands") lands taken away from peasant allotments or from the pasture or forests of the peasant community by the terms of the emancipation of 1861.

otrub (*otrubshchiki*, user of the *otrub*) peasant farm which consolidated scattered strips of land belonging to the household with the exception of the household plot and dwelling place, which remained in the village. Seen by the pre-revolutionary tsarist government as a transition to the more economically advantageous *khutor*.

podvornoe hereditary peasant tenure prevalent in the west and southwest of Russia. Various forms of collective responsibility as well as strip cultivation were generally retained. See discussion in Chapter 2.

Pugachevshchina term referring to the death and destruction associated with the years of the Pugachev rebellion of 1773–74.

skhod village assembly. See discussion in Chapter 2.

soviet first appeared in the Revolution of 1905 as a workers' council comprised of delegates from the factories of St. Petersburg, reappeared in February, 1917, as soviet of workers' and soldiers' deputies, and later expanded to include peasant delegates. By the end of 1917 soviets existed throughout the country.

SRs abbreviation of Socialist Revolutionary Party, formed through the unification of various populist groups in the 1890s and holding its first congress in December 1905.

Trudovik (pl. **Trudoviki**) a member of the group of peasants, radical intellectuals, and SRs who came together as delegates to the first duma of 1906 in order to fight for the transfer of land to the peasantry and the transformation of the duma into something approximating a constituent assembly.

uezd administrative subdivision of a *guberniia*, including several villages.

v narod (lit. "to the people") exodus to the Russian countryside of more than a thousand men and women, particularly students, in the spring of 1874. Their purposes were varied, and ranged from revolutionary agitation and socialist propaganda to projects for education and medical care.

volost administrative subdivision of *uezd*, usually including several peasant communes.

zemstvo elected assemblies created by an Imperial decree of 1864 to improve local conditions. Although all classes of the rural population were represented in these institutions, the gentry were dominant in the areas of leadership and administration.

Index